MANUEL
SCOTLAND'S FIRST SERIAL KILLER

MANUEL
SCOTLAND'S FIRST SERIAL KILLER

A. M. NICOL

PREFACE
BY
DONALD R. FINDLAY QC

BLACK & WHITE PUBLISHING

First published 2008
by Black & White Publishing Ltd
29 Ocean Drive, Edinburgh EH6 6JL

1 3 5 7 9 10 8 6 4 2   08 09 10 11 12

ISBN: 978 1 84502 241 9

A CIP catalogue record for this book is available from the British Library.

Typeset by Ellipsis Books Limited, Glasgow
Printed and bound by MPG Books Ltd, Bodmin

ACKNOWLEDGEMENTS

Many thanks to Donald for his advice, encouragement and
wisdom and to everyone at Black & White for their guidance
and patience.

CONTENTS

PREFACE

by DONALD R. FINDLAY QC

Two strikingly contrasting men were central to my decision to become a criminal defence lawyer.

One, as is well documented, was the actor Michael Dennison who played the title role in Boyd QC, an early black and white television drama about a barrister who displayed a passionate desire to secure justice for everyone he represented.

The other was Peter Thomas Anthony Manuel, once described as having the names of the saints and the heart of the devil.

In the late 1950s, when my school mates were into the adventures of Dan Dare and his struggles with the Mekon, my interests lay in a very different direction.

Peter Manuel stood trial for murder in Glasgow High Court in May 1958.

Nowadays, a murder trial may receive no more than a passing mention in the media. Over thirty years ago when I first started appearing in the High Court, murder cases attracted considerable attention. Public galleries would be occupied and the trials were widely reported.

But the Manuel trial was different. People queued to get in to observe the proceedings and virtually every word of the evidence was reported. The trial of Manuel was as unique as the man himself.

Peter Manuel was a serial killer, arguably the only true serial killer in the long and bloody history of our criminal justice system.

The trial and the man fascinated me.

I devoured every reported word and could recite the charges and names of the victims as other seven-year-olds would rattle off nursery rhymes. Following the guilty verdicts and sentence of death for the murder of seven people, Manuel unsuccessfully appealed in June 1958 and was hanged at Barlinnie Prison in Glasgow in July of the same year. Fifty years ago and yet I remember it all as if it was yesterday.

When I went to Dundee University to read law, the first thing I did was to go into the law library, excitedly remove the 1958 volume of the Session Cases and read and re-read the report of Manuel's appeal, the only aspect of the case to make the law reports.

Why this fascination?

At the time of the trial I certainly did not know. I remember my late father's embarrassment when people asked what the bairn was reading and he was forced to mutter under his breath that it was the Manuel trial. Seven-year-olds from Cowdenbeath were not expected to be interested in such matters.

Even today I do not really know the answer but hindsight has given me some insight.

For some reason I was destined to be a criminal lawyer. Defending the citizen against the power of the State is my profession and my passion. Whether that is because I believe in standing up for the underdog or am simply a bolshie so-and-so I will leave to others to reach a view on.

But for me, to have defended Manuel would have been the ultimate challenge involving, as it did, multiple murders and the spectre of the rope.

The life of a criminal lawyer is a strange one and I perhaps should not be as surprised as I am that most people do not understand what it is we actually do and why we do it.

A hallmark of a free society is that justice is dispensed in public. Any citizen accused of a criminal act should have that allegation examined in open court. The guilt or otherwise of a person so accused should be determined by randomly chosen members of the public – a jury – not by police officers, civil servants or lawyers. And since the State makes the allegation it is for the State to prove it. It is the task of the defence lawyer to make sure that the State does precisely that. Trials should be vigorously prosecuted and just as vigorously defended. It is the responsibility of the defence lawyer to examine the evidence in minute detail, to explore every possibility, to place every hurdle he can in the way of the prosecution case – whatever the nature of the crime may be and however horrific it may seem. In short, it is the duty of the defence lawyer to try to ensure that guilty people are convicted – but only guilty people.

PREFACE

That is why I would have relished the opportunity to defend Manuel.

I was once asked if I would defend Saddam Hussein. Without hesitation I replied that I would. A journalist tried to make an issue of this until one of his more astute colleagues pointed out that since defending people accused of committing horrendous deeds was what I did, this was no story at all. Had I been offered the brief and refused, that would have been a real story. When confronted with a client, the defence lawyer cannot permit himself the view from the moral high ground.

In my younger days I was in favour of the death penalty. Simplistically, it seemed to me that if you deliberately took the life of a fellow human being, you forfeited your own right to live. Over the years my view has changed. Execution is an act of revenge. No more and no less. I became convinced that a civilised country does not kill its own citizens and a country which does is not civilised.

From a personal point of view, I am constantly relieved that I have never had the responsibility of representing someone facing a sentence of death. It is stressful enough to stand before a man who has just been told that he may spend the rest of his life in prison. But what would you say to someone who knows the answer to the great mystery which confronts us all – the precise moment in time when the Grim Reaper will come calling?

And yet, I have often wondered how I would have handled the pressure of representing a man who faced the ultimate penalty. And would my fate have been the same as my distinguished predecessors who were instructed in Manuel's defence only to find their services dispensed with when Manuel decided to conduct his own defence – either an act of supreme folly or consummate arrogance?

A serial killer facing the death penalty would have been the ultimate professional challenge. Perhaps it is because I will never have this experience that I entertain this enduring fascination with Manuel. He was there in the world I have inhabited for these thirty years and more, but I was twenty or more years too late. And yes, I would have fought tooth and nail to try to save him because justice would have demanded it.

For long enough I have had it in the back of my mind to write a book about Manuel's life, times and crimes. Pandering to my own obsession – perhaps!

One day I was contacted by my friend, colleague and fellow

defence lawyer Allan Nicol. Over coffee, which I had to pay for, he explained that he had an interest in Peter Manuel. He had been researching his subject for some time and would I mind having a look at what he had written and offer any suggestions. I confess now that I had mixed feelings. I was envious that he had actually done something I always wanted to do. I was intrigued that someone else shared my interest. And I wondered. Could he recount this story, as horrible as it is bizarre, in a way which would be of interest to a wider audience than a few legal hacks steeped in the lore of Scottish criminals?

I read the early chapters and I was hooked. This was truly fascinating. Not only was Allan revealing detail I had never come across before, he was taking me back over fifty years and re-creating the atmosphere and the sense of fear which must have gripped parts of the West of Scotland while Manuel went about his terrible deeds.

I told Allan that he should finish the book and that he must try to get it published.

And here it is. The definitive work on one of the darkest chapters in Scottish criminal history and one of the most evil men ever to step into the dock of the High Court of Justiciary. But it does more than merely recount awful deeds. It is the story of Manuel's victims. The innocent people who suffered as Manuel butchered his way to infamy.

This book will shock you and move you – sometimes within a single page. It also made me think and should make you think. Given that no child comes into this world and has as his or her first meditation 'I want to be bad,' why do the Peter Manuels of this world exist? Allan Nicol provides you with the material. It is up to you to try to solve the puzzle.

I am honoured and delighted to have been involved in this project. I have tried to advise and encourage.

But this is Allan's book – and his alone. I hope that he is proud of it – he should be.

Now read on while Allan Nicol takes you back in time and introduces you to a man who shattered lives, killed without conscience and earned his place in the ranks of those who epitomise terror – the serial killers.

Meet Peter Manuel.

DRF

1

ENIGMA

Peter Thomas Anthony Manuel took his first breath in Misericordia Hospital in Manhattan, New York on 15 March 1927 and his last at 08.01 hours on 11 July 1958 at HM Prison Barlinnie, Glasgow. The extract death certificate records the cause of death as 'Judicial hanging as certified by DAR Anderson MB ChB.'

In the course of the thirty-one years four months between these two events, he progressed from minor theft to housebreaking, from indecent assault to a conviction for rape, and from simple assault to murder. He was convicted of seven murders and was undoubtedly guilty of murdering Anne Kneilands, though acquitted of that charge.

Days before his execution he is said to have confessed to committing three other murders, although to believe anything he said was unwise, as at that stage it was suspected he was either trying to convince the authorities he was insane in an effort to escape execution or he was hoping that he would be spared pending further enquiries. On top of that, the press had gone into a 'Manuel murder frenzy', ascribing almost every unsolved case within the time scale to the condemned man.

We also know that if by some nightmarish miracle he had persuaded the jury empanelled at his final trial in 1958 to acquit him of the capital murder charges – they convicted him unanimously on the serious charges they had to consider – police officers from Newcastle were waiting to arrest him for the murder of the taxi driver Sydney John Dunn. The evidence for this was tenuous and the allegation was probably part of the mythology surrounding the case. More recently, the press did the same to mass murderer Fred West when they sold countless copies of their newspapers on the basis of several stories now shown to be the result of editorial pressure rather than investigative journalism. At the time, it was thought Manuel could have killed as many as fifteen people. Nearly fifty years after his execution, it's difficult to come to terms with the enormity of what he actually did, and it seems clear that the authorities in wartime and post-war Britain had no idea how to cope with the monster in their midst.

When his parents returned to Britain from the United States, Peter Manuel was five years old. They first moved back to Lanarkshire then to Coventry. Then, aged twelve, young Manuel made the first of his many court appearances at Coventry City Juvenile Court where he was 'bound over' for twelve months for shopbreaking and larceny. Between then and 1946 he appeared again at Coventry, then in Ely, Cambridge, Darlington, Manchester, Southport, Hull, Beverley, Market Weighton in Yorkshire, Chatham and Glasgow, mostly for breaking into shops or houses and usually whilst on the run from approved school. He said that he ran away because he 'didn't like staying in the one place'.

Two convictions stand out.

On 24 June 1942, aged fifteen, he appeared at Southport Juvenile Court on three charges of housebreaking and a charge of unlawful wounding and was returned to approved school. He had broken into a house and made his way to a bedroom. Having stolen her purse, he woke up a sleeping girl so he could assault her and he used a hammer which he was holding with a handkerchief to stop the transfer of prints. Not only was that his first recorded conviction for violence, it was the first instance of nocturnal assault on a sleeping victim, something which he later refined to casual execution with a handgun.

Certain dates appear to be significant in his life. He would have been able to recall how he celebrated his sixteenth birthday on 15 March 1943 as he appeared at Market Weighton and was committed to Borstal for two years. The conviction was recorded as: 'Escaping from approved school. One case of robbery with violence; one case of larceny of a pedal cycle; one case cinema breaking; one case larceny from an offertory box; one case larceny from an attaché case; one case of not paying a railway fare and one case of indecent assault taken into account.' Apart from a total lack of respect for the offerings of a congregation, this was the point where the authorities took the inevitable but significant step of consigning him to the kill-or-cure effect of Borstal training.

In his case, it made a bad situation infinitely worse.

After at least two attempts were foiled, he was convicted of committing his one and only rape in 1946. Whether he was actually guilty of rape will be examined in a later chapter but after that date he does not appear to have raped or attempted to rape again, instead taking climactic satisfaction in his victim's terror.

Nearly half a century on, it is easy to be critical of the police and the penal system. He should perhaps have been arrested sooner, his psychopathic tendencies making him an obvious suspect for crimes committed in his locality, but the police just couldn't quite gather enough evidence.

To understand the case, we have to understand the times. In 1940s and 1950s Britain there was no DNA analysis, there were no crime 'profilers' and virtually nothing was known of what we now label serial or 'signature' killers. At a loss to explain him perhaps, some concluded he was inherently evil from birth and that nothing could have deflected him from his instinctive barbarism. Others regarded him as the ultimate attention seeker, convinced of his own invincibility and on a mission to demonstrate his intellectual superiority over his main, but not exclusive adversaries, the police. A psychiatric report prepared whilst he awaited execution at Barlinnie's D Hall in 1958 predictably concluded that he was a psychopath. His own sister even expressed that view and even after he was hanged, social commentators tried to categorise him.

One theory lay in the Victorian criminological 'science' of physiognomy which postulated that cranial characteristics mirrored the layout of the mind. Using this method, the study of facial features and head shapes allowed criminologists to tell at a glance who had criminal tendencies and who had not.

3

MANUEL

An uneven face pointed to criminal tendencies. Accordingly, a posthumous experiment was conducted where a mirror was placed down the centre of a photograph of Manuel's face so that the same side of his face was matched up and shown as whole. That was then photographed and the process repeated for the other half, and they were then compared. The results were described as 'most interesting'.

Can we assume he had two different faces?

Can we not further assume the same result might occur for many others who do not have criminal tendencies?

One writer added, without comment, an appendix to his book which showed that the dates of Manuel's later crimes, with one exception, coincided with the waxing phase of the moon, the one exception occurring on the cusp of a new moon. So was he a genuine lunatic?

For many young men who rebel and turn to crime, poverty and lack of parental care are often cited as crucial factors in their delinquency. Neither could fully apply in Manuel's case. The addresses he lived at in the Uddingston area at Viewpark and Birkenshaw were no better and no worse than many others in the area. His parents perhaps gave him too much support – his mother, Bridget, volunteering as a defence witness for him in a case in 1955. He rejected her on the basis that she shouldn't have to hear what awful allegations the police were making against him. Her appearance as a defence witness in Glasgow High Court in his final trial in 1958 seems to have been too much for her. His father Samuel, though, seems to have given him unconditional support in the face of increasing evidence of his son's progressive criminality. After all, Peter was usually well behaved at home.

In any event, young Peter could self-justify any vicious behaviour – outwith the family home – without fear of parental recriminations. One example tells a tale.

On the day he had been due to marry Anna O'Hara in 1955 – a marriage which did not take place – he abducted Mary McLachlan at knifepoint. She was lucky enough to survive and to complain to the police about what he'd done to her. Manuel, though, not only pleaded his innocence but defended himself and took full advantage of the large measure of tolerance the bench allow to party defenders. His acquittal even led some local people to question whether it was Mary McLachlan or Peter Manuel who was the greater social problem.

Later events were to be decisive in that regard.

No such doubt appears to have existed in Samuel Manuel's mind. The next time he saw her he spat at her, exhibiting either blind faith in his son's innocence or a dogged determination to ignore reality.

Yet Manuel could be charming, generous and almost caring, as when he was engaged to Anna O'Hara and he showered her, and her mother, with chocolates and other presents.

Friends and family were, however, often treated to presents he'd stolen in housebreakings. He also appears to have been genuinely fond of his pet Alsatian, Rusty and, incredibly, he must have returned several times to the house where the bodies of the Smart family still lay to snooze on a couch and to feed tinned salmon to the family cat.

There's also no question that Peter Manuel was of above average intelligence. In his court finale he predictably sacked his counsel in order to defend himself. The presiding judge, Lord Cameron, remarked that there was little doubt he had presented his own case with remarkable skill. Any satisfaction Manuel might have had from such a compliment was fleeting. Lord Cameron was soon to don the black tricorn and sentence him to death.

Long before his final trial, the battle lines between Manuel and the rest of society were drawn by the time he was committed to Borstal in 1943, aged sixteen. And after his conviction for rape in 1946, he apparently spent much of his incarceration in Peterhead reading up on reported criminal law. The cases of Moorov and Chalmers – one famously altering evidential proof in the prosecution's favour and the other regarded as possibly the high water mark of fairness in Scottish criminal law – must have fascinated him and led him to believe he could outwit investigating police officers. In particular, the latter case seems to have instilled a misguided belief that his confessions and actions at the time of his arrest would ultimately be excluded on the grounds of unfairness.

The police, however, ultimately won that particular battle of wits. They understood that his family was his one exploitable weakness, so when he was in custody on murder charges, his father was taken in for questioning on a relatively minor matter.

It did the trick.

The knowledge that the father was detained seems to have been enough for the son to confess to what is now termed 'special knowledge' of the crimes and to lead police to where one of the victims was buried. He appears to have been gambling on a little knowledge of the law saving him, but, of course, it turned out to be a dangerous thing.

Peter Manuel had also spent a lot of time trying to impress the criminal underworld but they, too, helped bring him down. They never accepted him and used to exclude him from the main business of the day, instead allowing him menial tasks and probably belittling him enough to convince him he had to earn their respect by way of more and greater crimes. One day in the Gordon Club in central Glasgow, where the crime bosses of the time met, he produced a handgun, no doubt to impress them. It did not have the desired effect. He was cursed for his stupidity then literally kicked out the front door.

Whatever motivated him, fifty years later he remains an enigma and a dark stain on the fabric of Scottish society.

2

THE EARLY YEARS

Samuel Manuel had been a welder to trade but found life difficult in 1920s Lanarkshire, so he emigrated to America. The image of the United States figures large in the Manuel story. Samuel, like so many others, saw the move as an opportunity to better his family's standard of living. In later years though, his wayward son Peter would boast of his American start in life, assuming others would be as impressed with Stateside gangsterism as he was. The Manuels left for America in 1925 leaving two-year-old James, Peter's older brother, with relatives, although they intended to send for him when settled. Samuel was good at turning his hand to various tasks to maintain the American dream for his family and he went from job to job with his wife Bridget, starting off in Detroit where he worked in a car body factory.

Peter was born in 1927, just before the economic collapse that led to the Great Depression and during the heyday of the Chicago gangsters. Even so, Samuel and Bridget must have been determined to stay, lasting until 1932 when Samuel took ill and they decided they would be as well starving amongst relatives in Lanarkshire as amongst strangers in the States. When they moved to Motherwell, near Glasgow, James and Peter met for the first time – James as quiet and reserved as Peter was brazen. Younger sister Teresa, who was born in 1934 and never married, eventually died in the family home at 32 Fourth Street, Birkenshaw, Uddingston in March 2008 aged seventy-four.

From the outset, Peter refused to conform to school discipline and spent his time complaining and causing trouble. Many youngsters can find schooling a problem, but Peter Manuel was different, seemingly determined to be noticed at any cost. He was disruptive in the class and often drew pornographic pictures to bemuse other children and shock teachers. He attended Park Street Roman Catholic School in Motherwell for a time in 1937, but skipped school when he could and started fights when he couldn't.

Still in search of work, Samuel then moved his family to Coventry where Peter embarked on his infamous criminal career. After being sent to approved school, he escaped eleven times and stole to stay alive, inevitably leading to further trouble and to the Borstal training imposed on his sixteenth birthday. Yet despite intermittent education, he later revelled in letter writing, mainly in connection with his perpetual war with authority. His spelling and punctuation were usually flawless, particularly after he engaged in some serious study in prison at Peterhead, although he often indulged in the flowery language of a layman trying to sound like a lawyer. Clearly, he considered himself intellectually superior to those around him – and no doubt in most cases he was, when compared to the inmates of the various approved schools and prisons he was to spend much of his life in. But his lifelong misjudgement was to imagine that because he was smarter than many of those in prison, the same applied to those outside – and to the police in particular.

In 1958, the year of his execution, the authorities examined him as to his 'fitness to plead' – meaning whether he was able to understand the charges he faced and to give instructions to his legal representatives – and at interview he claimed that he had won a scholarship to the King Henry VIII Grammar School in Coventry and that he had attended there for a year. Wartime bombing had destroyed records, and whether he attended grammar school or not, his education was disrupted after he was convicted of breaking and entering and sent to St Gilbert's Approved School at Woodbridge in Suffolk. By an early age he had been moved from the United States to Scotland then England and his mother later recalled a day when he came home from school in Coventry saying that he 'couldn't understand a word'. After that, he refused to go back.

Facing execution if convicted in 1958, he claimed that he had sustained a head injury during an air raid in 1943 or 1944 and that a piece of steel from a flying bomb had penetrated his right forehead. As a result he had been unconscious for some hours and his mind had 'been a blank' for four or five days after that.

His mother later recounted a different version he told her at the time.

And there was more.

In 1944 he said he had had an electric shock at work and three of his workmates had died in the incident. He himself had survived after he had been given artificial respiration, but his feet and hands were burned and since then he was prone to loss of memory, such as the time he drove a lorry from Blackpool to Preston in 1945 without being aware of his actions, or when he recalled starting a boxing bout but had no further memory until attending Bible class a few days later.

After conviction, he appears to have briefly feigned madness, so these claims have to be seen in context, but a psychiatrist who examined him found he not only had a scar on his right forehead but had one on his right hand 'consistent with a surgically inflicted wound to relieve a septic condition following a burn by electric shock'.

While he was serving his sentence, Manuel's family returned to Scotland again, mainly to escape from Luftwaffe bombing of Coventry where their house was destroyed. They settled in Uddingston, near Glasgow and by March 1945, Peter joined them, having been liberated on licence from Rochester Borstal Institution.

By that time, he was an experienced and violent housebreaker. His devoted parents must have fervently hoped for a new start for their troubled son. As parents often do, they worried they were in some way responsible for his criminal behaviour. They were, to some degree at least, and it's even been suggested that his father was frightened of him.

Whatever happened on his return, he immediately left Uddingston to go to Blackpool although still on licence from borstal. He slept on the beach in good weather and drifted from job to job. Sometimes he earned money as a street photographer, sometimes at the amusement arcade and sometimes helping run a back-street gambling school. He spent it on the 'promenade girls' and gained a reputation as a show-off who quaffed brandy, smoked cigars and carried a silver dollar which he would take from his pocket and continually flip. The local police knew him as a dangerous dreamer with an explosive temper. He imagined he was the gangster film star George Raft, but the fantasy ended when he was badly beaten up by a gang angry at his persistent attempts to charm one of their girlfriends. Being Peter Manuel, he reappeared with a gun which he was later relieved of when drunk. Before returning home he faced a charge of housebreaking which went to trial, but he was acquitted.

Whatever the effect his beating by the gang had, he could console himself that his attackers had been lucky that the gun had been taken from him before he could show them what he was made of. His first verdict of not guilty was the foundation for imagined future forensic invincibility, should he choose to challenge the facts.

On his return, Samuel and Bridget allowed him to carry on with his nocturnal activities and he was soon in court again, this time in Glasgow. Under a provision which allowed an early plea of guilty, known in those days as a 'section 31', he was sentenced to twelve months' imprisonment on 21 March 1946 for fifteen charges of housebreaking, two charges of housebreaking with intent to steal and a charge of attempted housebreaking.

While he awaited his court appearance, the Medical Officer in Barlinnie Prison, Glasgow passed him fit for 'Borstal treatment', but that was not imposed, as he had only recently undergone Borstal training, the effect of which was to totally alienate him from any prospect of rehabilitation.

In the course of the medical, the nineteen-year-old Manuel's chest measurement was noted as a mere 33.5 inches 'when expanded' and he was five feet four inches tall. Undoubtedly, there was ample scope for underestimating young Peter.

His early plea of guilty and his subsequent twelve-month sentence have to be viewed in the context of the circumstances, however. His decision to plead guilty, in itself an uncharacteristic move, and to start an inevitable custodial sentence, may have been an attempt to deflect attention from more sinister night-time activities. Indeed, had his ever-indulgent father not lodged £60 bail – quite a sum in those days – in relation to the housebreaking charges he was to plead guilty to, his son Peter would not have been at liberty to carry out sex attacks on three women on the nights of 3, 7 and 8 March 1946, the last leading to his conviction for rape.

But was it rape?

3

THE UNWELCOME GUEST

Samuel Manuel seems to have had a knack for choosing unlucky places for his family to live in. By 1946, though, it was the turn of the residents of Glasgow and Lanarkshire to have bad luck.

At that time, there was a succession of housebreakings in the Mount Vernon and Sandyhills areas of Glasgow, all with the same modus operandi. The culprit or culprits climbed up a drainpipe to break or open a window, but in so doing left fingerprints at the scene.

In February 1946, William Muncie, later Assistant Chief Constable of Strathclyde Police but at that time a Detective Constable, recalled in his memoirs the first time he met Peter Manuel. Having been called out in the early hours of a Sunday morning to yet another break-in, he discovered that the householder was on holiday and that there were fingerprints all over an attic window. After examining the scene he was later called to another break-in nearby. Again, the householder was on holiday.

This time a neighbour had a set of keys and the police searched the house. On top of a bed they found a pile of jewellery including a distinctive lady's gold lapel watch. Some items were taken for finger-printing and the police left. Muncie later remembered that a cup with fingerprints on it had been mistakenly left at the scene, so he and other officers returned to the house and as he dozed in the car, a colleague retrieved the key from the neighbour and went back in.

It was mid-day on Sunday 17 February 1946, and Manuel and Muncie were about to meet. When Muncie opened his eyes, he saw Manuel walking towards the car and he realised that he could only have come from one of the houses in the street, so he stopped him as he passed the car and asked him his name.

Manuel gave the correct name.

Muncie then claimed he'd seen him coming from the scene of the housebreaking – which was not true – but Manuel responded by saying he had been there but was 'only watching', and that another person, whom he named, was responsible. Indeed, he was still in the house, Manuel claimed, hoping that Muncie might fall for it and let him go.

Ignoring the legal niceties, Muncie searched him and found the distinctive lady's watch he had seen earlier on the bed. Either Manuel had entered a previously violated house after the police left or there was a more disturbing possibility.

When the house was checked again, the more sinister explanation came to light. Manuel had somehow discovered that the householder was on holiday and had used the house as a base to break into others in the area. He was either confident of avoiding an encounter with the returning house owner or he was ready to attack him or her before escaping.

It seems he was equally content to briefly co-exist with the owner, to later emerge like a ghost in the night, as it was discovered that he had actually constructed a bed from blankets, a quilt and a pillow next to water tanks behind wooden panelling.

How could he have had the nerve to do that?

Moreover, how could he possibly have found out about the sliding section of the panelling? This only emerged when the house owner reported bedding was missing and the loft was re-searched; it also meant that Manuel had discovered the sliding panel and the police had not.

Could it be that he enjoyed the thrill of hiding in someone's house?

How satisfied he must have felt when he thought he had eluded the police by staying put in his cosy little hideaway. What power he must have experienced when he treated a house as his own and what did it mean when he opened and ate tins of food and scattered some on the carpets, as he did with canned fruit in this case?

It was, of course, the first piece of the terrifying jigsaw the police would later have to deal with, but at this stage they must have had some difficulty reconciling his decent family with the long list of convictions they now discovered he had in England.

A further feature which became a Manuel trademark was his response when caught. He was most definitely not to blame and he could supply the name of the real culprit. Both lies, of course, but an insight into his total inability to accept any responsibility.

Given that fact, his next move might be seen as surprising – until seen in context. On 21 February when the court set bail at £60 and his father came up with the money, it led to his son being at liberty to carry out the three sex attacks between then and 8 March. Yet on 21 March 1946 he tendered pleas of guilty to the housebreaking charges and received twelve months' imprisonment.

Did he really think that the police would be so stupid as to forget that he was at large on the nights of 3, 7 and 8 March, or did he gamble that any sentence imposed for the housebreakings would 'cover' any further sentence for the three sex attacks he now carried out? It may even be that he committed the sex attacks in the knowledge that he was facing custody and their memory would sustain his fantasies during long nights of captivity. He may also have simply believed he would not be caught or convicted for the attacks and that they would somehow never come to light.

Given the peculiar approach the prosecution now took, he might have been proved right.

4

NIGHT ATTACKS – 1946

Samuel Manuel was a hard-working man, and an indulgent parent. He had clearly done his best for his family in trying times, so it might be that he was acting on that impulse when he raised the £60 necessary to keep Peter out of prison, whilst awaiting trial on the housebreaking charges. For others, and at least three women in Lanarkshire, it was a decision that would cause much pain, grief and sorrow.

A criminal enquiry is always more convincing to a jury when a suspect, unknown to the police at that stage, emerges because of a compelling piece of evidence. In modern times we have cases which have been solved by the discovery of DNA, linking some previously apparently law-abiding citizen with an often 'cold' crime. In 1946 Manuel was a whole new experience for the police. Of course by the time of his last few days of freedom in 1958, Manuel was 'in the frame' for every serious crime, with much justification. Yet, even at this early stage, it soon emerged he was rapidly becoming a 'usual suspect' in attacks on women at night.

There may have been others, but it's now recorded that he carried out three attacks. Manuel's hunting ground – nowadays accepted as often part of a 'behavioural pattern' – included Mount Vernon in Glasgow, just on the border, as it were, with Lanarkshire.

The first happened on 3 March 1946, when a woman with her three-year-old child walked along an unlit path between Mount Vernon Avenue and Carrick Drive at night. Because it was away from the street lights, she necessarily had to walk slowly and watch her feet, whilst watching out for her child. Manuel was waiting in the darkness, but what was he waiting for? If we assume it was for a passing woman, he must have made an instant decision that the child didn't matter, or at least wouldn't get in the way of his plans, whatever they were.

Despite the obvious terror she must have felt as he jumped out at her, she fought back and they slid down a hill, ending up against a fence which had barbed wire on it. Her child, meantime, was left on the pathway. The terrified woman screamed hysterically and he suddenly stopped the attack, she later told police. When he ran up to the area where her child was standing, though, she instinctively scrambled back to the path.

What he did next was unexpected and probably highly significant. He actually ran back in the darkness and repeatedly kicked her until she again fell to the ground before he ran off again. But why? Why attack a woman with a child in the first place? Why suddenly stop the attack when he might be expected to rape or indecently assault her at that point? And why risk a further opportunity to be identified by returning to beat her up?

It suggests that he was 'testing the water' and seeing where the attack might take him, in terms of whatever urges drove him on. It might also point to a need to test himself as to whether he could actually see the crime through. Was the unfortunate woman's obvious terror enough to stimulate him to the point of ejaculation, with the punishment beating at the end of the attack due to self-disgust or frustration? And was it significant that he went on to murder Isabelle Cooke on the same footpath on 28 December 1957, as if completing unfinished business?

Whatever the motives, the victim later recovered sufficiently to give a description similar enough to Manuel to cause police to regard him as a suspect. They had also found black hairs at the scene and a cap which had been altered by unprofessional stitching to fit a smaller head. Muncie saw a cap in the hall of the Manuel house later that day which had been similarly altered.

Evidentially, a reasonable start you might think.

Then Manuel disappeared for a few days.

Four, to be exact.

At about 9.30 at night, a young nurse finished her shift at hospital and was walking along Calder Road, Bellshill, about six miles from the scene of the previous attack. This time Manuel was really taking a chance, as this is a public road and there was always the risk he would be seen by passers-by. She saw him leaning against a fence as she approached, but had no idea she was in such danger. He must have decided it was safe to attack as there was no-one else about. Or so he judged.

He didn't even spring much of a surprise, because he simply ran across the road at her, giving her time to try to defend herself, which she did by dropping the suitcase she was carrying. She was struck in the face, then he put his hand across her mouth and warned her to be quiet. They ended up on the ground against a hedge at the side of the road, and at that point she managed to scream.

There are no details as to the identity of her rescuer, but he was riding a motorbike. In 1946, it would undoubtedly have been British and unashamedly noisy. As it neared, Manuel must have heard it and he ran off into the nearby woods. And by this time a pedestrian had also arrived on the scene.

His desperate gamble had not paid off.

Maybe he hadn't roughed her up enough to achieve satisfaction.

Now someone else was going to have to pay the price.

5

'RAPE' – 1946

Twenty-four hours later and only two miles away from the scene of the attack on the young nurse, a twenty-six-year-old woman alighted from a bus and started to walk along Fallside Road to her house in Ferry Road, Bothwell. Her husband expected her home at any time. She was a lady who had suffered bad health and apart from being a victim of tuberculosis, as so many were at that time, she had undergone a hysterectomy only three weeks before at Bellshill County Maternity Hospital.

Again, although it was a quiet public road it was risky for any would-be attacker, but Manuel was obviously as desperate on 8 March 1946 as he had been the day before.

He only lived a mile away and he didn't intend to fail this time.

She had seen him at the bus stop but had no cause to think she was about to be Manuel's next victim. After walking for a few minutes, she realised that someone else was on the pavement, and behind her, so she glanced back and saw the same well-dressed young man who had been at the bus stop.

Manuel seized his chance.

He ran up, punched her, pulled her to the ground, put his hand over her mouth and growled at her to be quiet. When she bit his hand, he became furious and he grabbed her head and banged it off the ground several times. This time he meant business. He ordered her to shut up, but she spoke, only to plead that he could take her money if that's what he wanted.

But of course it wasn't.

This time he'd taken more care not to be thwarted by knights on

18

less than shiny motorbikes. He pulled her up from the ground, twisted her arm and forced her over a fence to a railway embankment. He kept hissing at her to keep quiet and to get to the railway bridge, but she screamed nevertheless.

Nobody came to her help, though.

He made it clear what would happen if she did it again – he would kick her face in. He must have sounded as if he meant it, because the next time she said anything it was to plead with him that she was only just out of hospital. Knowing what we know of him now, it probably only gave him greater enjoyment that his victim was so vulnerable. And she wasn't to know what sort of monster he was.

Not that it mattered by that time, but her false teeth had now been broken and had fallen out of her mouth. One further indignity, though.

She was thrown to the ground where he tore off her clothes, and apparently raped her. He then tied her scarf round her eyes and ran off. When she could move, she made it up to the road and, too late, a pedestrian came to help her.

Again, the description this victim gave to the police fitted that of Manuel, and when the police called at his house on 9 March, he was arrested.

An identification parade was held that night and, in those days, the complainer had to walk down the line and to actually touch the man they were complaining about. Nowadays, instead of a line-up, there's an agreed DVD which the complainer views before possibly making an identification.

Little wonder, then, that one of the victims, the woman with the child from 3 March, fainted on seeing him again, which, in one view, could be seen as a positive identification. A definite identification came from the young nurse from 7 March, but the lady who had been attacked last failed to identify.

Manuel seemingly achieved on 8 March what he set out to do on the 7th.

With four days between the 3rd and 7th it could be that his urges were momentarily sated for that length of time, but that frustration from the previous night caused him to attack again on the 8th.

Whatever the cause, he was now locked up and unable to harm the general public until 1952. Yet, there is a suspicion it could have been longer if the Crown had not taken a strange decision about the prosecution of these three incidents.

They were linked closely in time. The nature and character of the first two were very similar and all three crimes were in the same area. There was identification, of a kind, for the first two crimes and the hair and cap evidence for the first crime must have had some evidential weight.

The decision was made, however, to proceed only with the rape allegation from 8 March 1946. The explanation at the time appears, unofficially, to have been that if he had been convicted of all three charges, the judge might have concluded that a psychiatric, rather than a custodial, disposal was appropriate, reasoning which now appears odd. In any event, Manuel made the first and less famous of his two appearances at the High Court of Justiciary at Glasgow, known as the Saltmarket, on 26 June 1946 in the South Court before Lord Russell, the prosecutor or Advocate Depute being G. Gordon Stott, a future Lord Advocate.

Manuel, nineteen years old by a few months, elected to defend himself.

He must really have had a good conceit of himself.

6

RAPE TRIAL – 1946

The 'new' High Court of Justiciary at the Saltmarket was opened in 1812 on the site of the previous court, which had a prison attached. To this day, the bodies of prisoners executed in a far more brutal age lie mouldering beneath the original portico entrance facing Glasgow Green. Later work on the building led to workmen finding some coffins, including that of the infamous Dr Edward, William Pritchard who died 'facing the monument' in front of a crowd of 100,000. It is said that he was identified by the good-class elasticated boots which were still encasing his bones – that is until one of the workmen promptly stole them and sold them on to a fellow customer in a nearby pub.

Whilst the exterior of the High Court in Glasgow has not changed down the years, the two oldest courts, the North and the South have, but not by very much. They were refurbished a few years ago and still retain many of the same features as when Manuel stood trial in the South in 1946 and in the North in 1958 – in itself something of a 'progression', as by tradition the South originally dealt with 'lesser' crimes.

Society, however, has most definitely changed. Today, the jurors who are cited to judge cases have different attitudes towards lawyers, judges, courts and policemen compared with their counterparts in 1946 and 1958. Back then, they were less cynical.

Justice, like many other blessings in Scotland, flows unstintingly from Edinburgh. Indeed, the historic position is that the only true High Court is in Edinburgh, all the others in reality only being justice 'on circuit' from there. Up until relatively recently, a fanfare of trumpeters led a procession of judges and officials down Glasgow's High Street to the Saltmarket to mark the beginning of the cases being heard on that circuit. Thereafter a man of the cloth would lead prayers seeking God's assistance in guiding the court to achieving appropriate justice, before a generous purvey, courtesy of Glasgow Corporation, was partaken of by those most intimately involved in the process of achieving that justice.

Another difference in 1946 was that the number of jurors was temporarily altered from fifteen to seven in terms of section 3(1) of the Administration of Justice (Emergency Provisions) (Scotland) Act 1939, which provided for 'the modification of the law relating to the administration of justice in Scotland in the event of the outbreak or imminence of war' and was dated 1 September 1939. Today a majority verdict of guilty is when eight or more out of fifteen agree, but under this wartime provision, which still applied in June 1946, a majority verdict of guilty was achieved when five out of seven agreed.

A story of the time relates to a jury of seven who had been directed that they could return a guilty verdict 'by five to two' and, of course, waited until 1.55pm before considering it appropriate to return to court.

A further provision was that two out of the seven empanelled jurors should be 'special' – having certain minimum property qualifications – as opposed to 'common' jurors who had none. This distinction dated back to the Jurors Act 1825 which stipulated that there had to be a minimum of five 'special' jurors out of the fifteen selected.

One institutional writer observed that 'lowering the standard' of potential jurors 'brought a class into the jury box, incapable, in a great variety of cases, of understanding the intricate and important questions which are submitted to them for decision. They become utterly confounded, in particular if the proceedings are protracted to any considerable length, and after four or five hours' attention to the evidence, are generally guided by the most able speech which is addressed to them on its import. Verdicts in consequence, both in the civil and criminal Courts, have become

much more uncertain than formerly, and the opinion has exten-
sively spread among practical men, that if you can only protract
the proceedings to a certain length, or the case is one of any
considerable intricacy, little reliance can be placed on the verdict
of the jury being conformable to the evidence which has been
laid before them.'

Clearly, the hoi polloi had to be kept in check, even in 1946.

If criticism can genuinely be levelled at the police for being less
than diligent in arresting Manuel or at the prosecution for electing
to try one out of the three possible charges, it has to be accepted that
they investigated and prepared a solid case for the trial.

The Indictment read as follows:

You, PETER THOMAS ANTHONY MANUEL, did on 8 March
1946 in Fallside Road, Bothwell assault A B, beat her with your
fists, knock her head on the ground, grip and twist her arm,
force her over a fence to a railway embankment and did there
throw her to the ground, pull down her knickers, lie on top of
her and you did ravish her.'
          (Signed) Douglas Johnston A.D.

Manuel had, of course, started his twelve-month sentence by the
time this trial began, so the time limits which applied to holding him
in custody on the present charge were no longer pressing. At that
time, Scots Law decreed that if a prisoner had been remanded in
custody for a trial, that trial had to be completed within 110 days of
his first appearance in court.

On any view this is a demanding stipulation, and looks particularly strict when compared with today's benchmark Human Rights
provisions. Indeed, in one High Court case, the Crown got their sums
wrong by one day and at 10am on the 111th day, defence counsel
pointed this out and his client walked free from the charges.

Forever.

From Glasgow's Barlinnie Prison, Manuel wrote to the prosecution in his characteristic quasi-legal style:

23

905 Manuel 12 mos.

To Whom It May Concern

––––––––––––––

I Peter Thomas Anthony Manuel, Hereby put into writing a statement, to the effect that I intend to hold my own defence at the forthcoming trial on Tuesday, 25th day of June 1946, at which I am indicted at the Instance of one, George Reid Thomson, His Majesty's Advocate.

(Sgd.) Peter Thomas Anthony Manuel
19th day of June 1946

The police enquiry had started by physically retracing the route the victim had been forced to take. A broken dental plate was found and two distinct sets of footprints could be traced down to an area of flattened grass; thereafter the footprints went in different directions, tending to corroborate the victim's story. A cast was able to be taken of the apparent male print which matched the heel of a shoe seized from Manuel; red and green fibres on his clothes matched threads from the victim's scarf, and when his shoes were examined, the following was found – the mixture of dust and mud was 'consistent with being at the locus, strengthened by the presence of carbonaceous grains and red sandstone conglomerate, none of which was found anywhere else in the vicinity'.

Having chosen to defend himself, he seemingly earned the praise of the court – surely, with hindsight a dangerous precedent which must have only further fed his ego – and he elected not to give evidence although he did address the jury, pleading his innocence as he had done to the police when arrested.

They convicted him unanimously and he was given a sentence of eight years to commence at the end of the twelve-month sentence he was already serving.

That conviction represents the only time he was charged with actual rape and, despite the verdict, it has to be questioned. It was certainly said of him that, for physical and psychological reasons, he found it difficult, but not impossible, to achieve full sexual relations. The build-up to the 'rape' conviction appears to show an escalation in his violence towards women, and, with the exception of the abduction of Mary McLachlan in 1955, what followed this conviction was a further escalation in violence, and now not solely confined to random females.

The clear implication is that he achieved sexual relief through violence, and required a stronger stimulus after each attack. How then could he have been convicted, and unanimously, by a jury of actual rape?

The victim undoubtedly testified to her belief that rape had occurred, and by violently tearing at her skirt and underwear there seems little room for debate as to his intentions. However, the victim was understandably hysterical and no doubt dazed after being punched and having her head repeatedly battered against the ground. In her medical condition, she must have been prone to genuine pain when she moved vigorously, let alone if, say, he had digitally penetrated her.

When the case is studied in depth, however, two important facts emerge – there was no fresh injury to the vagina and a vaginal swab did not reveal the presence of semen. Indeed, none was detected on either her pants or her underskirt.

It was a different picture when his clothes were examined. What were described as 'complete spermatozoa' were found on his trousers, shirt and singlet. Was Manuel – technically – not guilty of rape, but guilty of an attempt to rape? Was he, in fact, pandering to his own violent urges to gain satisfaction? And what effect did this have on him? After all, his dark secret meant that he did not actually commit the full crime. A defence based on the truth – he would have raped his victim had he been capable – was unstateable and his only alternative was to go to trial and hope for the best. For him, there was never any likelihood of simply accepting culpability. And in 1940s Lanarkshire he would probably have been unable to confide in anyone about his peculiar condition.

Better to serve a sentence and keep quiet.

7

PETERHEAD

Incarceration can do one of two things to you. It can make you reflect on what got you there and make you decide you don't want to come back. Or it can make you bitter, particularly if you're not being honest with yourself.

Peter Manuel was never any good at reasonable self-appraisal. At nineteen he was facing nine years in jail, and Peterhead Prison was where sex offenders went then, and still do. For the newcomer, getting established in the prison hierarchy is important. Psychologists will tell you that convicts who have committed the most despicable of offences have one comfort left – sex offenders are an even lower form of life than they are. In the knowledge that society in general agrees with that assessment, they righteously go about making life hell for the SOs, with threats, gestures and violence or by defiling their food in ways best not discussed. Outside of prison, tabloid campaigns against real or imagined paedophiles are often then pursued further by persons whose own contribution to a better society is questionable. It makes them feel good about themselves.

Manuel's conviction involved sex, but no child was involved, so he was not automatically fodder for the tender mercies of the inmates who were in charge. In his favour was that he looked younger than his nineteen years, so his youth spared him much of the usual Peterhead welcome. Once he settled, he seems to have generally behaved well. He was studious by the standards of others and often enjoyed helping some of them with their reading and writing. He wrote stories and had a talent for sketching. And, of course, he was the best barrack room lawyer amongst hundreds.

Left to himself, he appeared deep in thought, and probably was. Was he re-running the crimes he'd committed and experiencing remorse or satisfaction? But the only true measure of possible remorse is the nature of behaviour on liberation.

Inevitably, he had run-ins with prison officers, but in the early part of his time, nothing too serious. There was one incident, though, that stood out, when he reacted violently to an individual it was better to let have his own way. But instead of this foolhardiness leading to retribution, it brought a new-found respect, and it's said that a bunch of safeblowers – surely 'the cream' of Peterhead inmates in the 1940s – began to look after him.

In his imagination, he probably saw himself as Jimmy Cagney or Mickey Rooney and he certainly lied that he had won a Golden Gloves award in the boxing ring in the United States.

His gangster credentials were developing.

To start with, he was American, wasn't he? Even though his family had returned to Britain when he was a child, he was able to emphasise or extinguish an American twang, to suit. It's said that he boasted about his father being a mobster who met his end on 'Old Sparky' and there were dark hints of previous work for intelligence agencies on both sides of the Pond.

If he was in talkative mood, he had to be somebody – and somebody important. If he was not for talking, it usually meant trouble, his pent-up anger about his true self and about being locked up predictably boiling over.

The next piece of the gangster jigsaw is to show that they could never break you. When a box of knives went missing in March 1951, the Principal Officer discovered Manuel was to blame. In best Cagney fashion, he immediately admitted he'd stolen it, just for the hell of it. That he was dealt with leniently only further confirmed his view that he was well ahead of the game. Placed on rations of bread and water, his next step was to really show them who the boss was, so he attacked a warder, smashed up a cell, escaped into the corridor and destroyed as many bowls as he could before being restrained by several other warders.

His strength was said to be remarkable for such a small man.

Now he had made it.

He was somebody to be reckoned with – in Peterhead anyway.

Placed in isolation, he was given no recreation. A well-meaning Catholic priest spoke to him and quickly discovered he was irretrievably outside the pale of the faith.

A psychiatrist concluded he had a 'persecution complex', but a fellow inmate was probably closer to the mark when he said that Manuel was 'steeped in American gangster lore, and he seemed to realise he was sexually queer and there was nothing he could do about it'.

Another inmate – who was to turn against him when he saw what he was capable of in later years – wrote an article in the now defunct Glasgow *Evening Citizen* in June 1958, shortly before Manuel's execution. In it, he described meeting and quite liking him. He was earning 1/6d per week more than he was, as a blacksmith, and he spent less on tobacco than other prisoners, preferring to buy chewing gum, hair oil and toothpaste. He often travelled with him to and from the quarry near to the prison, when Manuel talked about the American underworld. He could apparently 'recite the lives of Capone, Dillinger and Baby Face Nelson'.

Dillinger too could be charming and he too convinced himself that he had been given a raw deal when he got his first jail sentence, which in his case was fifteen years. Dillinger wrote to his father that he had gone into prison a 'care-free boy' and come out bitter about it all. He was seen as a 'Robin Hood' to poor farmers in the Great Depression and he reserved his violence for policemen, FBI agents and bank clerks. Like Dillinger, Manuel died in his thirty-second year, and like Baby Face Nelson, Manuel was a five-feet-four-inch-tall psychopath.

Cinema crowds cheered when Dillinger was mentioned in news broadcasts in 1934 as Public Enemy Number 1, and booed when Federal Agents were interviewed about him. Today some choose to celebrate 22 July as John Dillinger Day.

PETERHEAD

As yet, no-one has felt the urge to nominate a Peter Manuel Day. He was let loose on society again in the spring of 1952, and for a while at least, there seemed to be a possibility of rehabilitation rather than revenge.

8

RELEASE – 1953

Against expectations, Peter Manuel gained full remission from his sentence.

The man in the street usually views remission as a treasonous act perpetrated by the prison authorities on a soft society – unless of course he's serving a sentence himself. The reality is that remission is given in exchange for good behaviour in prison which must continue whilst back in society, an incentive even for Peter Manuel.

By 1953 he was twenty-six and had developed a muscular frame, although he never grew taller than five feet four inches. His father, Samuel, managed to get him a job with the Gas Board, and for a while he worked with British Railways before returning to the Gas Board. For a budding Jimmy Cagney it was a bit mundane, but he kept his fantasies alive in various ways.

He could be polite and was always impeccably dressed and well mannered. He played piano passably, was said to have a good singing voice, and had an interest in astrology. He had a thing about gloves – beyond their usefulness at the scene of a crime – which others commented on. In pubs and clubs, he could be heard talking about crimes reported in the newspapers in a way that hinted he knew more about them than he could reasonably reveal, especially point-scorers like hold-ups or safe-blowings.

Murders others committed, curiously, were never commented upon.

He rarely swore, drank sensibly and looked after himself. He bought a typewriter and let it be known he was intending to become a journalist. And a direct method of boosting his ego was to become involved with the police again, this time as confidant. Subconsciously, he desperately wanted them to acknowledge his wisdom and worldliness – better still if they relied on him for help in solving cases.

To begin with, though, he went to Bellshill police office to complain to Detective Superintendent James Hendry about perjury by police officers at his trial in 1946. Hendry noticed a difference in him. He was more assured and his accent had become more refined. It seems that after serving a stretch in Peterhead, he had reinvented himself and become more polished and confident.

For Manuel, Peterhead was his university and his chosen subject was 'legal matters'. In his new role as someone important, he offered to 'play ball with them if they would play ball with him' and to provide 'information' about murders in Soho and Stirlingshire. He also gave the name of the perpetrator of the crimes – later found to be someone totally unconnected with them and someone he simply didn't like. On investigation, as the police were required to do, all the allegations disappeared without trace, although the pattern of blaming others and alleging perjury would be seen again at his final trial.

A good example of his need to impress the police – without appearing to want to – was later revealed by Detective Superintendent Hendry in a newspaper article after Manuel's execution. He said Manuel rarely looked him in the eye when they spoke but he was far more confident when writing.

When two men escaped from Saughton Prison in Edinburgh in 1955, they misguidedly sought help from Manuel, who advised them to shelter in a hayloft at Haughhead Farm near Uddingston. He then informed the police where they were and claimed his reward for 'performing a public duty'.

He then wrote a letter to Hendry which reveals just how much he wanted to be 'a big shot':

32 Fourth Street
Birkenshaw
Uddingston
20. 12. 55

Dear Friend?

I see in tonight's paper that you snared a couple of sleeping birds last night with the aid of a rather large perch.

It is quite possible that the two birds in question may feel (quite wrongfully) that I was the cause of their downfall.

Subsequently they may pass their opinions along the 'Grapevine'.

Therefore I feel it would be in the best interests of the public if you informed the Press that in the evening of the 21st of Dec you detained and questioned Peter Manuel for two hours on the strength of a tip you received implying that I had aided the two??

This will take care of a possible mistake via the grapevine and will ensure that any information I receive in future will be used as I already stated in the best interests of the public. Incidentally keeping these two characters locally situated cost me personally the best part of a fiver. I feel that I should not suffer a financial loss in performing a public duty, and anyway it's Christmas.

Yours Sincerely
P. Manuel

P.S. Seasonal feelings urge me to wish you a Merry Christmas and a prosperous New Year but honesty compels me to admit that I won't lose a great deal of sleep if you don't see another Christmas.

What else could he be hoping to achieve apart from acknowledged kudos? The suggestion that the police should inform the press, 'in the best interests of the public', that they had questioned him about the incident makes no sense whatsoever, but can be seen for what it is – an attempt to have the police do something he wanted them to do and, at the same time, have his name in lights.

He, of course, kept his criminal activities alive, although in relative terms, to a restricted degree. When acting as a shunter with the railways, he suggested to a criminal acquaintance that they should steal from some wagons in his care at a goods siding. The accomplice later recalled Manuel's insistence on emptying their pockets of anything which could be dropped at the scene which might give their identity away. He also mentioned his usual fetish for gloves. Manuel stood in his railwayman's uniform watching for the railway police whilst the wagons were looted.

He seems to have totally misjudged another job, though, when he tried to impress a safe-blower. He described a small safe in the railway office, but when they broke in, the expert realised that Manuel had allow free rein to his hyperactive imagination. The safe weighed half a ton.

Despite all of this, there was one lifeline to a normal existence – falling in love and settling down with a good woman. And he actually met her in 1954.

9

ANNA

It was one day in the summer of 1954 that Manuel first met a 'lovely wee bus conductress' at the bus terminus at the Mossend goods yard where he then worked. The third time they met, he asked her out. She had no difficulty in accepting the offer. He was soft-spoken, restrained and respectful. She was Miss Anna O'Hara and she came from Carluke, also in Lanarkshire.

The same criminal colleague who wrote about their night-time theft from the railway wagons described meeting Manuel that summer.

'He was dressed to perfection, and he was with a very attractive girl. I would have defied any judge of character to have seen in Peter Manuel a man who had served time in prison. He told me he was engaged or about to be to engaged to this girl. He did so with pride in his voice. He was obviously in love, and I was convinced that he had found the one who might persuade him to leave the criminal life.'

If that was right, there was one difficulty. He never told her about it.

Instead of revealing his past, he turned on his charm, and for a while it definitely worked. Since then, it's been a matter of debate whether he could have settled down with Anna, and if so, whether she was in any danger.

Oddly enough, the answer to both questions is by no means clear.

He could, of course, be very charming. The O'Haras were a close family and protective of Anna, and Manuel was under scrutiny.

At first he sailed through. At Christmas they exchanged presents and he was generous. The rest of the time, Anna and her mother were regularly given boxes of chocolates when he visited their house in Glenburn Terrace. He spoke very well, was serious and considerate. The family, and Anna, liked him.

The relationship developed and they spent all the time they could doing what courting couples in the Lanarkshire of the 1950s did – went walking, listened to the radio, went to dances and sometimes to the pictures. With his good singing voice, he could manage a passable 'Unforgettable' by Nat King Cole or 'Oh! My Papa' by Eddie Fisher. Other singing stars of the time were Tony Bennett, Perry Como and Al Martino, who sang 'Here In My Heart', a Manuel favourite.

They saw films like *High Noon* with Gary Cooper – the song 'Do Not Forsake Me' a hit for Frankie Laine, although Tex Ritter sang the film version – and *Singin' in the Rain* with Gene Kelly. That era also produced *The Big Heat*, *From Here to Eternity* with Burt Lancaster and Frank Sinatra, and *On the Waterfront* with Marlon Brando.

In 1950s Britain, most things American were cool, probably even more so than today. With his sweetheart beside him, Manuel's American tough guy persona must have empathised with Gary Cooper or Alan Ladd taking on the baddies.

Their relationship conformed to the times. A son or daughter would normally only move out of the family home if they worked away or got married. Naturally there was never any suggestion of sexual activity, and in Peter and Anna's case, that did actually seem to be the case. The couple became engaged on 20 May 1955 and a wedding date was set for 30 July that same year.

Throughout the courtship, he behaved particularly well. He even appears to have gone straight, by his standards. The old Peter was still to be found out there, though, in the dangerous world he inhabited.

One of his favourite haunts was the Woodend Hotel in Mossend. After the engagement was announced, he was with some associates and he told them how he'd fooled his fiancée into thinking she was wearing the ring she'd wanted. In the jeweller's, she noticed one that she said was lovely but too expensive, so he made a show of insisting she got it. Before she actually got it, though, he bought a cheap imitation, gave her that and returned the real one to the jeweller's. Even if he was indulging in a bit of macho bragging and had actually bought her the expensive one, it was still demeaning.

His 'them and us' approach clearly extended to including Anna, though. She was safe in his company, was treated well and had no real reason to suspect the monster within. Peter Sutcliffe, the Yorkshire Ripper, exhibited the same dichotomy – his wife and relatives genuinely appear to have had no idea about his horrific extra-mural activities. And they did not seem to be in any danger either.

Maybe he hoped that Anna would be as understanding as Bridget, his mother, was about past misdemeanours. Even so, how was he to break the news of his criminal past to her?

Previous commentators have concluded that the anonymous letter Anna received about him was also sent by him, and was no more than an exercise in attention seeking. They could be right, but there was more to it than that. The letter said he was American by birth, had travelled to Russia with the Secret Service and that his real father had been executed in the electric chair. After she burned it, she mentioned it to him. He made light of it and said not to worry about it, as he knew who would have sent it.

On another occasion, when she asked about the rumours that he had been involved in serious criminality, he said his brother was the one who had been in trouble, and they were always being confused with each other.

What was he trying to achieve? He undoubtedly wanted to marry her and there was no way round it – she would find out about his past. What better way than to break the news in a way that exaggerated and obscured the facts? He employed this tactic in his court cases to mix up fact and fiction and create doubts. He may have been hoping that they could go ahead with their plans with Anna thinking, 'yes, there's something in his past, but I'm not sure what to believe any more.'

Ironically, it was not because she discovered his criminal past that Anna O'Hara did not marry Peter Thomas Anthony Manuel, although it was a factor. The main reason was religion. Or Peter's lack of it.

His family were Roman Catholic too, but he had long since given up any pretence of practising. To the O'Haras, it was crucial that their daughter's intended was able to partake of Communion at the forthcoming Nuptial Mass, something which required him to have confessed his sins. As he had not been to confession, that would have meant another sin was added to the list. Moreover, he refused to go to confession rather than simply pretend, which is interesting, since he was prepared to be cavalier with the truth in most other circumstances. He might even have gone through the motions and done what was required to keep the family happy, but that he did not suggests that he still had some regard for religious truth.

The consequences were, at first, predictable, and the engagement was called off. He sent presents to Mrs O'Hara but to no avail. Anna had decided and that was that. He had lost out because of her doubts about him. Whether an excuse or not, she decided they could not marry because he failed to meet the accepted practices of the religion they ostensibly shared. And from there, he rapidly gave up on any notion of social compliance with a view to settling down.

The same criminal associate who had seen him at the start of his happiness with Anna saw him after it had ended. He was drinking alone in the Woodend Hotel. He had on his railwayman's uniform and he needed a shave, something no-one could normally have said about him, even in Peterhead. Before they headed off to steal again from the goods wagons, he asked him about his romance. Manuel sounded bitter. He said it was on the rocks and he said something else, too. 'You're better off keeping away from women, they would get you hung!'

10

ATTACK ON MARY

For 30 July 1955, there was one entry in Peter Manuel's diary: 'On this date Anna and Peter will be united in holy matrimony.' This was discovered after he was arrested for abduction and indecent assault.

The date of the crime was 30 July 1955.

In 1955, there were people like John Buchanan in every town. He ran a small wooden store at the side of the road near to the Manuel house in Birkenshaw. Mr Buchanan lived in a 'caravan' beside the store.

Another who lived near to the Manuel house was twenty-nine-year-old Mary McLachlan. On 30 July, Mr Buchanan was at home and Mary was coming home from a failed rendezvous with friends at a dance in nearby Blantyre.

Sometime about 11 o'clock that night she made her way into the lane called Lucy Brae. Although it was a summer's night, it was dark, but as she was to prove, Mary was a girl with nerve and composure when it mattered.

Peter Manuel sat brooding at home that night, until he suddenly got up and left the house. He had a knife this time. He waited until she walked by in the darkness, then he sprang out and covered her mouth with his gloved hand and pushed the tip of the knife to her neck.

She had nearly made it home.

Manuel growled at her to keep quiet and to keep walking. She tried to frighten him off, saying her husband was just behind her. He countered the bluff. 'You're by yourself, I know 'cause I followed you.'

He made her climb over a barbed wire fence into the field near to Mr Buchanan's store. She cut her leg and finger and this time she shouted for help. He warned her that if she did it again, he would cut her head off. But this time he said it in such a way that Mary fully understood the situation. He definitely meant it. She was now in the worst-case scenario – rape then murder was her expectation. Even a quick-witted woman like her has a breaking point, and she started sobbing and asking him to let her go.

He punched her on the mouth and cut her lip.

The alert Mr Buchanan had heard her cry for help and not only had he asked someone to go for the police, but he had started to search with a torch, and others joined in. Then two policemen arrived to search the area. They discovered a young couple and when they enquired, they said that they had heard the screams as well. They searched to within a few yards of where Mary lay with Manuel firmly holding a knife against her throat, then they gave up. It was decided that it maybe had been the young couple fooling about, after all.

All the others searching gave up too and one by one they returned to their homes, unwittingly leaving a terrified woman to her fate.

She wasn't to know, but the necessary excitement process for Manuel to achieve satisfaction had begun with them lying together in the field. He had seen the torchlights and he had again warned her she would 'get the knife'. She lay in fear and silence for more than an hour, and as the searchers' voices tailed off, she gave up hope, on both counts.

She was now at his mercy.

As he graphically outlined her fate – her head was to be severed and buried – he groped under her clothes and forced kisses on her. His eyes bulged and his mouth contorted in pleasure as he growled his threats. She sobbed pathetically and pleaded with him, pretending that she had children who would miss her.

Suddenly, he stopped.

She thought the reference to her imagined children had struck a chord with him.

She was wrong.

It made no difference to him then, as it had made no difference on 3 March 1946 when his victim actually had her child with her. All that had mattered was that he had vented his anger and lust by a crescendo of terror, and she had unwittingly played her part.

He stopped groping her and sat back.

His attitude had changed.

She now had to assess her situation, and she was intuitive. The first danger seemed to have passed – she had escaped rape, though his grabbing her and his vile talk had been bad enough. The next worry, being realistic, was that he would now have to carry out his threat and that her body and head would be separated and buried where they were.

Meantime she sat in abject silence, shoulder to shoulder beside this maniac with the knife. It was over an hour later when he next spoke, and she immediately noticed something else – his accent had gone from put-on to local.

To her great credit, she tried to regain some control of the situation, and she suggested that she go home. A real gamble. He could easily now reward her insolence by carrying out his threat. Instead, he told her she was going to have to stay there all night. A partial success then. At least he had moved on from the decapitation scenario.

Her true mettle emerged now. She sensed she might talk him round. Look, if you're in trouble, I might be able to help.

He waited awhile, then said he had been drinking and had lost control and felt he had wanted to murder somebody.

Had wanted.

She gained courage.

And Manuel started to talk, like only he could.

He gave her the truth as made up by Peter Manuel, a mixture of fact and fiction twisted to suit and put him in a better light. He said he was to be married that day but that his intended had called it off the day before, causing him to feel he wanted to murder somebody, so he got a knife. He then decided to drown himself instead. At the banks of the Clyde, though, he went off the idea as he remembered he could swim! He had seen her and she bore a strong resemblance to his fickle fiancée, but he would not have done anything to her if her hair had been a different colour.

In other words, it wasn't his fault, but he had been let down by a cold-hearted lover and had been driven to near – but not actual – suicide. As she had looked like the treacherous fiancée, he had no option but to do as he did.

So it was actually Mary's fault. And again, not his.

He asked if she knew him. She had to be careful again, and said no.

He asked her name and she gave a false one.

He asked where she worked and when she told him, it could have gone fatally wrong for her. He mused that they must therefore travel on the same bus in the morning, which was true, and after she refused his offer of a cigarette, he lit one himself and in the light of the match, she knew who he was, though not by name.

She felt relief as he told her he wouldn't now be on the Monday bus, after what had happened, but her terror rekindled as he lazily reached into his inside pocket and took the knife out again. He looked at it for a while as Mary considered she now knew too much to be allowed to live.

She was not to know that she was about to become the last of Peter Manuel's victims of violence who would be allowed to live to testify.

He toyed with the knife, then, amazingly, threw it into the under-growth on the railway embankment they were beside, saying, 'There, it's away!'

At last she could relax a bit more and she asked if she could go home, and – as only he could do – he asked her if she wanted him to see her home!

They got up and started back over the field, and he asked if she was going to report him, because if she was, he would go with her to the station – you see, he hadn't done this sort of thing before!

She coolly informed him to forget it, just as she was going to.

Like a genuine couple, they parted at First Avenue, she going home to Third Avenue and he to Fourth Street, Birkenshaw. When she made it home, she broke down and told her mother and sister what had happened. It was after three in the morning and there would be no sleep for any of them that night.

For Mary, the indignity of indecent assault and the terror of knife-point threats and violence were over, and she had survived.

But it was to be the start of a new, forensic, ordeal.

And again, it was Manuel in control.

11

ACQUITTAL AT AIRDRIE

All things considered, Mary McLachlan had no option but to go to the police. The only remarkable fact was that she didn't know exactly who her attacker was or know about his reputation. After all, they lived close to each other and often saw each other on the way to work.

A policeman went on the Monday morning bus with her and only Samuel appeared, but it was enough to confirm the identity of the suspect.

At the locus of the crime, they found the knife, with his finger-prints on it where she said it would be, and that night Manuel was picked out at an identification parade, then charged and remanded in Barlinnie Prison.

Initially, he offered an alibi, using the details of a real incident and changing the date. At the time of the allegation, he claimed he was with a woman in a pub in Uddingston and then he spent the night at her house.

The lady confirmed his story in every detail except one. His overnight stay was definitely on 23 July rather than 30 July. The reason she was so resolute in her memory being correct was that her husband was home on 30 July, but not on 23 July.

So much for that line of defence.

The case was gaining strength, particularly when blood of Mary McLachlan's type was found to be on his clothes.

The week before his trial, he wrote to the Procurator Fiscal at Airdrie to inform him his intention was to defend himself.

In typical Manuel jargon, he wrote:

My solicitors have informed me that they have notified you that I no longer desire them to conduct my defence. I hereby give you formal intimation that I intend to conduct my own defence. I was interviewed today by a member of the office staff here, and he informed me that the Sheriff Clerk at Airdrie has cited three people to appear on my behalf to appear as defence witnesses. I am also bringing forward my mother, Mrs B. Manuel, as a defence witness.

Since my pleading diet I have been informed that one of the Crown witnesses has made an open and public statement that implies perjury.

However, as perjury can only be committed under oath, I shall have to await trial and see what develops. I give you this information before the trial that it may be clearly established that there has been no collusion or complicity on my part.

I would also request permission to interview my witnesses before trial commences.

Yours sincerely,

Peter T. Manuel

Evidently, the accused man who had been arrested the day after the crime and had come up with a false alibi was now anxious to see justice done!

Today, in cases of a sexual nature, an accused is barred from conducting his own defence, but not then. When the trial started on 17 October 1955, he therefore had the added thrill of personally cross-examining his victim, who gave her version of events and then stuck to it. He managed to score a few points over the police who had initially searched for the distressed woman, and sympathy from the jury for the party defender started to grow. The store owner, Mr Buchanan, stayed on after giving evidence and noticed them warming to him, as he gestured and hammed it up. One of the police said they were in plain clothes and the other said they were in uniform, and the jury enjoyed the spectacle of the underdog confusing the professionals.

What he then had to do was concoct a story to fit the facts. No difficulty there for a man with his prodigious imagination.

The next problem was to get his story to the jury without having it destroyed by the prosecutor in cross-examination.

Again, there was a way – and he seized it.

Of course, the purpose of cross-examination is to put your case to the witness where it differs from his version. Using his experience from defending himself before, he knew that the judge allowed latitude to party defenders, particularly in front of a jury who might react badly to an unrepresented accused being railroaded by professional lawyers.

His plan was to miss out the awkward bit – where the witness has an irritating habit of disagreeing with your version of events – and to somehow blurt out his version without taking the oath. His letter to the Procurator Fiscal showed he knew exactly what perjury was, namely telling lies on oath, so he would have to get round that, which he did by electing not to give evidence, but to continually make *ex parte* statements to the jury when addressing them at the end.

In other words, he could put an alternative case forward without being asked about it and without it being properly tested.

Despite well-founded objections by the prosecutor, the Sheriff allowed him to tell his version of events. He told the jury that he knew Mary and that they had been going out together but had a fall out. They met earlier on 30 July than she had said in her evidence and in the course of an argument he hit her and cut her lip. He apologised and they immediately made up then she went with him to check on rabbit snares he had set, but she had cut herself on the barbed wire fence. They sat down, he lit a cigarette but then saw Rusty, his Alsatian, was in danger of being struck by an approaching train, so he threw the knife he had with him to attract the dog's attention.

All this should have been put to Mary in cross-examination, but was not.

It's not difficult to imagine how she would have reacted to the suggestion that they had been dating each other or that she had gone snaring rabbits with him and his dog.

Nowadays, the prosecutor could seek to lead 'evidence in replication' where evidence has actually been given, but this was not available in 1955, and in any event, he had not taken an oath to tell the truth. Had the jury been told that no trains ran between 29 July and 1 August, they would have realised the bespoke nature of his defence. As it was, they elected for the 'bastard verdict' of Not Proven by a majority.

Mary was inconsolable and now had to face up to a whispering campaign from the Manuel family and the spitting encounter with Samuel at the bus stop. She likened it to her being on trial and Manuel being the victim, and found that some neighbours shunned her and now believed she was a troublemaker. Within a few years, of course, all that was to change, but at least she had discovered who her friends were.

At the end of the trial, Manuel was patted on the back by his family and friends, members of the public applauded, and, to his eternal embarrassment, a police officer on court duty shook his hand!

No-one could stop Manuel now.

He was invincible and the authorities had better realise it.

And another thing.

In case he couldn't wangle the same non-perjury routine next time, it was better that witnesses were not in attendance.

Live ones, anyway.

12

THE EMBASSY, THE FBI
AND THE ORGANISATION

After his release from his nine-year sentence in 1952, Manuel bitterly complained of perjury and collusion by the police. It was to be the same old routine before his final court appearance.

In a psychiatric report prior to his 1958 trial, he denied all charges and said it was all part of a grand conspiracy against him by Lanarkshire Police. Being unable to trace the real culprits, it seems the uniformed conspirators met up and agreed to pretend it was Manuel who had committed eight murders, thereby allowing the real perpetrators to remain at large.

He pointed out that in 1955, despite legal advice to plead guilty, he defended himself and was acquitted, and since then, the Inspector involved in that case was out to get him. Presumably, the real culprit or culprits were still out there for the crimes of 1946, 1956 and 1957, and, of course, Mary McLachlan was just a girl with a problem.

As he saw it, the police force and he were out to destroy each other. He was convinced he would triumph, then the conspiracy against him would be revealed and the plotters would all be disgraced.

The psychiatrist reported that Manuel appeared confident, which is no surprise, and, with scant regard for punctuation, he noted, 'In the circumstances, therefore, I would not say that the accuser's accusations are of the character of insane delusions, but there is no doubt that his relations with the police have a highly emotional significance to him and, from his conversation one would almost think that his main object is to revenge himself on certain police officers and to humiliate them at whatever cost to himself and, although I do not regard the accuser's suspicions of, and accusations against, the police as delusions – because such ideas are not incompatible with the beliefs of men of his character and way of life – it did occur to me that in the case of the accused his suspicions of the police may have been magnified and distorted to the degree that these ideas came to dominate his mind so that they may have the significance of a paranoid system in which the accused sees himself in the role of a master criminal engaged in a struggle with the police which he confidently expects to win, and I thought it possible that his motive in some of his criminal acts might be the pursuit of self-satisfaction and aggrandisement.'

John Dillinger with a dash of Professor Moriarty.

Down the years, he had told some whoppers, but of course if you are going to lie, those are the best currency. Faced with egregious allegations of a police conspiracy, the jury might conclude that what he said in his defence was so outrageous it must be true.

The same psychiatrist recorded another incidence of his 'memory loss' condition. Manuel was far too shrewd to come out and say it, but he was obviously concocting a plan 'B' if convicted of the capital charges, along the lines of memory loss and diminished responsibility.

Whilst concluding he was 'sane and fit', the psychiatrist noted that he actually did believe that Manuel suffered from memory loss when he said he did!

Convincing the psychiatrist can be regarded as a pretty good start.

Manuel related the time in 1956 when he claimed he took a girl to the cinema to see *Richard the Third*. It was a Tuesday. When he next saw her, in his house, she was cold towards him and he asked her what was wrong. She told him it was because he had not turned up for a date on the Thursday, as he had promised to when they were out together on the Tuesday. He suddenly realised that he had no memory of either going to see the film or of the arrangement afterwards. He went to see it again and had no recollection of it at all, although he could predict the outcome of some of the scenes.

All very mysterious – until the girl he had named was asked about it and she said nothing of the sort had occurred. No visit to the pictures, no date and no huff.

He refused to be ordinary.

Amazing things had to happen to him.

On 7 December 1954, he went to the American Consul in Woodlands Terrace, Glasgow, ostensibly to enquire about American citizenship and about returning to the country of his birth. They knew nothing about him and he was plausible. To underline his importance to Uncle Sam, and to demonstrate his vicarious loyalty to the cause, he hinted at being privy to vital information about American national security.

His self-importance was boosted when they became intrigued enough to fly him to the American Air Base at Ruislip, near London. Interrogated by an FBI agent for three hours, he was easily caught out as knowing not a lot about America, let alone about her security in the era of reds-under-the-bed and McCarthyism (McCarthy had been the subject of a censure vote in the Senate only five days before). The best he could come up with was a fuzzy story about his involvement in a £40,000 gold bullion raid at London Airport in September 1954. The FBI listened to his story then summarily flew him straight back home. As an afterthought, they notified Scotland Yard he was some kind of fantasist who might be able to help them with their enquiries about the bullion raid. Quirkily, officers from there came to interview him at Ruislip after he had been flown out, and so it fell to Lanarkshire police to follow it up.

When he came into Uddingston police office, he was in best Hollywood mode, talking freely, if generally, about the bullion raid, but clamming up in traditional B-movie style when a notebook was produced.

In his mind at least, the authorities were dancing to his tune. He was someone.

He told police that after he had been released from Peterhead, a man approached him and told him he was impressed with the way he had behaved whilst serving his time, and he suggested that Manuel come and work for him. There was one important proviso, though – he was never to ask any questions.

He agreed and was immediately given £250, which had then been followed by £50 per month ever since. Letters started arriving from all over the world for him, but there was never any sender's address on them. They told him to carry out certain 'jobs'. Then one day, he got his orders to go to Euston Station in London and to wait to be identified in the buffet there. A French couple turned up and made contact – he sort of recognised the man, who was called 'Leon' – and they went to a house in Willesden.

'Leon' left him for a while with the woman, and when he returned in a black car, Manuel drove it to Feltham in Middlesex and parked it. A van appeared with four men in it and they transferred four heavy suitcases into the car. No-one spoke. 'Leon' then told him they were now to go to Liverpool, which they did. Once there, the cases were transferred into an American Buick and he was told they had to be at Stranraer early next morning. With Manuel at the wheel, they made it in time, of course, and another van met up with them and relieved them of the cases. He then drove to Carlisle and 'Leon' took over the driving and told him he now had to get himself home, which he did without being seen, jumping on the guard's van of a train and jumping off again at Law Junction in Lanarkshire. When he got home, he read about the raid and realised that that was what he had been involved in.

The police officer, James Hendry – who was listening to this story – couldn't resist butting in. Gently mocking him, he pointed out the unfairness of it all – Peter had driven them all over the place and they had abandoned him in Carlisle! It's probably indicative of his child-like nature, but Manuel – to Hendry's amusement – became earnest and confided that 'the organisation was like that – you just did as you were told.'

He then told of a meeting in Dublin where one of those present was found to be a traitor and 'the boss' walked in and shot him.

You learned not to ask questions.

Apart from the improbability of the police not being suspicious of a large, gas-guzzling, heavily laden Buick being driven about Wigtownshire in the early hours of the morning, there is an impression of Manuel watching some crackly black and white movie and transposing himself into the action.

Hendry marvelled at how Manuel coped with being found to be telling a pack of lies – he didn't mind.

Once he'd said it, it became fact.

Specifically, Hendry caught him out by the simplest of means. He checked the dates he'd been given and found that Manuel had been at work on all three days, but Manuel was not at all embarrassed he'd been rumbled.

At work, he told his workmates that he had been flown to New York with G-men whom he had helped trace a suspect to an airport and that he had then witnessed a gunfight in which the suspect had been killed.

In April 1954, three years after the country was rocked by the revelations about the spies Burgess and Maclean, Manuel told Hendry he had information about them. Arrangements were made for the Special Branch to interview him, but in the course of it, they quickly discovered that their would-be informant lived in a world with a population of one.

In another incident, after a bank raid in Ibrox, Glasgow, in July 1955, the detective in charge received a call to say that the brains behind the raid was a Peter Manuel from Uddingston. The detective phoned Hendry, asking if he knew of him. Hendry asked if he knew the source of the information, and when he found out the call had been anonymous, he told his colleague not to bother about it, and explained it would have been Manuel who had gone to the trouble of putting himself in the limelight.

When this was later confirmed by Manuel, there was no sign of remorse, self-consciousness or humiliation. It's little wonder that the real underworld had no time for him, and he only made it worse by trying to impress them.

Add that to his sexual violence and his war with authority, and you have the build-up to a fatally explosive finale. If the world hadn't realised by now that Peter Thomas Anthony Manuel was a man of influence and power, then he'd just have to go out and prove it.

Each innocent death was designed to precipitate a showdown with the police.

If they were up to it.

13

ANNE KNEILANDS

On 5 January 1956, the newspapers reported a break-in at a store in Ballachulish in Argyllshire the previous day, where three raiders had stolen a safe containing £1,000 before driving north. The police at Fort William gave chase, the car was abandoned and the occupants made for the hills and escaped. An RAF Mountain Rescue team joined the hunt, temporarily, before they had second thoughts and eccentrically decided that a Sheriff's warrant should authorise their involvement. When that failed to materialise they returned to base, ending a truly surreal night in the Western Highlands.

It was just the sort of fanciful scheme Manuel would have loved to brag about being involved in, particularly as the abandoned car was a black Buick. In fact, if he had not returned to work on 4 January, it might be imagined he actually had something to do with it.

Plainly, though, he did not. But two things are certain. He definitely did return to work on 4 January. And he had obvious fresh scratches on his nose and right cheek.

On Thursday 5 January 1956, the newspapers reported a brutal murder on East Kilbride golf course, Lanarkshire. It was quickly termed the '5th Tee Murder', and in the manner of the day, it was also reported that the girl had been 'criminally assaulted', meaning that apart from being brutally murdered, there was a sexual element to it.

The victim was a seventeen-year-old machinist from nearby High Blantyre, who had been missing since the evening of 2 January and had been found at 3pm on 4 January. Her name was Anne Kneilands, she was five feet ten inches tall, fair haired and the second eldest of six children. Her workplace was a factory in Howard Street, Glasgow and her little corner there was decorated with a picture of Glenn Ford, to which Anne had embroidered tinsel round the frame.

She had been very much looking forward to the break at Christmas and New Year. Her family knew she was going out on the Monday to keep a date with a man she had met at a dance in East Kilbride Town Hall the previous Friday. Her sister Alice had also been at the dance and she was able to describe him. The would-be date was now under immediate suspicion.

The girls had danced with two men in particular, and at the end of the dance, the men had seen them home. Alice had been escorted by a James Harrow and Anne by Private Andrew Murnin of the Parachute Regiment, based at Aldershot, but home for the festive season. Anne later told Alice that she and Andrew had agreed to meet again at Capelrig bus terminus at East Kilbride at 6pm on the following Monday, their intention being to catch the 6.15pm service which ran from East Kilbride to Glasgow. Anne must have had doubts about it, as she told her sister she would come home 'if he didn't turn up.'

If only she had.

She stayed at home the entire weekend and left for her date at about 5.20pm on the Monday. When he failed to show up, she decided to catch the next bus at 6.45pm, probably hoping he was late rather than forgetful.

In the meantime, she went to visit family friends called the Simpsons at Capelrig Farm. There were seventeen children in the family, ranging from a girl aged eighteen to twin boys aged eight months. Mr and Mrs Simpson had both been married before and had imported no fewer than ten children from previous relationships before adding a further seven of their own.

Anne spent some time in the house and told them she had missed her bus, but was going to catch the next one. Mrs Jean Simpson recalled Anne leaving at 6.40 that night, in time to catch the bus at the stop nearby.

Anne did not tell any of the Simpsons that she had been stood up, and for a while after her body was discovered, police were unsure of her movements. They initially worked on the assumption she had gone dancing anyway, and the following Friday, dancers at the Co-operative Hall in Blantyre were treated to a detective taking over the microphone and interrupting the dancing with a plea for information about what she had done when she left the hall on 2 January. The dancing then resumed with a quick-step as police waited for witnesses to come forward. They failed to do so – for one extremely good reason – Anne was never there on 2 January.

Police, however, had followed up an alleged sighting. Someone said they had seen her dancing with a tall, heavily built man on the night of the 2nd, but when this was investigated, the gentleman in question was found to be innocently dancing with his wife, who resembled Anne. They later also established that Anne could not have afforded to go dancing anyway, having only a pathetic four pence in her purse when she left home.

Obviously, her date was going to have to pay them in to the dance.

When traced, Andrew Murnin was quickly cleared, having celebrated Hogmanay in traditional style and failed to meet with Anne. He could account for his every move, mainly because he was with friends and family, and on 2 January he had returned home from a friend's house at 7pm and stayed in for the night. In fact, he had drunk too much and gone to bed.

Anne's parents had gone to Glasgow on 2 January and they were not unduly concerned when she did not appear that night as she could easily have stayed at a friend's house at that time of year. The next day, however, they began to worry and by the 4th they reported her missing.

Later that same day they were told the terrible news, their agony complete when they realised they must have driven by her body on their way home from Glasgow on 2 January.

What Anne did and why she did it can now never be known.

Maybe the last thing a disappointed young girl is going to do is come straight home to face the inevitable barrage of questions leading to the revelation that someone simply forgot to turn up to meet her.

Pride was undoubtedly at stake. She was not streetwise, and had been out aimlessly passing time, unaware of her world having people like Manuel in it, or the awful danger she was in.

There were sightings of her on the bus and outside the Willow Cafe in East Kilbride, which was closed. She obviously did not want to go home, despite the cold weather. The police had no real leads and they quickly eliminated all of the Simpsons, fourteen of whom had obliged by being at home the night Anne called.

Detectives also had to check a story from two children who were returning from the cinema when they noticed that a man who had boarded their bus at Clarkston Toll in Glasgow – not particularly close to the murder scene – was not wearing shoes. They described him as 'tall, thin, having black hair with grey streaks' and his light grey suit was 'covered with dark stains'.

What film had they seen?

The body had been discovered at 3 o'clock in the afternoon of 4 January by a George Gribbon, who was in the habit of walking on the golf course with his dogs and passing the time looking for lost golf balls. At first he thought he had seen someone lying sunbathing in a little hollow in the ground, an improbability at that time of year and on very damp ground.

When he got closer, he found out the awful truth. Anne's skull had been broken into pieces, a further fifteen of which were found at another spot.

He hurried to phone the police at a nearby farm. On the way he told some road workers and they too went to the scene then phoned the police as well.

When the crime scene was examined, it revealed a truly horrific scenario. The tall elegant young victim had been remorselessly hunted down by an older man six inches shorter than she, but with a strength borne of sexual frenzy. She must have been petrified when she first realised his intentions, and she ran for her life down a steep embankment and up the other side, leaving a ballet-type shoe embedded in the mud.

Even with the passage of time, her last hours can be pieced together. Excited about her date, she left the house with virtually no money but with obvious expectations of dancing and had put her dancing shoes on, little realising that she would be pursued across a muddy field.

After losing her right shoe in the chase, she had run into barbed wire in the darkness, which had caused multiple lacerations, then she had lost her other shoe before being caught and brutally finished off. She had eventually run in abject terror across a muddy field for hundreds of yards in her bare feet, as evidenced by bare footprints in the mud.

Given that police thought she was dancing at the time, they did not at first realise the significance of what a Hugh Marshall had heard at about 8.40pm on 2 January. He had been walking his dogs and was at a fence at the side of the golf course in Maxwellton Avenue when he heard the sort of noise someone would make when being struck, an 'Oh!', which he also heard a second time. He later took part in an experiment where a police officer blew a whistle at various parts of the golf course, and he seemed to pinpoint the murder spot as the likely source of the noise he had heard.

There could, however, be no doubt where the murder had occurred. The ground there was saturated with blood and littered with pieces of skull, but the body was found at a different spot, inclining police to the view that her killer had either spent some time beside the body before moving it, or had possibly returned and moved the body to a more secluded spot.

And to take satisfaction from his brutality.

Another Manuel trait was that her underwear had been torn from her as had a stocking, but there was no physical evidence of sexual interference.

And of course he had scattered her meagre possessions around the area, possibly to try to outwit police, but more probably on account of some strange compulsion. Her blood-soaked headscarf, her watch, an earring, some beads and a French five centime piece were found in different places, and 340 yards from her shoes.

At a loss to explain what weapon had caused the injuries, the police took a tree stump from the scene on the basis that it might have been used. With Manuel, though, there's always a twist.

On 4 January, thirteen-year-old Elizabeth Simpson was using a shovel to clear up ashes at the back of Capelrig Farm when she found a purse which had metal spools in it. It was Anne's and was recognised by Mary Simpson.

Why had he put it there?

Perhaps he had stalked her from when she left the farmhouse that night and after the murder he returned to leave it there to try to focus suspicion on someone inside.

She may even have told him she had been there.

In his confession two years later, he claimed they had met and spoken and that she had insisted they walk home along dark roads.

In his eyes, people like Anne Kneilands asked to be victims.

14

MANUEL IN THE LIMELIGHT

Rather than enjoying a quiet stroll with his dogs and perhaps coming across a few lost golf balls, Mr Gribbon's afternoon had gone somewhat awry. After rushing to Calderglen Farm and contacting the police, he had been administered the age-old panacea of a strong cup of tea. The police had gone straight to the murder scene, and it seemed logical they should now want to speak to Mr Gribbon.

At that time, East Kilbride was rapidly becoming a 'New Town' and part of the 'Glasgow overspill'. Today the area bears little resemblance to the layout in 1956, though the spot where Anne Kneilands was slain has not been developed.

A policeman traced Mr Gribbon to the farm and took a statement from him as he finished his tea. Proper procedure initially demands that no-one is ruled out, and the unfortunate walker who finds a murder victim is necessarily subjected to subtle scrutiny. Like Mr Murnin and the entire Simpson clan, Mr Gribbon was briefly suspected but then seen to be totally unconnected to this vicious crime.

Experienced police officers trawled through their list of potential suspects, and Manuel was on it.

Apart from the scratches on his face, something else should have focused the enquiry on him. At that time, he was actually working alongside the golf course with a squad from the Gas Board, helping in the construction of the New Town. He must have privately basked in his secret knowledge as the awful story broke around him.

And then a chance presented itself for him to take centre stage.

Constable Marr, the policeman who was on his way to take Mr

Gribbon's statement, had stopped to speak to Richard Corrins, who was Manuel's foreman. Gribbon had originally told some workmen of his gruesome find, and the police officer was making enquiries of workmen in the area as to where he was now, so he described Gribbon to Corrins.

Listening in, the labourer standing beside the two seems to have concluded that the police now regarded Gribbon as a suspect. He asked Marr if the man 'didn't come quietly and started a fight, would it be alright to hit him back?'

The curious labourer was Manuel, and he was indulging in his compulsion of drawing attention to himself. Or was he laying the foundation for a later defence by gambling on the possibility that should the police charge him with the crime, he could protest it was only because he had made himself conspicuous by this remark?

Or, as previous commentators have concluded, was he simply the owner of a big mouth?

Constable Marr had no time to reflect on Manuel's peculiar request, and he went on to speak to Mr Gribbon, and matters rested there for the moment.

The police, though, were back at the site on Friday 6 January about a report of a theft of wellingtons from one of the workmen's huts, probably stolen by Manuel to keep the pot boiling. On the Monday, Constable Marr and another officer again spoke to Mr Corrins, the foreman, and again Manuel was powerless to stop himself from adding his twisted twopence-worth.

He approached them and gave them a fictitious account of not just him, but Corrins too – and he said this in front of him – chasing an unkempt, unshaven man from a partially built house. The sinister figure had quickly made off and avoided capture by these two right-minded and determined Gas Board employees, anxious to capture the wellington thief and bring him to justice.

The wellingtons were both left feet and of little use – but the fictitious story was helpful in focusing suspicion on its author.

Corrins said it was complete rubbish.

He went on to tell police that Manuel had been convicted of rape in 1946 and they now became interested in Manuel's movements on the night of 2 January.

On 12 January, ten days after the murder, Detective Superintendent Hendry called round to the work site and interviewed Manuel, and in a foretaste of future tactics, other officers co-ordinated simultaneous interviews with his parents. As ever, paternal loyalty came to the fore and in a clearly rehearsed party line, Samuel stoically informed police that his son had definitely stayed at home on the night of the 2nd, exactly the same story his son was telling Hendry.

Even so, Hendry himself later searched the house and took away the clothes and shoes Manuel said he was wearing. It had only been twelve weeks since Manuel's underhand forensic triumph at Airdrie Sheriff Court in the Mary McLachlan trial, and it was 1950s Britain. People had fewer possessions and clothes were clothes. Because of the McLachlan trial, the police were aware what clothes he owned, and a particular jacket and pair of flannels were now missing. In his father's presence, Manuel blithely lied that he had given them to a friend and did not want the police to bother him. Both knew it was a lie, and Samuel's involvement now becomes truly culpable; he could have said that his son was in fact wearing the clothes in question when he went out on the night of 2 January, and that when he came home he had facial injuries. He could also have added that the blazer and flannels were never seen again.

Samuel Manuel also knew that his son's claim that he had received the scratches in the course of a fight in Glasgow at Hogmanay was nonsense, but nevertheless his impulse was to cover up for his son and to ignore the increasingly obvious truth.

Astonishingly, twelve days after the murder, Manuel's stolen wellingtons tale appeared in the press. The *Scottish Daily Express* actually ran a front-page story on 14 January 1956, complete with a smiling picture of Manuel, headed, '5th Tee: Gas men lead police to a hut.'

The picture is interesting. It came from a previous photograph on file and had been cropped to miss out both the police car he was emerging from and the policeman standing beside it and clearly related to a previous arrest.

The story went on to say that a sawn-off pickaxe handle had been found under a hut used by workers from the Gas Board and that

Police were led to the hut after two gas board workers reported that a pair of gumboots had been stolen on Monday night.

The two were thirty-five-year-old foreman Richard Corrins and twenty-eight-year-old assistant mains layer Peter Manuel.

Peter Manuel of Firth (sic) Street Uddingston said last night: 'Detectives came to the shed and searched the area. They found the half pick shaft under the shed. None of the workers here had seen it before.

'Last night detectives called at my home and questioned me for four hours. The detectives said it was only routine questioning.'

Manuel was taking a chance.

That the photograph of him stares out from the page beside the story either means the police were playing him at his own game with the newspaper's connivance, or that he was never actually in East Kilbride on 2 January and was confident no-one could identify him.

Whichever it was, he certainly thought he had laid the foundations of a false trail and when he gave evidence twenty-seven months later, he couldn't wait to mention the article.

He also enjoyed a further little mind game in late 1957 as he was cruelly 'assisting' William Watt with solving the murder of his wife, daughter and sister-in-law. Watt's solicitor, the renowned Laurence Dowdall, had agreed to meet Manuel as he claimed that a man he knew had confessed to the crime. In the course of their discussion in a Glasgow restaurant, Manuel casually produced a photograph of Anne Kneilands, so that Dowdall would see it, and asked 'Do you know her?' Dowdall said he did not. Manuel then slowly tore it into little pieces and placed them into an ashtray.

He later did the same to Watt.

Why?

Did it give him extra pleasure to toy with Watt and Dowdall, and was he playing his favourite game of evidential brinkmanship? After all, tearing up a murder victim's picture does not amount to proof of involvement.

It does, however, give additional satisfaction to an aspiring serial killer.

15

THE KNEILANDS CONFESSION

With hindsight, it's puzzling that the police did not act on what they had. Manuel was working very close to the murder site and evidence at the crime scene suggested that the terrified young girl had been chased from the roadway at Maxwellton Avenue – where the Gas Board were working during the preceding days – down a road under construction, where she had lost her headscarf and an earring, before losing a shoe and coming to grief. Manuel was freshly injured on 4 January, some clothes he owned were missing – and he could not account for their present whereabouts – and he had behaved strangely when the police had first started their enquiries.

There was possibly an element of 1950s Dixon of Dock Green style fair-play, now gone from police thinking, that if his father was going to resolutely alibi him, then that was that. Even so, there remains a suspicion that they somehow failed in their appointed duty, even although they continued to search at and around the murder scene and even used a powerful magnet to dredge for possible murder weapons from the nearby river, charmingly called the Rotten Calder. If they had given up on proving Manuel's involvement, that fact was not for the public to know, and those critics of the enquiry have to accept that even with Manuel's later confession to the crime, Lord Cameron still regarded the Crown case as insufficient for the jury to have to deliberate upon, and directed them to acquit.

What we cannot fully appreciate in today's Britain, however, is the awfulness of having to decide whether an accused should be executed or not. Juries were often decidedly faint-hearted in that respect, and whilst no-one would remotely dream of applying that description to Lord Cameron, it has to be said that judges quite rightly needed to be extra certain of evidence leading to a pronouncement of doom.

At his trial in 1958, there was even an unexpected piece of evidence from one of Manuel's labouring colleagues from the Gas Board. John Lennan of Uddingston exchanged smiles with Manuel when he was asked if he could identify him in court, then confirmed he had noticed scratches on his face at about 5 o'clock on the evening of 4 January 1956.

The Advocate Depute then asked, 'Were they recent scratches?'

Mr Lennan answered, 'Yes, quite recent. It seemed to me as if the scratches had been inflicted by fingernails.'

Mr Lennan's expertise in that field appears to have been unchallenged.

When Manuel's freedom came to an end on his arrest in January 1958, he hand-wrote a confession to the crime, in the following terms:

On the first of January 1956 I was in East Kilbride about 7pm in the evening. At about 7.30pm I was walking towards the Cross when I met a girl. She spoke to me and addressed me as Tommy. I told her my name was not Tommy and she said she thought she knew me. We got talking and she told me she had to meet someone, but she did not think they were turning up for the meeting. After a while I asked if she would like some tea or coffee. She assented and we went into the Willow Cafe. I do not remember how long we were there but it was not long. When we came out, she said she was going home and I offered to see her home. She said she lived miles away and I would probably get lost if I took her home. I insisted and she said 'All right'. We walked along the road up to Maxwellton Road. From there we went along a curving country road that I cannot name. About halfway along this road, I pulled her into a field gate. She struggled and ran away and I chased her across a field and over a ditch. When I caught up to her I dragged her into a wood. In the wood she started screaming and I hit her over the head with a piece of iron I picked up. After I had killed her I ran down a country lane that brought me out at the General's Bridge at the East Kilbride Road. I do not know where I flung the piece of iron. I then ran down to High Blantyre and along a road that brought me to Bardykes Road. I went along Bardykes Road and over the railway up to where I live. I got home about 10.15pm. I went up to East Kilbride from Hamilton about 6.30pm in the evening.

Leaving the circumstances of the giving of the statement aside, it is a mixture of improbability and known fact woven together in such a way as to suggest that Anne had virtually invited her own demise.

Would she really have gone up to a man twelve years her elder and mistaken him for someone else? Would she have persisted with her misidentification, saying that she thought she knew him, and then volunteered the information that she was meant to meet someone, although it looked like they were not coming? She hadn't even told Mrs Simpson.

The press coverage would have given him the fact of the failed meeting, and possibly even the Willow Cafe episode, but two things stand out; she assented to go to the cafe – not agreed.

Manuel in lawyerspeak.

Secondly, he claimed they actually went into the Willow, which was closed from 31 December to 4 January.

Here was he being too clever by half?

Anne then apparently compounded her foolhardiness by her surprising insistence that if he saw her home, she was concerned only that he would get lost on the way back!

So, all things considered, her actions were so reckless as to warrant what happened next.

After he pulled her into a 'field gate', she sealed her fate when she stupidly struggled and ran away, and when she started screaming it was evident he had no option but to hit her over the head with a piece of iron he just happened to have 'picked up'.

In his eyes, a fall-back defence, involving a reckless young girl prone to unjustified hysteria.

If the jury firstly accepted the statement was fairly made – a different argument, involving inducements about his father being freed in exchange for him writing it – they might decide it was flawed. After all, the cafe was shut, and he had specified the date as the first, not the second of January. If these bits were wrong, the rest of it might be too.

If neither of these strategies worked, they might very well decide she was guilty of contributory negligence – the empty-headed young girl being suicidally careless in her aimless wanderings that night. Anything could happen when he entered a courtroom and bamboozled witnesses and jurors.

As matters stood, he had experienced at least two notable victories against the police. Not only had he won the McLachlan case, he claimed to have triumphed against a charge of burglary in Blackpool in 1945, although no record of that seems to exist.

As 1956 wore on, he grew increasingly confident that he was exempt from the rules that govern other peoples' lives.

There was still much to do to balance things up, of course. The police still had to acknowledge they had tangled with the wrong man. He would not be content until he had gained revenge on them. Attacking ordinary members of society would underline the incompetence and powerlessness of a police force floundering in his wake.

With a reliable supply of off-the-peg defences from Samuel, he saw himself as invulnerable and unlikely to be convicted of any crime now, no matter how vile. Of course, his imagined admirers were not to know that his courageous all-or-nothing combat with the police was only really a symptom of the problems arising from his deep-rooted sexual difficulties.

16

THE COLLIERY CANTEEN CAPER

It might seem odd to ascribe such motives to a psychopathic serial killer, but one aspect of Manuel's behaviour which should not be underestimated was his need to be accepted by the underworld. Violence and crime were rife in many parts of Lanarkshire and Glasgow, and safe-blowing, bank hold-ups and illegal gambling were common. A London connection existed to take care of everyday matters from simple grudge beatings right up to assassinations. It worked on a quid pro quo basis. London gangsters would send someone to do a job in Glasgow and vice versa.

Razor-gang members were ten-a-penny and generally useless to the more organised criminals, because of their tendency to brag of their accomplishments if allowed into the big league.

Discretion was vital.

Manuel failed dismally on that score, boasting in local pubs about his real and not-so-real exploits.

He never really understood that crime bosses despised a show-off with a loose mouth, and it only drove him to be all the more extravagant in his claims, and thus further away from acceptance.

He had been a loner from the start, with some genuinely scary habits. His nightmarish hiding tactic – after he had broken into your house he stayed there – seems to have been perfected from an early age. At Christmas 1942, aged fifteen, he escaped from an approved school, and carried out a hammer attack on a school employee's wife before indecently assaulting her. Then he disappeared again, and for an entire week he hid behind the school Nativity scene during the day, emerging at night to scavenge for food and valuables.

A sex-offending gangster is also an anomaly, according to the code, so he was barred on that ground too.

Not only did he further distance himself from career criminals when he started shooting innocent men, women and children, but he now earned their genuine contempt, and they eventually and uncharacteristically did what they could to assist the police in snaring him.

He had cunning but not common sense.

Having seemingly survived intense police pressure in January 1956, he regarded himself as now worthy of proper respect in the right circles, and began to work with others in petty crime.

Time passed and people started to come to terms with the awful happenings of 2 January 1956, although the Kneilands family never could. The construction of the new town of East Kilbride continued and life went on. The police knew, but could not prove, that Manuel had killed Anne Kneilands, and he knew they were waiting for a break in the investigation. He seemed to imagine that other criminals were admiring his cat-and-mouse game with the police, and he decided to share his undoubted expertise at breaking and entering with fellow predators, which turned out to be a grave error for the would-be master criminal, and incomprehensibly naive. To date, trust had been a family experience, more particularly parental and to a greater degree paternal.

Unusually for him, he decided to team up with an acquaintance and break into a canteen at a colliery in nearby Blantyre. Somebody tipped the police off about the job, and they were waiting, with some satisfaction, to capture him in the act.

Just before midnight on 23 March 1956, their information proved correct when they saw two figures in dark clothes approaching, and they quickly moved in after the two were seen to try to force their way in. His colleague was caught without a struggle but Manuel took off and escaped.

Even with a tip-off, a fair number of officers and the element of surprise, he had proved as slippery as ever.

Except for one thing.

As he made off, he caught his clothes on a barbed wire fence and police were able to retrieve the fabric for a match, so the next stage was to wait outside the Manuel abode in Birkenshaw for the return of the prodigal son with torn clothes. This time they caught him and arrested him amidst the usual domestic protests of victimisation. He appeared the next day at Hamilton Sheriff Court, was granted bail and trial was fixed for 2 October 1956.

Awaiting trial, he revelled in the fact that he was able to take up a job on the nightshift at the very same colliery. After one night's work he had made his point and never returned.

Anyone else facing an inevitable custodial sentence might realistically view the intervening six months as an opportunity to reflect on where all this was taking them. Manuel's thoughts turned to the challenge society had offered, and if they were going to lock him up again, he was going to give them something to think about in return.

The clock was ticking and simple citizenship qualified you to a measure of Manuel's revenge; the closer in time to his imprisonment, the greater the danger. With the clear vision of hindsight, it is possible to identify the build-up of murderous likelihood, the major component being the approach of incarceration.

July 1956 was probably far enough away from the trial to place his activities in the 'mildly dangerous' category and at that stage, small-time theft and housebreakings sufficed. On the 28th, police received a call about two individuals acting in a suspicious manner at the back of a house in Uddingston and when they attended, both fled from the scene by leaping from a wall. One of them fractured his heel in the jump and was arrested, but Manuel had done it again and escaped, this time without a case against him, unless the captured man spoke up.

He was called Joe Brannan, and from that point on he played a major part in tightening the noose around Manuel's neck. Of course, at first he became the temporary custodian of extended Manuel family trust. Was he going to rat on him or not? Manuel sweated it out, still new to the concept of trusting non-blood-tie associates.

For his part, Brannan too represented the small-time operator hoping for a break into the big time, although he knew and understood the rules. The ultimate justification for any behaviour was that 'economic necessity' drove a man to hold up a bank or blow a safe. If a have-a-go hero got in the way, then it was acceptable to deal with that situation as you had to, up to and possibly including murder, although it was always to be avoided if convenient. Women and children were simply not in the equation, and murder for the sake of it was as mystifying to Joe Brannan as it was to Superintendent Hendry. Sure, he had heard the rumours about Manuel and how he had never gone by the rules, but without proof rumours remained rumours.

Behind the scenes the police scoffed at Joe's loyalty to Manuel. What did he owe somebody like that? He was a pervert. He was a killer of young lassies – she could have been related to you for God's sake man! He's as big a danger to you as he is to the rest of us – maybe even bigger, as you're teamed up with him now.

Brannan didn't crack.

Or that's what Manuel was led to believe, and the psychological battle of wits had started.

Manuel thought he'd done it again and got away with another minor victory against his hated enemy, the police. As October and a probable jail term approached for Manuel, both sides took stock. On one side, Lanarkshire Constabulary still had the unsolved Kneilands murder on their books, and in truth, must have realised that the chances of proving that Manuel was the killer were diminishing as time passed.

Against that, if and when their self-appointed adversary was safely off the streets for some time, it would at least allow some time to evaluate the best way to progress the case, particularly if the Joe Brannans of the world were redefining old allegiances and were prepared to actively assist them.

But Manuel always had the element of surprise, with the police only able to react to whatever his next move might be. By now, they knew what he was capable of, but his next outrage surpassed even their most cynical prophecies.

17

A FISHING TRIP GONE WRONG

The *Scottish Daily Express* for 25 June 1958 exclusively ran the first part of William Watt's story.

'Why Manuel Hated Me' described Watt's relief that Manuel's appeal had failed and that he was now definitely going to be executed. The article ran with a photograph which typifies why, to this day, there are dark hints of Watt's complicity in the horrific shooting of his wife, sister-in-law and daughter as they slept at home.

A mere twenty-one months after the murders, it shows a carefree, smiling older gentleman hand-in-hand with his obviously younger fiancée, Miss Lorna Craig. In the course of the trial, he had confessed to being less than the perfect husband, having succumbed to extramarital temptation more than once in the course of his marriage. In the style of the era, newspapers had latched on to that fact and made mention of Mrs Watt suffering 'poor health' – implying there might be some justification for his marital infidelity.

In post-war Britain, news editors felt compelled to offer an explanation for such mystifying conduct. The media also made much of Watt's supposed wealth, being the owner of a chain of bakery shops. But there was more to it than mere jealousy or moral disapproval.

In one of the most stunning investigative own goals ever scored in recent British criminology, Watt was charged with the murders of his wife, daughter and sister-in-law, eleven days after they had happened in September 1956.

He must have had an inkling of the authorities' forthcoming faux pas, though, when police frogmen appeared where he had been holidaying at the time of the murders, the Cairnbaan Hotel, near Lochgilphead in Argyllshire and started methodically searching the shallow waters of the Crinan Canal for a handgun.

Rumours of his guilt had escalated and a large crowd gathered a few days later outside Rutherglen police office in Glasgow when it was announced that 'a man' had been charged with the murders. The *Scottish Daily Express* reported that Superintendent Hendry, who had been working sixteen hours a day since the murders, came out of the police station and announced the arrest, then he went back inside to re-emerge ten minutes later to 'drive off in his shooting brake for tea'. It was also reported that Watt was inside the building, and that two constables were seen leading a whimpering black dog – they told reporters it was a stray – from the station to a pen on waste ground opposite. Official fiction was thus maintained until the next day, when William Watt appeared on petition at Glasgow Sheriff Court, the usual masses heaving and pushing outside. He was then remanded to the grim confines of Her Majesty's Prison, Barlinnie, Glasgow for sixty-seven days before collective sanity returned and he was released without any further procedure.

At his trial, Manuel milked this stunning misjudgement for its full worth and tried to bolster his defence by allying himself with the erstwhile view of the prosecution that for some unknown, unspecified and deeply puzzling reason, this otherwise caring and responsible businessman had driven overnight from the Crinan Canal to his home in Glasgow, slaughtered his nearest and dearest, then hurried back to continue his fishing holiday.

The authorities might also have reflected that the crime had occurred well within 'Manuel country' and that they now had two dangerous murderers living in the same patch.

At Manuel's trial, defence counsel cross-examined Watt, as his duty obliged him to in terms of Manuel's instructions, to the effect that he was the murderer of his own family.

Watt's responses were poignant.

In between bouts of tears, he described the deceased as 'my beautiful girls' and when pressed further to admit his guilt he famously shook his head and retorted, 'What a profession, what a profession!'

Indeed.

The same profession he himself had needed so much when he was arrested, and the same profession that had got it so wrong that he was locked up in the first place.

If convicted, Watt would undoubtedly have gone to the gallows in Barlinnie, probably relieved to take his leave from a society gone mad.

Posthumous pardons, however, do not resurrect the innocent.

So what, if any, was the excuse for the prosecution to get it so horribly wrong?

The Watt family had moved into 5 Fennsbank Avenue, Burnside on the south side of Glasgow on 13 July 1956, two months before tragedy struck on 17 September. The family had looked forward to moving into an area which was a step up the social ladder, and Mrs Marion Watt's health had improved following a heart operation. Vivienne Watt was sixteen years old, and like most teenagers, had strong views of her own. Mother and daughter had gone for a short recuperative holiday together and on their return, it was father's turn to take a break. As he done several times before, he went to the Lochgilphead area in his maroon Vauxhall Velox, taking his black Labrador, Queenie. His destination was the Cairnbaan Hotel at the side of the Crinan Canal, a particularly scenic spot and ideal for fishing. As well as his fishing gear, he had taken his shotgun. As a man with an unblemished past, and indeed having served as a police reservist, he had no difficulty in being deemed responsible enough to own such an item.

He left home on 9 September 1956 and drove the ninety or so miles along Loch Lomondside seeking a relaxing week or possibly two weeks' holiday. He wasn't to know that when he left that morning his life had changed for ever and his family's had all but ended.

In an effort to 'prove' Watt's guilt, a police driver was later able to demonstrate it was possible to cover the route in two hours four minutes, Watt having told them he usually took two hours fifteen minutes.

Fifty years after the event, it might be thought that technical advances in motor engineering and possibly more user-friendly roads – anyone who has driven Loch Lomondside or Loch Longside might question the latter proposition – would lead to a time reduction in the journey. On the other hand, the volume of traffic on the roads has increased hugely.

The Automobile Association website, though, tells you that the journey from Fennsbank Avenue, Burnside to Cairnbaan is 90.7 miles and takes three hours eleven minutes, abiding by the speed limits. It can only be assumed that covering the route in two hours four minutes in 1956 was achieved without technical mishap, which was something of a consideration in those days.

The police had used a Ford Zephyr for the test drive and claimed they had managed an average forty-five miles per hour. Anyone old enough to remember being in a car in the 1950s will, however, recollect continual breakdowns and puncture stops.

To carry out a well-planned triple homicide, Watt presumably had to act normally before the event, and he excelled at this. He spent the time fishing, meeting old friends, watching television in their houses and having a dram or two with the hotel owners, who were personal friends.

On 16 September, he filled his car with seven gallons of petrol and arranged for the local mechanic to have a look at the engine, which was not running properly. He also complained that the lights were flickering on and off, and it was arranged for the engine and wiring system to be properly checked the following day. It was an appointment he did not have a chance to keep.

Filling with fuel on that date could be a telling factor against him; postponing the rectification of the lighting and engine problem, though, suggests less than ideal preparation for a lengthy clandestine overnight drive.

He had phoned home to Stonelaw 4055 every couple of days, and on the 16th he did so again at about 10.30pm, speaking to his wife, Marion, who told him her sister, Margaret Brown, was staying with her that night and they discussed whether he should stay an extra week. Marion said it was up to him, and it was left at that. The only other call that night was made from Stonelaw 4055 to the operator asking for an alarm call at 7am. It was timed at 1.26am and was probably made by Mrs Watt.

Of the four who were in the house at the time of the incoming call, only one lived to tell the tale. She was the nineteen-year-old neighbour, Deanna Valente, who had spent the afternoon and evening with Vivienne and recalled Mrs Watt and her sister Mrs Brown sitting in the front room listening to records. The girls themselves had indulged in the well-known teenage ritual of the time of listening to the 'Hit Parade' on Radio Luxembourg late on Sunday night, with Vivienne leaving the house at about 11.40pm.

She later recalled that Vivienne had spoken to her father on the phone and after the call, she said, 'Oh, I am mad, Deanna, my father hasn't given me my money this weekend. He has promised to double it when he comes back.'

When a person is charged with a serious offence, the tiniest detail is often considered significant.

Could Watt, 'the ladies' man', have an additional motive for the crime by falling out with his daughter? Was he so mean-spirited that he 'forgot' to give his daughter her pocket money in order to save a shilling or two, and was his promise to make it up to her an empty one?

From the starting premise that he was guilty of killing his family, the police looked closely at what else they could 'prove'. He had sat up until 12.30am on the Monday morning, drinking with Mr Leitch, the owner of the Cairnbaan Hotel and a former colleague in Glasgow's Eastern Division police, then he let Queenie go for a walk before he went to his room, having – more in hope than expectation – announced his intention to get up at 6.30am to go fishing.

In a newspaper article he later claimed he had been drinking with

Leitch until 'about 2am', which certainly would have increased police suspicion, particularly as two witnesses, one being the local mechanic, claimed that they saw Watt at his bedroom window at 1am when apparently checking the weather before retiring to bed.

In order to rise early, he had borrowed an alarm clock from the kitchen of the hotel and set it to go off at about 6am. However, when he later told police he had switched it off, this was found to be wrong. He may have thought he had switched it off, but it seemed very much that he had simply slept through its ringing.

Or he simply wasn't in his bedroom when it went off.

He was next seen at 8.10am by the waitress from the hotel clearing frost from the car windscreen. He said he had risen at 7.30am to drive to the river he was later to fish – the Add, which runs near to the historic Dalriadic fort at Dunadd – to check how the water was running, before taking breakfast at 8.30am.

Suspicious?

When the news of the murders broke, two things happened.

The first was a disgrace.

A journalist phoned the husband of the murdered Margaret Brown. He was at work and did not know of the tragedy. The journalist asked him questions about where he lived and whether his wife was at home. Understandably, Brown did not give out any information, but was curious and went home anyway. When he came back to work, the tactless reporter phoned again, causing Brown to phone the police. He then found out that the police were coming to interview him and when he phoned Watt's brother, John, he eventually found out about the murders.

In all probability, it was the same dangerous hack who phoned the Cairnbaan Hotel at 11.20am claiming to be 'a business acquaintance' of Watt's. Mrs Leitch put it down to some sort of crank call when the 'business acquaintance' actually asked what Watt's first name was, at which point she hung up.

The second thing to happen was that Watt's brother, John, phoned the Cairnbaan Hotel about 11.30am and spoke to Mrs Leitch, giving her the terrible news about events at Fennsbank Avenue. She then sent a local taxi driver to drive Watt back to the hotel and when he was told of the murders he initially failed to understand what she was saying. Then, after a phone call to his brother's secretary, he broke down and wept, whilst others packed his belongings. Someone even polished his shoes as Watt changed out of his fishing gear.

Had Watt polished his own shoes, it would undoubtedly have added weight to the case against him, and it's not difficult to imagine headlines along the lines of 'Cold-hearted Killer Calmly Polished his Shoes'.

Watt resolved to drive the ninety miles home himself, but then sensibly decided against the idea and a local man drove him to Alexandria, taking him sixty-eight miles of the ninety, where a Sergeant William Mitchell – who took part in the timed driving experiment – from the Lanarkshire force, took over. During the first part of the journey, Watt tried to compose himself and succeeded to the extent of being able to attempt a smile on meeting the sergeant.

A terrible blunder.

Mitchell immediately became highly suspicious and reported that his expectation was to convey a broken man home and instead he met 'a man with a smirk on his face and no tears'.

Up to this point, no-one seems to have harboured any doubts about Watt's lack of involvement in the crime. After this, however, events avalanched.

He had been occasionally unfaithful, and it was now seen as an extension of such conduct that he had slipped out of the hotel sometime after 1am, bundled the dog in the car, started it, driven home, broken the glass at the front door to deflect the blame, executed all three within, then driven back to the hotel, keeping up a good average speed despite large banks of mist that night. He had presumably been content to run the risk of being seen, but on the other hand, fate and the elements had kindly supplied a layer of overnight frost on the windscreen of the Vauxhall on the Monday morning.

A risky business, you might think.

And the alarm clock told its own significant tale. After being returned to the kitchen, it had gone off, briefly, at about 6pm, twelve hours after being set to go off the first time.

Police then spent hundreds of man-hours scrutinising his domestic situation. Apart from admitted lapses of occasional unfaithfulness, there was nothing else of obvious concern.

They also tried to establish how he had managed to drive 180 miles without apparently lowering the fuel level. All garages in the area were checked to see where he had filled up and whether he had done it between 7.30 and 8.30am. Or perhaps he had a secret fuel cache, using cans? They searched all over the local countryside to find it.

They pushed a silent car on the gravel path outside the hotel to confirm that the noise could not be heard from Mrs Leitch's bedroom, which it could not. A few days later, frogmen dredged the Crinan Canal and searched for the murder weapon and bloodstained clothing.

Unsurprisingly, neither were found.

The clothing never existed and the gun was in a different stretch of water ninety miles to the south.

A spot of blood found on his hotel bed sheet became noteworthy and fitted neatly into the mindset of officers more and more convinced they were on the trail of a brutal killer. The theory seems to have been that he had driven back in the night spattered with his family's blood and a spot had somehow been transferred. Watt's explanation to his solicitor that he had cut a corn from his foot and that a small amount of blood must have come from there, started to sound like the unconvincing and desperate explanation of a murderer rightly brought to book by good old-fashioned sleuthing and intuition.

After a suspect has been charged, the psychology alters dramatically.

He now has to explain the evidence against him and cope with the 'weight of the prosecution', as represented by many citizens who sincerely believe that 'if he's in the dock, he did it'. Coincidental happenings and unconnected events magically transform into further proof, and in what psychologists call 'confirmation bias', 'evidence' is gathered which then substantiates the newly arrived at assumption of guilt.

From such origins, the case gained strength and it was reasoned that someone must have seen Watt in the course of his homicidal journey through the night. Police appealed to the public and suddenly found themselves with two seemingly solid nuggets of good hard evidence to present to the Procurator Fiscal.

And to the present day, both are still difficult to explain away.

18

WHO SAW WATT?

There has been a ferry service between Yoker on the north bank of the Clyde and Renfrew on the south for over 500 years. Today's ferries are light passenger-carrying vessels with room for one vehicle only – an ambulance.

The ferry service in the 1950s was a great clanking blue platform which crabbed its way across the Clyde, sometimes dangerously close to massive newly built ocean-going liners and warships, pulling itself on vast chains which then dropped behind it and settled back onto the sludge of the river bed. At certain times, it became packed with shipyard workers – to the exclusion of vehicles – anxious to get home. At other times, it was useful if your journey was from the north to Paisley or certain parts on the south of Glasgow and vice versa. The 'new ferry' ran day and night from 1952 until 1984, by which time new bridges and a tunnel under the Clyde largely undermined its value.

The thorough but misguided investigation which aimed to prove Watt's guilt led police to question everyone on all possible routes between Cairnbaan and Glasgow. Despite Watt maintaining he had not actually been on the Renfrew Ferry since the 1940s, and there being no great logic to taking that route, police checked anyway.

They struck prosecutor's gold.

The ferryman, John Taylor, said he could distinctly recall a lone male driver taking his car from Yoker to Renfrew at about 3am on 17 September 1956.

If Watt had left Cairnbaan at about 1am, it was near perfect timing.

According to Taylor, there was also a dog like a black Labrador in the car. He had noticed this when he spoke to the driver as he bought a ticket. This was an amazing break in the case, but would it stand up to the next test, that of identification? It did, spectacularly, and on all counts.

Taylor picked Watt's Vauxhall Velox out of a 'parade' of twenty-four cars and he followed that up when he identified Watt himself at a more conventional identification parade of nine men, saying he could have picked him out of a group of 100! Finally, he topped that by identifying Queenie as similar to the dog he had seen that night. The only unfortunate thing from the investigators' point of view was that Taylor had failed to note the car's registration number, something he often did in order to assist police trying to trace stolen vehicles. Had he done so, and Watt's registration number was on the list, Watt would surely have hanged.

When questioned by the police, then by journalists, Taylor said he was only telling the truth and that he had not seen any of the many pictures of Watt or his car in the papers.

There is little doubt that lack of motive for the murders baffled the police. That the truth was that a complete stranger had broken in and 'murdered for kicks' did not feature largely in the 1950s investigator's matrix. Safer to follow known behavioural patterns and spotlight the husband.

When Laurence Dowdall was engaged to represent Watt, he later wrote that another factor in Watt's arrest was that instead of quietly leaving the investigation to the CID, Watt 'fulminated' about the police being unable to catch the killer, and told anyone who would listen, including the ubiquitous journalists, that if the police couldn't do it, he would. The police began to resent him and members of the public began to dislike him, despite his loss. When he was remanded for the murders, Watt's misery was compounded by fellow inmates delighting in gesturing with an imaginary noose and shouting at him that he was going to hang.

When Dowdall investigated Taylor's statement, he told him that Watt was definitely the driver. The first break came, though, when

Taylor then told him that the car was definitely a Wolseley, not a Vauxhall. Indeed, he was sure of that because he could remember that when the lights of the car were on, the radiator badge lit up, a feature found on Wolseleys but not Vauxhalls.

The police appealed to anyone else, apart from Taylor, who could help and a Roderick Morrison told them an interesting tale. He was travelling north to Fort William with his wife and was on Loch Lomondside at about 2.30am on the 17th, when he noticed a car speeding southwards towards him. Again, the timing tied in.

The road was then notorious for bad bends and sudden dips. That night there were mist patches too, and Morrison was alarmed enough to warn his wife about the speed of the approaching car. Suddenly it disappeared and for a moment he thought it had crashed off the road. He then saw it parked at the roadside, its lights off. Lest the driver was in some sort of trouble, he stopped and approached the other car, which had one male occupant who was sitting smoking a cigarette wedged between his index and second fingers, the index finger crooked over the cigarette.

The man also shielded his face from the glare of the lights of Morrison's car with his other hand. Before he could get close enough to speak to him, however, the mysterious driver quickly switched the lights back on and drove off. Morrison thought that the car was either a Standard or a Vauxhall, and of course one explanation for the driver pulling over was that the lights had temporarily failed, the same fault Watt had reported to the local mechanic at Ardrishaig.

Morrison attended a thirty-strong identification parade and he requested that the participants hold a cigarette. He was then able to pick Watt out as being the driver on that misty fateful night, because he was the only one out of the thirty who held the cigarette like a pipe!

And anyway, why did the driver shield his face and drive away so suddenly?

Detective Superintendent Hendry had obtained a warrant to search Manuel's house shortly after the Watt killings, but with the evidence of Taylor and Morrison, the enquiry was now centring on Watt.

In a later article in the Glasgow *Evening Citizen*, entitled, 'I did not feel right about arresting William Watt', Hendry wrote, 'It is never a very pleasant task probing the movements and motives of people at the heart of a tragedy. But it is all part of a policeman's job, and I would like to make one thing clear in the public mind . . . Mr Brown [the brother-in-law] was investigated every bit as closely as Mr Watt.'

At his trial, Manuel lost no time in personally asking questions of Hendry, having sacked his counsel by that time.

He asked, 'Did you feel when you were arresting William Watt that you were arresting a man who had murdered his wife?'

Before Hendry could answer the question, Lord Cameron told him not to, on the basis that it sought to elicit an opinion, but in the article, Hendry was to write that his answer would have been that although the evidence pointed to Watt, he did not feel it was right.

On his release from Barlinnie, Watt asked to meet Hendry and, surprisingly, he agreed. Watt asked him, 'How does it feel to talk to a man whose life you tried to take away?'

Hendry, it has to be said, ducked the question with the clichéd reply that 'it was no part of a policeman's job to decide on a man's guilt, he merely collects evidence and seeks the truth.' Hendry also expressed the view that no jury would have convicted Watt, but that perspective is not only risky but dangerous. If a reporting officer has private misgivings about an accused's guilt, it's probably wise to keep them private rather than publicly suggest that it would have worked out well in the end thanks to the jury. Juries often convict in 'thin' cases. And there's no margin of error in capital cases, particularly after sentence.

Of course, Watt was never tried, but as a matter of fairness, the whole outlandish episode had to be explored at Manuel's trial.

What of the 'evidence' against Watt?

At Manuel's trial, Morrison had to concede that he never had a clear view of the face of the other driver, something he had never actually claimed.

Taylor, though, stuck manfully to his identification of Watt. By that time, however, he had altered his evidence from the car being a maroon Vauxhall to a red Wolseley, exactly as he had said to Dowdall. However, he lost further ground when his story changed to not really noticing the colour as much as a scrape on the car, mentioned, it seems, for the first time. In cross-examination, his position deteriorated further when he illogically claimed confusion and deafness had caused him to say 'Wolseley' when he actually meant 'Vauxhall'.

Even if Morrison was doing his best to stick to the truth, questions were raised about Taylor. It was suggested that his identification of Watt was 'just one of those things' and it was never really satisfactorily explained.

One possibility which fits all, of course, is that the Watt lookalike never actually existed and Taylor, like the rest of the population, did see newspaper reports and pictures of Watt and could easily pick him out as a result; if that was the case, he might also be in a position to identify a maroon Vauxhall Velox, and his performance in court was a sudden loss of nerve under pressure. If that proposition was extended, it might then be wondered why he failed to note the registration number of the car, as he normally did after 1.30am. He claimed that this omission was because he was not scheduled to work that particular nightshift, but why note car numbers at all, unless anxious to help the police?

Yet, at the time of the investigation into Watt, no-one appears to have had any doubts that Taylor was telling the truth.

The suspicious Sergeant Mitchell confirmed that Watt had said something like 'Do you think I did it?' when he told him it was best not to discuss it on the journey from Alexandria. As for the comment about the 'smirk rather than tears' on his face, he said Watt had said, 'I believe you're right,' and he had retorted, 'I know I'm right.'

The sergeant had, of course, been one of the officers who had conducted the test drive from the Cairnbaan Hotel. However, the route they timed did not include taking the Renfrew Ferry, which would actually add time to the journey, particularly if the ferry happened to be on the opposite bank at the time of arrival. Coming off the A82 and driving to the north embarkation point does not seem to give any logistical advantage, although Mrs Leitch agreed in cross-examination that you would take the ferry if you were going to the south of the city. A cast-iron reason not to take the ferry, of course, is to avoid contact with potential witnesses.

Watt would have known that the back door of the Cairnbaan Hotel could be left open at night, so he would have to have calculated that no-one was about as he crept up to his room on his return. As for him pushing his car away from the building prior to starting the engine, Dowdall claimed that even doing that made a loud crunching sound on the gravel. Arriving back, at say 6 or 7am, having completed the first part of the scheme, it would have been ultimately disastrous if Mr or Mrs Leitch happened to look out of the window to witness such eccentric behaviour on his return.

What if Queenie barked?

And what about the Glasgow end of the plan? Do you park in the driveway of your own house, or do you risk parking and returning to your car in the early hours of the morning in a built-up area, particularly if you are hitherto a normal law-abiding citizen deficient in Manuel's unique nocturnal cunning? Certainly, the police theory of Watt's guilt postulated he had parked the Vauxhall in a quiet street near to the family house.

By the very act of giving evidence for the Crown at Manuel's trial, Watt was automatically immune from prosecution, but by that time he had been cleared of involvement anyway.

By most people.

When Watt himself appeared at Glasgow Sheriff Court a few weeks after Manuel's execution, Dowdall tendered a plea of guilty to a charge of driving through the then notorious Gorbals area of Glasgow on 23 December 1957 whilst under the influence of drink so as to be incapable of having proper control of his vehicle. The solicitor explained to the court that there was no truth in the widespread rumour that Manuel had been in Watt's car that night. Sheriff Frank Middleton, whose reputation was that of a martinet anyway, disqualified Watt from driving for five years – this being his second such offence since January 1955 – and fined him £50.

In the course of passing sentence, the Sheriff had characteristically enquired why Watt had not tendered a guilty plea at the outset. Dowdall proffered an unconvincing explanation rather than admitting that the last thing Watt needed prior to Manuel's trial was more forensic fuel for Manuel to add to the glowing public debate about Watt's erratic behaviour.

19

ENTER DOWDALL

How would Manuel have reacted to the conviction and execution of William Watt? Previous commentators have agreed that he could not bear others to 'get the credit' for his actions, hence his approach to Laurence Dowdall to 'help' Watt. From that point of view, he would probably have been unable to simply ignore any court proceedings against Watt, and would have tried to inveigle his way into a starring role.

Alternatively, beating the serious crime system was getting easier for Manuel. They had failed to pin the Anne Kneilands murder on him, and when they did bring live witnesses, like Mary McLachlan, he was too smart for them. Then they obliged him by charging an innocent man with the murder of his own family.

He now had to demonstrate his total control, and in so doing, he brought himself into the limelight and, in his mind at least, taunted the authorities, Watt and Dowdall.

It's not hard to imagine that his primary motive in making contact with Dowdall was self-aggrandisement. He would be seen as heroically stepping forward as a defence witness at any future trial Watt might face, his knowledge of one man's innocence and another's guilt compelling him to act. Manuel would envisage himself giving evidence which mesmerised the jury – he said he liked ladies on the jury as he 'had a way with them' – after which he would be fêted as a dangerous but principled operator, regardless of whether Watt was acquitted or not.

Indeed, Watt's fate was of no consequence to Manuel.

Manuel had first made contact with Dowdall in typical style:

ENTER DOWDALL

Dear Sir, Last Tuesday, October 2nd, I was sentenced to eighteen months imprisonment in Hamilton Sheriff Court. Today I lodged an appeal and I decided I should like you to represent me. I wish to obtain Bail during the period as appellant and desire to have this accomplished with all urgency. I would like you to come and see me on Wednesday. The proposals I have outlined are to our mutual advantage, mainly due to the fact that I have some information for you concerning a recently acquired client, who has been described as an all round athlete.

Yours sincerely,

P. Manuel.

Dowdall attended as requested. After all, the author desired his wish for bail to 'be accomplished with all urgency'. He quickly realised that Manuel was fully aware that he had no prospect of a successful appeal, and that his real motive in writing was to talk about the 'all round athlete', the newspapers having described Watt as a one-time successful competitor in Highland Games.

When Manuel said he knew who had committed the murders, Dowdall considered the situation, then advised that he should tell the police.

Manuel's response was described by Dowdall as 'expressing profound disapproval of the police' in an 'inelegant copulative sentence of exactly three words.'

So how exactly did Manuel's path cross so poisonously with Watt's?

Retired sisters Miss Margaret Martin and Miss Mary Martin left their house at 18 Fennsbank Avenue, Burnside, Glasgow for a holiday in Wester Ross on 15 September 1956. Shortly after they left, Manuel smashed the glass panel of their front door, let himself in and turned the place upside down. He lay on a bed and dirtied it with his boots, before burning a carpet with a cigarette and pouring a tin of soup on another one. Manuel then stole a pair of nylons to wear over his hands to ensure a lack of fingerprints in his next venture.

Classic Manuel.

How did he know the owners were away? Perhaps he heard

people talk, or more likely he couldn't care, as he used the Misses Martin's house as a base to attack the Watts' house. He was already armed with his .38 revolver, so the ladies were indeed fortunate they were away and did not come back. He specialised in the defence-less.

When they were told of the break-in, the Misses Martin returned from holiday and eventually discovered that two distinctive rings were missing – in evidence, Miss Margaret Martin estimated that she had told police that fact on or about 20 September. Manuel later blamed another man for the theft and made a point about the timing of the knowledge of the missing rings, which was described by no less than Lord Cameron as 'shrewd'.

What is certain is that he crept out of number eighteen and over to number five in the early hours of 17 September 1956, smashed the glass panel at the front door, went into Mrs Watt's bedroom and shot her in the head as she slept. Mrs Brown, who had been sleeping next to her sister, he then killed with two shots, strongly suggesting she had stirred after her sister was killed, and Manuel had to quickly disable her with the first shot before making sure with the second. Mrs Watt's nightdress was pulled up and her sister's pyjama trousers had been torn from the waistband down her right leg.

Vivienne died a different death.

There were signs of a struggle in her room and she had been knocked out by a blow to her chin. It's also probable that her hands had been tied behind her back. Her black pyjama bottoms had been ripped from her and several buttons were scattered on the bed and floor. She had been wearing a pyjama jacket and a cardigan, the buttons of which had been torn off, and the ripped trousers were lying on top of the bed. Her bra was found on the bedroom floor. It had a tear at the front and the straps were torn, but it was still fastened at the back. Either he had torn it from the girl during the assault or he had toyed with it in the afterglow of the attack. Given that when she was found, she was wearing the pyjama jacket and the cardigan, he probably wrenched it from her body whilst she was fighting for her young life or removed it by force shortly after she was shot, which might account for her arm extending underneath her body.

Exactly when he shot her was not fully established; he either shot her, then tore her nightwear off, or tore it off and leered at her after she had been knocked unconscious, perhaps waiting for her to come round before shooting her, to maximise his pleasure.

Before he left he covered the bodies with the bed sheets.

He does not appear to have taken anything from the house, but he did light a cigarette before trampling it into the carpet and burning it.

The murders were discovered the following day when the daily help arrived at 8.45am and could not get in, or rouse anyone inside. The postman became involved, entered the house and discovered the crime scene. Both witnesses heard three or four terrible snores coming from Vivienne's room. The postman thought the family pet Queenie had made the noise, before it was realised that Vivienne was still alive.

She died shortly thereafter.

Just how long did he keep the terrorised girl alive?

He must have been well away by the time the operator tried, on three occasions, to rouse Mrs Watt with the alarm call she ordered for 7 o'clock. With his eerie tendency for lingering at the scene of the crime, who can tell when he finally left?

After the police were called to the murder house, it was discovered that there had been the break-in at number eighteen as well. It was a reasonable assumption that, whoever violated number eighteen may have broken into number five, and Manuel's signature was on number eighteen. Police went straight to 32 Fourth Street, Birkenshaw with a Sheriff's search warrant for a .38 revolver, arriving at 2am on 18 September.

Samuel came up with the same old threats of complaining to his Member of Parliament about harassment and Peter moaned about them blaming him for everything that happened. That the police did not seek a warrant for clothes but merely made a cursory examination of cuffs and pockets was later criticised.

Manuel simply refused to co-operate at all and to give any information as to where he had been at the vital times, and, unsurprisingly, the gun was not found. They did not take him to the station as a suspect and, anyway, they had no knowledge at that time of what, if anything, had been stolen from either house. Manuel could now start his sentence on 2 October smug in the knowledge that he had once again given the police a headache. He would also be able to recall and savour his handiwork as he served his time.

The master criminal had made a mistake, though. He failed to consider the possibility that anyone except the police could be a danger to his deadly game, particularly the cronies he drank with and boasted to in the Woodend Hotel.

On the same day the murders were committed and discovered, however, one of them contacted the CID and told them what had happened the day before. He said he had been drinking with Manuel on Sunday 16 September when Manuel told him he was going to do 'a Jew's house' that night as there was a 'stack of money' there; in case of difficulty, he said he had something 'to stop anybody' and tapped a bulky item in his inside jacket pocket. To further impress his drinking partner, he told him he knew that it worked as he had already tried it out on a cow, shooting it through its nostril.

Getting close enough to a cow in a field to shoot it at such close range could be difficult, but it happened there had been a cow found dead that week in a field near to Birkenshaw which had been tested for anthrax. It was found to be clear of the disease, after which the carcass was released to be processed for bone meal. It had been bleeding from the nostril when examined, so matching any bullets from the dead animal and the crime scene suddenly became important.

Had Manuel seen the dead creature from the bus, as others had, and decided to invent the tale, or could this be a breakthrough? He might have shot it as it lay dead, of course, but that was of no consequence, as long as a spent bullet could be retrieved for comparison.

A policeman's lot is sometimes truly not a happy one, and several officers from the Lanarkshire force now spent four days combing through vats of flesh and offal, and examining machinery in case a bullet had slipped through. They found pieces of wire and even some spent shotgun cartridges, but no .38 bullet.

As if to underline just how misplaced Manuel's trust was in those around him, a second informant then told police Manuel claimed he had tried some target practice in woods near his house. The police scoured the local trees for signs of bullet marks in bark, but again to no avail.

Or was Manuel amusing himself and secretly enjoying all the misspent police activity?

Deanna Valente had told officers that she could hear Vivienne's radio on in the kitchen until the early hours of the Monday morning. She had heard Doris Day singing 'What Will Be Will Be', a song which became a football anthem for reasons unknown, but which was then at number one in the Top Twenty, so its airing could be timed to after 12.30am.

Police were baffled as to how the wireless was audible yet no-one seemed to have heard the fatal shots. They test-fired seven shots inside the house and were mildly surprised when they found that they could not be heard from outside. The house at 5 Fennsbank Avenue was solidly built.

Deanna's mother then found a gun at the back of her house, which was handed to the police. In a Pythonesque moment, some papers frenziedly reported that a gun had been found near the scene of the crime, but they hastily dropped the story when Mrs Valente told them it was a child's toy and asked reporters camped in the street why they were making such a fuss.

A cast of footprints found at the rear of number eighteen was taken and further evidence of that common urban phenomenon – a single shoe – was discovered, but the erstwhile owner never revealed himself, as he never seems to do with all the other single shoes which puzzlingly litter certain streets.

Dowdall now had the task of demonstrating Watt's innocence by proving that Manuel was guilty, and even with all the information in the public domain, he managed to uncover more, which helped return the investigation to its proper course.

20

MANUEL MEETS DOWDALL

Dowdall's first meetings with Manuel were in the unsanitary and overcrowded precincts of Barlinnie Prison, Glasgow, where he was confined from 2 October 1956 until his release on 30 November 1957. From the latter date until his arrest six weeks later on 14 January 1958, Manuel embarked on an unparalleled killing binge.

He also 'signed in' with a couple of housebreakings in Uddingston and Mount Vernon shortly after his release. Ensuring that the message was clear, he cooked himself meals in the violated properties, which let his old adversaries know he was back.

However, one of the first things he did was to approach several newspaper offices to offer 'exclusives' on the Watt killings, and from a modern perspective, it's interesting to note that none appear to have been tempted, hopefully but probably not due to journalistic standards.

Manuel also found time to continue his self-indulgent taunting of Watt, who had been released on 3 December 1956. In one of the most bizarre encounters in recent criminal case histories, and exactly a year after Watt's release, on 3 December 1957 Dowdall arranged they should all meet in Glasgow's Whitehall Restaurant.

He arranged to meet Manuel at 6pm and told Watt to give them half an hour together before he arrived. When he entered the restaurant, Dowdall immediately noticed Manuel sitting at a table reading a paper. No-one would have guessed he had just been released from a year's stretch in prison. He was wearing charcoal slacks, a dark blue blazer, a white shirt and fashionable tie. As usual, he was immaculately groomed with not a hair out of place. Dowdall sat at the table and spoke to Manuel, who was calm and assured.

When Watt arrived later, he approached the table and immediately threatened to 'tear Manuel to pieces' should he discover he had anything to do with the murder of his family. Dowdall reasoned that Watt was physically capable of carrying out the threat, but he managed to restore calm to a surreal situation by getting Watt to sit down.

Manuel reacted by sitting bolt upright and snarling, 'People don't do that to Peter Manuel.'

After things calmed down and the spectre of violence receded, Dowdall eventually left the grieving husband and father with the killer of his family.

The next time Dowdall and Manuel were to meet was in the North Court six months later.

Manuel's initial story to Dowdall in Barlinnie was the usual weave of known fact and fantasy arranged to place him in the best light. Now he was turning the screw on Watt and playing out a warped role in his own unique version of reality.

In this instance, the character he was playing was that of criminal consultant.

He told of a character whose name he refused to divulge who had come to ask him to assist in a break-in at Fennsbank Avenue. The man said there was a lot of money and only women in the house, but Manuel refused on principle, such cowardly behaviour obviously being no part of his repertoire. The mystery man had even returned to see him the same morning after he had committed the murders 'in a hell of a state' and 'in the horrors'. He had a Webley revolver with him, the lanyard ring of which he had broken off and thrown away. Then, for some unfathomable reason, he requested Manuel get rid of the weapon for him and he had obliged by throwing it in the Clyde. He then gave Watt a detailed description of two rings – very much like those owned by the Misses Martin – that the rattled assassin had also given him to dispose of and said he had dropped them down a drain. The mystery killer could obviously have done these things for himself and Manuel could not explain to Watt why he acted in this eccentric fashion.

It was to be the first of several meetings between them, and Watt knew what he had to do to make the unsavoury arrangement pay dividends.

Dowdall had sought advice from a friend in the police who knew Manuel well and it was decided that the best strategy was to play to his considerable ego. Accordingly, on a return visit to Manuel when he was still serving his sentence in Barlinnie, Dowdall cast doubt on his story and Manuel reacted as hoped by giving a detailed description of the interior of 5 Fennsbank Avenue, which he claimed had been passed to him by the deranged but observant perpetrator.

It matched exactly.

The same tactic at another meeting yielded more results.

Dowdall listened to more information, and then suggested that it could easily have been culled straight from the newspapers. Manuel was then provoked into telling how the wrongdoer told him he had broken a glass panel at the front door with the gun, gone into the room on the left and shot two women. After that, he said that a girl had run out of a bedroom screaming and he had knocked her out with a punch on the chin, tied her hands behind her back and put her on her bed. The madman had then acted suspiciously like Manuel himself as he ransacked the house, then opened some tins of food and had something to eat. After that, he heard the girl stirring, so he shot her and then shot one of the women a second time as she appeared to still be alive.

If what he had said before was bordering on 'special knowledge known only to the perpetrator', he had now definitely crossed the line. No information had been given out as to how many shots had killed the victims. And no-one appears to have noticed that the killer had eaten food in the Watt house.

The effective drip-feeding of Manuel's ego continued.

It was reasoned that having held himself out as the omniscient master criminal, Manuel would be disappointed if the fantasy suddenly stopped.

If that was correct, he would be compelled to make the next approach.

Dowdall did nothing, and sure enough Manuel made the subsequent move.

His letter started 'Dear Lawrence' [sic] and was signed 'Peter'.

Dowdall reflected on how he had managed to be in a situation where he was now on first-name terms with a deranged psychopath. Manuel obviously craved acceptance by Dowdall and was clearly hoping for Dowdall's acknowledgement of him as his intellectual equal.

At their next meeting, and in the face of continued scepticism from Dowdall, Manuel obligingly drew a picture of the Webley revolver which Dowdall slipped into his file as he left the prison.

The drawing became a Crown production at his trial.

With equal doses of scepticism and praise, more and more details were teased out. He explained that he had declined to take part in the easy job at Fennsbank Avenue for the very good reason that he knew for a fact that the gunman meant business. He knew that because he had been at a run-of-the-mill housebreaking in Bothwell with him a few days before the Fennsbank job, when one of the housebreakers – a female – had lain on a bed and expressed disbelief about the gunman being able to use the gun. His reaction when doubted had been swift. He quickly produced it and fired into the bed she was idling on.

Manuel must have realised that he was supplying evidence to Dowdall, so his need to be acknowledged as central to events outweighed other considerations, such as the precaution of distancing himself from the crimes. Had he kept silent about the gun being discharged during what was later recognised as the Platt break-in, the link with the Watt murders might just have failed to materialise.

Although surprisingly malleable with Dowdall, he had not given up on taunting the police. After the story of the lanyard ring being thrown away emerged, officers went straight to 32 Fourth Street, Birkenshaw and dug up the garden. They found nothing, and as he often boasted that he could 'con the coppers into digging his mother's garden' whenever he wanted, it may have been that he was giving out some false information simply to amuse himself. Even so, he now knew for certain that Dowdall was passing it on to the police, yet something compelled him to continue with this entertaining diversion.

After Dowdall left the dapper Manuel and the tortured Watt together in the restaurant, violence of some kind might have been the expected outcome. Watt had already demonstrated he was capable of supreme self-control, even to the point of originally creating suspicion against himself.

Now he was to use it to better effect.

The unlikely pair met several times in Glasgow bars and once at Watt's brother-in law's house. Perhaps sixty-seven days in Barlinnie had made Watt think twice about ridding society of Peter Manuel by his preferred means.

True to form, Manuel gave Watt some further extra detail. He now revealed the identity of the crazy gunman as a Charles Tallis and the female housebreaker with the tendency for breaking in and going to bed as a Mary Bowes. Along with a Martin Hart, who had served time with Manuel in Barlinnie, Manuel said the three had gone to 18 Fennsbank Avenue and broken in. They then cased the Valente house which, to Hart's certain knowledge, had a safe in it containing between £5,000 and £10,000 in cash. They had then tragically mistaken the Watt house for the Valente house after seeing Deanna there – the fact she spent the Sunday evening there was well publicised in the newspapers – and when they returned later, Tallis smashed the glass door panel with his gun to gain entry. The plan had been to execute all but one of the occupants who would then be forced to reveal the location of the safe, before they too were to be murdered.

Watt's exemplary self-control was tested to breaking point when Manuel supplied further detail about his house.

Why would the real offender tell Manuel about the positions of the display cabinet, the cocktail cabinet, the standard lamp and the photograph on the piano? Watt held himself in check but told Manuel he knew he had done it.

Manuel calmly denied it and stoically and repeatedly blamed Tallis, and in keeping with his usual routine, he supplied more information on the Platt housebreaking, but this time with a different spin: Mrs Bowes had fired the gun at Tallis after he had playfully thrown her onto the bed and then jumped onto it himself; he had been grazed by the bullet fired by the outraged lady.

Manuel correctly observed that if that bullet was traced and it matched those from the Watt crime scene, it would certainly and finally let Watt off the hook. Manuel's evidential brinkmanship carried little risk of self-imploding as far as retrieving the gun went – 'the Clyde' is a fairly unspecific search area. The Misses Martin's rings would not be easily traced either, and to this day never have been.

At the trial, Watt also mentioned that Manuel produced a photograph of Anne Kneilands which he tore up – just as Dowdall had reported had happened – and placed in an ashtray in a public house in Glasgow. In Watt's case, the ritual was preceded by a cruel reference to Vivienne.

Manuel plainly got pleasure in reliving his exploits in dangerous circumstances, and perhaps that helps explain why he talked so much.

For what it's worth, some inmates and former inmates at Barlinnie claimed that Manuel had already mentioned the layout of the Watt household to some of them before his release, but it has to be noted that stories of journalists rewarding information about Manuel with cash led to an unseemly scramble by 'former cellmates' eager to claim inside knowledge.

But should a bullet be traced from a housebreaking in Bothwell in mid-September 1956, it could trap him.

21

THE PLATTS AND THE MISSING BULLET

On 12 September 1956, the Platt family set off from Douglas Drive, Bothwell for a fortnight's holiday in the Lake District in England. On 15 September, police were called to their house, where they found a break-in with a familiar pattern to it.

A deed box had been forced open and its contents scattered. In the kitchen, an empty soup tin was lying beside a pan with some soup in it and the rest appeared to have been poured over the floor. An empty pear tin was lying on the floor, the pears scattered on a carpet. In an upstairs bedroom, a jug with soup in it was lying beside the bed and the intruder had deliberately wiped his filthy boots on the bedspread. A pair of scissors lay on the floor beside the bed and there were tears and cuts on the bedclothes. The mattress had an eight-inch slit in it.

The family came home six days after setting off and told police that some tools, a stopwatch, a wristwatch and an electric razor were missing. The razor had been a present for the sixteen-year-old son of the house, who must have been the only adolescent at the time with such a technological wonder – it was one of fifty of a prototype and was not on sale to the public.

The Platts were a family who made the best of what they had. They cleaned up the mess and tried to forget about the intruder, although it has to be said they had moved to Fife by the time of Manuel's trial in May 1958. Mrs Platt was a thrifty housekeeper who sewed up the slash on the mattress and it remained one of the Platt family's possessions.

Waste not, want not.

About a year after that, a lump in the mattress was investigated and it was found that the missing watch had been there all along. Then in December 1957, Mrs Platt again found the mattress a bit uncomfortable and in the process of smoothing out the lumps and bumps discovered that one of them turned out to be a spent bullet.

The Platts' sangfroid knew no bounds – they were 'curious' but paid little or no attention to it and put it in a drawer. It was only when they realised that the police were looking for a .38 revolver in connection with their investigations into the Watt murders that Mr Platt measured the unusual find and then took it to the police. That someone had carried out a triple murder a few miles away possibly just two days after his house had been broken into does not appear to have weighed heavily on his deliberations.

When ballistics experts examined the cartridge, the unique striation marks made when the bullet exited the barrel of the gun matched those of the bullets from the Watt murders.

It was a bad break for Manuel. Mrs Platt's curiosity had helped place a noose around his neck.

A puzzle remains, though. Did Manuel anticipate that the cartridge might be found and so decide to get his story about Tallis and Bowes in first? Alternatively, when it was not discovered straight away, it might have been better to keep quiet as, after all, it might never surface. On this occasion, however, he had been too clever by half.

Perhaps he had tried to retrieve the incriminating cartridge and had cut the mattress open and when he failed to find it, attempted to lay a false trail by leaving the watch. Whoever found the watch might then just leave it at that. Against that, and apart from being careful not to leave fingerprints, he was generally cavalier about his crime scenes. Sometimes he appeared to be blatantly reckless and determined to leave his calling card.

Just why did he shoot the mattress, though?

The obvious answer appears to be that it was a dummy run prior to carrying out the real act a few nights later. If the Platts had been asleep at home, they would undoubtedly have been his victims.

Or, as no victim was available, perhaps he was acting out a fantasy and was playing out a scene from some long-forgotten black and white gangster movie.

What he did, though, on 15, 16 and 17 September 1956 further illustrates the characteristic behavioural build-up to an anticipated period of imprisonment in early October, the key being escalating violence. His final fling, at the end of 1957 and the beginning of 1958, by necessity, had to be flamboyant. Each thrill had to outshine the previous one in order to make it worthwhile.

The slow build-up of hard evidence against Manuel was small consolation to Watt. Gossip and innuendo translated into an economic downturn, just short of ruin, for his business.

But in small measures, the tide was turning. The main players in the underworld recognised that Manuel was a major liability to the smooth running of normal business and they helped in his downfall. Informers told police that James Tinney O'Neil had sold him a gun, but when questioned he initially denied it. O'Neil – nicknamed 'Scout' – later testified at Manuel's trial that Manuel had approached him and told him that he needed a gun for a hold-up in Liverpool. He had then put Manuel in touch with someone called Dick Hamilton, who could supply it. After Hamilton and Manuel met up a 'close' in Glasgow city centre, O'Neil weakly claimed Manuel said nothing to him about actually having a gun but patted his jacket pocket knowingly a couple of times. The revolver and seven or eight rounds cost £5 and the date was 10 or 11 September 1956, just before the Watt murders.

This evidence electrified 1950s society, and after the trial ended, various newspapers vied to 'expose' Glasgow low-life.

Lord Cameron was on their case before that, though, in the course of the trial.

At the end of 'Scout's' testimony, Lord Cameron sought clarification from him on a personal level. The *Bulletin* noted Scout's 'several long scars' and the fact that he was asked to speak more clearly on several occasions before His Lordship asked him if he was working on either of the occasions he met Manuel – undoubtedly a yardstick of a fellow's standing – to which the answer was, of course, 'No', he was living courtesy of the National Assistance Board.

The actual seller of the gun, Hamilton, described himself as a 'book-maker's clerk', clarified in cross-examination as a 'bookie's runner' – in other words, someone who took money for illegal street bets. He said he had got the gun from Henry Michael Campbell, who testified he had 'found' it in an officer's hut whilst serving in the RAF in 1952.

His Lordship interjected, 'You mean you stole it?'

Campbell took a deep breath and then said, 'Yes, Sir.'

An *Evening Citizen* investigation after the trial revealed that an amnesty after the Second World War brought in 1,723 guns and revolvers in a single year in Glasgow alone. After the First World War, returning troops were, surprisingly, allowed to keep so-called 'trophy guns' but they were strictly licensed so that by 1958 only twenty-eight such licences still existed. In a strangely contemporary note, it was observed that the use of a gun to protect property was frowned upon, and it was pointed out that some years before, a Glasgow lawyer had shot and killed an intruder in his house. He was then tried for murder, but acquitted.

The Manuel trial highlighted just how easy it was to get a firearm in 1950s Glasgow. The transaction took three or four days and cost £5 with no questions asked. The article continued, 'the dregs of Glasgow have a way of life of their own' and that there were 'hundreds of people' in Glasgow who seemingly needed a gun once or twice in their lives as decent men 'want a frock coat for a wedding'.

Yet it was that very stratum of undesirable criminals that helped turn Manuel in. He had been an outsider in America and England and when his parents returned to their roots, he was a misfit there too. In jail in Peterhead, he was a loner. His one chance to be accepted was his engagement to Anna O'Hara, but that failed. And in the 1950s, if you were unmarried, social mores, lack of housing and shortage of money dictated that you continued to live with your parents, which Manuel did, yet he somehow grafted a ghoulish nocturnal second life onto a seemingly ordinary existence. But even the 'dregs' of the city with their own agenda had no understanding of the one Manuel planned.

22

SYDNEY JOHN DUNN

The early hours of Sunday 8 December 1957 were wet and stormy in the area of Newcastle upon Tyne. The central station was busy with passengers braving both the weather and the swirling smoke from trains coming and going.

That morning, the 'Paddy train' had arrived at 4.05 am. Its local name was due to the large number of Irishmen who arrived in the area looking for work, having travelled on steam packets across the Irish Sea to England and then taken the train from Carlisle. For the time of day, it was especially busy, with the London to Newcastle arriving at 4.29am and the Bristol to Newcastle at 4.38am.

Two taxi drivers who knew each other well and who both lived in St Thomas Crescent, Newcastle were working that morning. Thomas Green was waiting for a fare at the taxi rank underneath the portico at the side of Newcastle Central. He noticed two men who emerged from the station at the same time. One of them asked to be taken to the Newburn area and the other to a village called Edmondbyers in the moorlands of County Durham. They appear to have spoken to Green at the same time.

Just then, he spotted the pre-war Austin 18, registered NVK 935, driven by his colleague and neighbour, Sydney John Dunn, coming into the pick-up area, and he arranged for the second passenger to take Dunn's cab for the twenty-two-mile trip to the small moorland community near Consett, whilst he took his passenger the six or so miles to Newburn.

Dunn was thirty-six years old and single and ran the taxi business with his mother and two brothers. He was described as sober and hard-working, and during the war he had served in the RAF, surviving 'the worst of the fighting'.

His luck was about to end.

His mother later recalled him being 'on edge' before he left for work on the night of Saturday 7 December. Unusually, he had left to start work at 8pm, two hours earlier than normal.

He had been seeing a widowed lady from Gateshead, usually on a Saturday night, but his family had not been introduced to her at that stage. That weekend, the plan had been changed to the couple meeting on the Sunday night and he had gone to work instead.

That Sunday night, she turned up to meet him as planned, but he didn't appear.

Green recalled following Dunn's cab some distance until they parted company at Scotswood Bridge, with Dunn heading off towards the bleak moorland, his cab lashed by gale-force winds, blinding rain and sleet.

What happened after that is as much guesswork today as it was in 1957.

The twenty-year-old upright Austin, although not easily spotted from the road, was seen by passers-by in a gulley off the main road to Stanhope at various times throughout daylight hours that day. The first sighting was later reported at shortly after 8am that Sunday morning. In the course of the day, several drivers and their passengers noticed it but no-one stopped to investigate, even though a scarf and peaked cap were seen to be lying on the ground beside it. Most of them either decided that it had been abandoned at the scene or, incredibly – given the weather conditions – that it belonged to 'picnickers'. Whatever reason, even if just reluctance to become involved, no-one thought it appropriate to delve further, until a member of Durham Constabulary was cycling by and decided to investigate.

The car was at right angles to the road. The interior and exterior lights were smashed, and both the front and rear driver's-side doors were lying open. There was blood on the steering wheel, and it looked as if there might have been a road accident and the driver had been injured. The policeman decided that the darkness and the weather, combined with the barren moorland on both sides of the road, made an individual search pointless. He cycled the two miles to Edmondbyers and checked whether there were any reports of an accident or whether anyone had been admitted to hospital with head injuries, but drew a blank on both.

He then quickly organised a search team and a quarter of an hour after they started searching at eight o'clock that night, a tracker dog found the body of Sydney John Dunn lying in the heather about 150 yards north of the car. He had been dragged there by the tails of his coat, which had been pulled up and left over his head. His wallet was found nearby but it still contained a few pounds. Nearer the roadway, a pencil, a lighter and some coins were also found.

The *Durham County Advertiser* for Friday 13 December 1957 reported the authorities' confusion about the circumstances of the case. Calling it the 'on-off-on' murder enquiry, it told the story of the passenger going from the station to the moor, and then of the taxi sitting seemingly abandoned all that day at the roadside.

Initially, and unbelievably, the police issued a statement saying that Dunn had an injury to the neck but that foul play was not suspected!

About an hour later, the 'foul play' pronouncement was withdrawn when the police discovered that Dunn's probable last act was to uplift the passenger from the station. Referring to that, and in a surprisingly gentlemanly tone, a police spokesman then announced, 'The police are anxious to interview this person, and if he would kindly come forward, it would assist our enquiries considerably. It is desired to emphasise that the passenger whoever he may be has nothing to fear.'

The averment that the passenger 'has nothing to fear' was also later withdrawn.

At 7.30pm on Monday 9 December, a third police statement said that a post-mortem revealed that death was due to a bullet wound to the head.

The bullet was described as either a .32 or .38 British make which had probably been fired at a distance of at least twelve inches and from 'a very worn revolver'.

Thereafter the deceased man's throat, somewhat unnecessarily, had been cut, leaving a five-inch gash.

Door-to-door enquiries at Edmondbyers and Stanhope brought no leads, nor did a thorough search of the moorland and outbuildings between the two communities. Members of the Durham Light Infantry, amongst others, assisted police in searching for the murder weapon, the area being sectored off into 'string avenues' and the searchers being directed by loudhailer. A group of refugee Hungarian soldiers, stationed nearby, appeared with mine detectors to try to seek out the murder weapon.

The Newcastle *Evening Chronicle* reported that falling snow hampered their efforts, and that one embarrassed dog-handler fell into a 'bog-hole', his dog having the good sense to jump around it. He shouted for help and four of his colleagues eventually pulled him to safety, but had they not been nearby, it was reckoned he would have gone under and perished.

The *Chronicle* wondered if such a fate had fittingly befallen the killer.

The moorland was to reveal no more clues, and the denizens of the villages of Stanhope and Edmondbyers gave no hint of any knowledge of the crime or help in solving it. In particular, no-one came forward to tell of either seeing or giving a lift to an inappropriately dressed man walking along the side of the moors in the teeth of a gale. In reality, there would have to be a genuine risk of exposure for anyone foolhardy enough to try to walk from where the car was found to a place of shelter. Speculation mounted as to why the killer had not driven away in the car. Could it be that he was either unable to drive or unable to restart the car after the assault?

A further conundrum was that the angle and concentration of bloodstaining in the car strongly pointed to the killer sitting in the front passenger seat at the time of the shooting.

Seventeen days after Manuel's execution, a nine-man coroner's jury at Shotley Bridge in County Durham took twenty minutes to conclude, 'We find Dunn died from a gunshot wound in the head. He was murdered by Peter Manuel and the charge is capital murder.'

Their verdict was based on the following evidence:

a) The taxi driver Green, who had spoken to Dunn's passenger together with another driver, Albert Younger, who had seen him, attended an identification parade at Hamilton police office in January 1958. They both identified Manuel by placing a hand on his shoulder. It was reported that when Green picked him out, Manuel 'mockingly' bowed and introduced himself by name.

b) Grass found in the turn-ups of a pair of Manuel's trousers was found to be similar to that found on the moor known as Edmondbyers Common.

c) A button with thread attached recovered from the running board of the Austin could have come from a coat belonging to Manuel.

d) Two red fibres entwined in the button could have come from a maroon jumper belonging to Manuel.

e) A yellow thread entwined in the button could have come from a brown suit belonging to Manuel.

Manuel had been in the area around the time of the murder. It was known that he had been in Newcastle for an interview with British Electrical Repairs Limited on the morning of Friday 6 December 1957, having been released from jail the week before.

Although blood-staining in Dunn's pockets told of some kind of search of the victim, there seemed to be no solid motive for the killing. If Manuel had pulled the trigger, the crime stood out singularly as being well away from his normal 'comfort zone' with quick and easy access to his home base in Birkenshaw.

Dunn's earlier pre-work edginess must surely have been unrelated, as the fare he had picked up was obviously a random act – if indeed he was the murderer. It could be that the passenger had been dropped off and that something sinister had then happened to Dunn, but in that case, why did the innocent traveller not come forward?

As the crime had occurred in such an isolated area, the police and press initially decided that the killer had to be a local man, the taxi lying two miles from Edmondbyers on the road to Stanhope. Turf and soil were found to clog the car's exhaust pipe, suggesting that it had trundled backwards into the earth, and although the meter was switched off, the ignition was still on. That the lights were smashed possibly meant that the killer had no knowledge of where the light switch was located on the dashboard and had panicked on seeing the lights of an approaching car.

Speculation arose that smashed glass found further along on the road to Stanhope came from the Austin as a result of being rammed by another car, causing it to turn round in an effort to get back towards Edmondbyers.

Police later thought it more likely that all the lights had been smashed where the car was discovered and that the glass on the road was unconnected. Yet no-one could say why the car was found two miles beyond Edmondbyers if the passenger had specifically asked for that destination.

The *Newcastle Journal* hinted that the attack could have been sparked off by the sort of behaviour not mentioned directly in 1957, when it suggested that the area could have been specifically chosen by the passenger 'to give new and ominous instructions' to the miserable driver.

Because of the method of the killing, the press also speculated that the perpetrator might have been trained as a commando. The nature of the wound at autopsy suggested that the deceased had in fact been shot from a distance of eighteen to twenty-four inches 'by an expert revolver shot'.

Could a shot from that distance be distinguished as either 'expert' or 'amateur'?

The old car was not a custom-built taxi but rather a solid old work-horse of a family saloon, and as a result, there was no partition screening between driver and passenger, assuming he had decided to sit in the rear of the vehicle. The method of killing – shooting then throat cutting – resembled the sort of excessive violence taught to certain special forces during the war when dealing with enemy sentries. The *Newcastle Journal* for 13 December 1957 went so far as to declare that because of the nature of the murder, if the killer was as young as twenty-five, as had been suggested, he would have learned his deadly art during a stint of National Service, a proposition unlikely to meet favour with those who served such a spell, their time consisting mostly of marching, polishing floors and peeling potatoes with little time for mastering the essentials of sentry assassination.

The combination of the Paddy train's arrival very shortly before the murder and the brutality visited on Dunn led to press conjecture that the killer could be an Irishman belonging to 'an illegal organisation across the Irish Sea', where possession of knives and guns was 'commonplace'.

The IRA theory emerged after it became clear that there would be no speedy solution to the mystery, but it ran counter to what Green had originally said in at least one important respect.

He told police the man had a local, 'North Country', accent but when the question of Irish involvement arose, the witness altered his view and agreed that the accent could have been Irish after all!

Interestingly, the passenger conveyed into the moors that morning was described as male, aged twenty-four, five feet eight inches tall, swarthy, with greased-back hair (possibly parted to left), medium build, dark single-breasted suit, possibly blue, no hat, light shirt, dark tie and dark grey loose overcoat.

Police also described themselves as 'anxious' to trace and speak to a 'swarthy' man who was seen to drive slowly by the spot, possibly in another taxi, where Dunn's cab was found.

Green had gone into hiding fairly quickly after the event, fearful that his knowledge might make him a target for the killer. When Dunn was laid to rest, fellow drivers attended in force, but Green remained hidden.

The theory seems to have been that Manuel had stayed on in Newcastle until the Sunday morning, when he emerged like a nocturnal ghost to murder Sydney John Dunn either for the sheer hell of it, or out of anger because he had ordered him to take him to Edinburgh rather than Edmondbyers. Then, having dispatched Dunn, he made off over the moors to escape justice for the time being, leaving the car in the gulley as he was unsure of how to drive it. Prior to leaving, he indulged in tell-tale 'scattering behaviour' with the unfortunate man's few possessions.

Any effort to make sense of the known facts inevitably leads to the uneasy realisation that the verdict of the coroner's jury's was only a possibility. Had any prosecution case been properly tested in a criminal court on either side of the border, a conviction would have been by no means certain.

That Manuel was in Newcastle on the Friday before the murder seems beyond doubt; from the realistic starting premise that a serial killer with a penchant for using guns happens to be in your neck of the woods around the time of a shooting, the identifications by both Green and Younger are but a short step towards an automatic assumption of guilt.

He was obviously capable of the murder, and may also have had a morbid curiosity about decapitating a victim, something he gruesomely outlined to Mary McLachlan. He would answer to 'swarthy' and the hairstyle would fit – as it would most of the male population at the time – although he never used hair grease.

The grass found in his clothes would have to have been there for about five weeks and there is no evidence – presumably as there couldn't be – that it was an unusual or unique strain. Many photographs of Manuel and events surrounding his final trial still exist and there is one of a policeman taking his clothing from 32 Fourth Street, for 'forensic analysis'. It shows a man in an overcoat, slightly taller than those in the curious crowd round about, approaching a van clutching a mixture of clothes and two pairs of shoes; the inside of the van looks grimy and the clothes are all bundled together. There is no sign of anything being 'bagged' and the officer is not wearing gloves. Presumably, the concept of cross-contamination did not exist in 1958.

The 'corroborating' strength of the other evidence, literally, hangs by a thread. Was the mottled brown button of a commonplace design or colour, and could it have been found on thousands, possibly millions of other garments worn by the male population in post-war Britain? Furthermore, how could a red fibre come from a man not apparently wearing a red or maroon jumper and a yellow fibre come from a suit described as 'possibly blue' rather than brown?

Surely there would be little room for error or confusion if Manuel had uttered more than a few words to Green? His accent was unmistakably West of Scotland, and, just as importantly, his height was well documented as five feet four rather than five feet eight inches. His build was 'stocky' rather than medium, and at thirty-one, he might not have been easily taken for a twenty-four-year-old.

How many times had taxi drivers in 1957 been hired to drive to Edinburgh from Newcastle, and why should he go to Edinburgh at all? Such a fare would have to have been agreed beforehand on a fixed-price basis. Whoever had asked to go to Edmondbyers apparently asked both Green and Dunn separately for that destination, unless both made the same extraordinary mistake. Finally, the pronunciation of the two places is entirely different, particularly in a West of Scotland accent, which truncates the capital city to something like an undignified 'Embra'.

Any examination of the area quickly reveals that without a strategically placed second vehicle, there was no alternative escape route. Manuel did have experience of train travel with his work, and he would have been resourceful enough to board a train without the need for a ticket, but the main Carlisle line lies well beyond walking distance from that isolated spot. Apart from that, what reason could there possibly be for choosing the moors as a starting point for a flight from authority, especially if no provision has been made for an alternative method of escape?

If he had shot Dunn elsewhere and driven to the moors, why did he not dump the body there and drive to a more convenient place to leave the car before catching public transport?

The more likely explanation for Dunn's few possessions being 'scattered' is that they fell out of his pockets as he was being dragged through the heather to where he was found.

Rather than Manuel simply surfacing in the middle of the night at Newcastle Central, a more likely explanation for the killer appearing when he did was that he had come off the train which had just arrived – the Paddy train. The definite impression at the time had been that he, the killer, had been on the train with the man who had gone on to Newburn in Green's taxi. In one of their official statements, the police had actually said that the supposed killer 'may have had a friend with him.'

If so, why did he never come forward to help clear up the mystery? The murder was well publicised in all the local papers. Even if he wasn't actually with him, the 'Newburn' man must have been able to shed some light on the appearance of the supposed killer, as he must have seen him at the station.

As has often been observed, eye-witness identification can be surprisingly suspect. The basis of the charge against William Watt provides a perfect example. That said, how could Green and Younger both select Manuel at the identification parade despite the details Green at least originally provided? Other witnesses also later claimed they had seen him in Newcastle between 6 and 8 December. Did Manuel's notoriety go before him? Was it even possible that there had been behind-the-scenes discussion beforehand – even innocently and between police officers from the respective forces – which unwittingly helped to get the 'right man'?

In the aftermath of the Watt murders, Lanarkshire CID had circulated Manuel's details to all forces in Britain together with the information that he was a suspect and that a .38 had been used; to begin with, there was an expectation that the same weapon had been used in both murder scenes, but that was not borne out. However, Manuel's photograph was shown to witnesses in Newcastle to try to trace his movements. As in the Oscar Slater case, did the main witness eventually alter original details to conform with subsequent police intelligence?

For what it was worth, Manuel was adamant that the two had misidentified him. Ignoring the unintended meaning of the double negative, his response when cautioned and charged was a denial, 'I don't know nothing about it.'

He went on to give details of his movements that weekend but the police dismissed these as 'uncorroborated' and 'containing certain discrepancies', although these were not made public. After Durham police left Barlinnie Prison, he turned to another prisoner and asked, 'What the fuck was that all about?'

That his story was unsupported is not quite true.

When his mother was later relating her story to a newspaper as her son lay in the condemned cell, she accepted he was responsible for many horrific deeds, but she singled out the murder of Sydney John Dunn as the one she thought he did not commit – she was convinced he had made it home that weekend instead. Had she been simply clutching at straws, she might have been expected to complain that he had been charged with the Kneilands murder, of which he was acquitted.

Of course, when charged with offences, Manuel was habitually guilty.

Down the years, he had developed two main strategies; he either admitted his guilt – even as a bluff and to be retracted later – or he kept his powder dry pending knowledge of the prosecution evidence in order to concoct a made-to-measure defence.

His reaction in this instance, like the geographical location, doesn't quite fit the bill. Manuel's trademark was stealth when committing the crime followed by a show of contempt – the killer here was clumsy in risking identification before the commission of the murder.

The 'worn revolver' makes no further appearances, has no known history and was not apparently subjected to the inevitable disposal in the river that he later confessed to in respect of both the Webley and the Beretta he had used in other murders.

Previous commentators have casually accepted that Manuel was guilty of Dunn's murder, mainly, it seems, because he was in the area at or near the time and because he was unquestionably capable of it.

From the condemned cell at Barlinnie Prison in June 1958, he wrote a farewell letter to a friend which sarcastically noted that he was in the frame 'for every unsolved murder since Cain killed Abel.'

He finished it, 'I wonder where I was that night?'

23

ISABELLE COOKE

At mid-day on Christmas Day 1957, the Reverend Alexander Houston and his wife Frances locked the front door of their house at 66 Wester Road, Mount Vernon, Glasgow and went to visit friends. When they came back a few hours later, they found that back and front doors were open and a window was smashed. Missing was a camera, a pair of sheepskin gloves, a sock and £2 taken from a collection box for missionaries. The gloves were a present from friends who lived round the corner in Carrick Drive.

Eleven days later, the Reverend Houston was appealing from the pulpit for volunteers to help search for a girl who was missing from the same drive.

Mr and Mrs Cooke lived at 5 Carrick Drive, Mount Vernon along with their four children: a girl, seventeen-year-old Isabelle, who was a pupil at Hamilton Academy, and three younger boys. Their house was in a cul-de-sac a couple of hundred yards from the footpath where Manuel attacked the mother and child in March 1946.

Nearly twelve years later, on 28 December 1957, Manuel had returned to a tried and tested crime scene to wait for the milieu he was comfortable in – darkness.

That date could also be significant for another reason – it was the day Chief Superintendent James Hendry retired.

Mr and Mrs Cooke had left home at 4pm that afternoon, leaving Isabelle, her brothers and Mr Cooke's mother in the house. They returned just before 8pm, by which time they knew their daughter had left to meet a boyfriend and go to a dance in Bellshill, as she usually did on a Saturday night.

By that time, however, she was dead.

She had left home at 6.45pm to meet up with a sixteen-year-old called Douglas Bryden. He later gave evidence that he had waited forty-five minutes at a bus stop in Uddingston for her before he gave up and went directly to the dance by himself.

Isabelle never arrived at the dance either.

Mrs Elsie Gardner lived close to the path Isabelle would have gone along, and her evidence suggested that the young girl walked out of the house and straight into Manuel's clutches. Mrs Gardner had been in her garden in the 'early evening' of the 28th, when she heard a female voice shouting out as if 'someone had got a fright'. Her dog had heard the noise and barked, running to the gate and continually barking until it calmed down and no further noise was heard.

Perhaps Isabelle was dead within five minutes of leaving the security of her own home.

For teenagers like Isabelle in the 1950s, the main recreation was dancing, and like Anne Kneilands, she looked forward to going out on a Saturday night, before the country effectively closed down for the Sabbath.

Isabelle had gone dancing in 'sensible' shoes but carried her dancing shoes in a vanity case which also contained a cosmetic bag – the indictment called it a 'pouchette' – a brush and a fan. All the girls did the same, the aim being to effect an air of glamour like the film stars of the day. She had a fur stole, 'Eiffel Tower' earrings, and a spray of artificial flowers on her dress.

Like Anne Kneilands, she was tall, pretty and seventeen. She was also on a date, but unlike Andrew Murnin, Douglas Bryden had turned up at the agreed tryst, then gone on to the dance, but he too was quickly eliminated as a suspect.

The Cookes endured the same indescribable agony the Kneilands had suffered as they awaited their daughter's return, but unlike Anne, Isabelle had apparently just vanished. The minuscule comfort of their daughter's body being quickly found was not even granted to the family, hence the Reverend Houston's appeal from the pulpit and the employment of hundreds of volunteer searchers. The minister was later recruited by the police to break the sad news to the Cookes when their daughter's body was eventually found in the early hours of 16 January 1958.

On the day she vanished, Mr and Mrs Cooke had gone to bed around midnight, puzzled as to why she was not in. Shortly after that, Mr Cooke found he was unable to sleep and he got up and searched with a torch at the very spot where his daughter had been attacked a few hours before.

By then she was buried in a field a quarter of a mile away.

The family phone was out of order, and in that dreadful situation, they took comfort in the notion that she had had to stay over somewhere and could not get in touch.

At their wits' end, the family reported her missing the next morning.

Hopes rise and dash in a tortuous fashion when a loved one is missing; knowledge of the unsolved Kneilands case hovered in the background, and when a policeman came to the door at 4.30pm they were tortured with worry, but anxious for good news.

It was bad news.

Her cosmetic bag had been found; a few hours later her under-skirt was found, then her coat, her flower spray, her pants, her vanity case, her brush and her stole. They were all identified by parents devastated with the certain knowledge their girl was never coming home.

Police activity was brisk and they co-ordinated a search of the River Calder with the Fire Brigade, British Rail and the National Coal Board all co-operating to lower the level of the river, and leading to the discovery of some of her clothes. Hundreds of volunteers searched the area and because the path was close to a railway line, every single goods wagon in Britain was checked in case she had been dumped on a passing train, an idea possibly owing something to the plot in the 1955 film *The Ladykillers*.

Manuel's homicidal impulse had trailed off in typical fashion, with him scattering trophies from his victim all around. It's thought that such behaviour is triggered by a desire to lay false trails, and whilst there may be some truth in that, it does not fully explain such actions.

Again, it has to be imagined that he gained some strange after-pleasure from behaving in that manner.

He definitely seems to have laid a trail with the buttons from her coat, leaving them near to an old mine shaft. When that was searched her vanity case was found, but, of course, her body was not. What is clear is that he must have spent a lot of time, post-murder, moving the lifeless girl about, digging not one but two graves, and planning out where he was going to leave his beloved false clues, in the shape of the dead girl's meagre belongings. Significantly, the scattered possessions were found in a straight line running between the Cooke house and the Manuel house, starting with the ring, then the vanity case, then some buttons, after which was her grave. That her shoes, her petticoat and her coat were found further along the line and closer to Birkenshaw presents a macabre image of a corpse being undressed by a killer loath to part with his trophies until only a few minutes from home.

By now he must have genuinely thought he was untouchable.

Mary McLachlan, Anne Kneilands and now Isabelle Cooke – and the police were powerless to stop him. In his own mind, he was firmly in control and they were dancing to his tune. When he later saw them searching the River Calder he commented to a friend that what they were finding was 'only a red herring' and when they were searching on a railway viaduct his view was that 'one of the bastards hanging by his neck from it' would be a fine sight, 'preferably if it was one with stripes on his arm'. Perhaps that observation was poignant and shows the stakes he was playing for in his 'me or them' mentality – the loser to hang.

His reliance on fellow offenders was naive, however. They did not admire the senseless slaying of innocent women for two possible reasons; for a start, there was no commercial gain, and anyway it was downright cowardly. Not that Manuel saw it that way. In his scenario, he was Cagney coolly 'plugging' little people who deserved to die. He could not expect other felons to understand his sexual difficulties, so he tended to keep the details of his attacks on young girls to himself. Nevertheless, he did open up to Joe Brannan, who then reported to the police every night at midnight. In the Cooke murder, it did not pay dividends, but it would the next time he killed.

Manuel fantasised he was a champion boxer in his desperate craving to be acknowledged as a 'hard man'. Indeed, some previous writers have gone as far as describing him as one of 'Glasgow's Hard Men', which apart from being geographically incorrect is nothing short of a complete misrepresentation.

One incident ten days before he was arrested for the final time sums it up.

It can be safely assumed that if the Misses Martin or the Reverend Houston and his wife had been at home, he would have executed them without much compunction. When a Mr John McMunn was awakened in his house in Uddingston in the early hours of 4 January 1958, he experienced something most of the population would rather forgo.

Hearing a noise, he switched the light on to see Peter Manuel sneering at him and his wife round the bedroom door. Had he known who it was, Mr McMunn might not have reacted as he did, but he showed commendable composure in shouting 'Who is it?' and 'Where's the gun?' Mrs McMunn was as quick-witted as her husband and she shouted 'Here it is!'

Manuel had thrown the Beretta in the River Clyde by that time and he was without the comfort of a weapon, so he ran for his life as Mr McMunn chased him downstairs and out of an open window. Ruthless serial killer he might be, but self-preservation was clearly still dear to him.

The Cooke murder enquiry ground on with no obvious results, but Joe Brannan's information was about to pay dividends. Not, however, before more innocent citizens were executed.

24

SMART KILLINGS

In his celebrated book about a criminal psychopath from 1944, *Rebel Without a Cause*, Robert M. Lindner explained the difficulty with the term 'psychopath'. He wrote, 'All those characteristics which, by any count, may be considered the negative of qualities suitable for current civilised communal living, have at one time or another been assigned to the individual called 'psychopath'. And, in truth, there is no other way in which he can be described except by reference to the social order in which he happens to exist.'

He argued that the difficulty with attempting to define the term is that psychopathic behaviour 'can be measured by no other rule than that of the prevailing ethic and morality', so that in 'a society where total abstinence [from alcohol] is mandatory . . . inebriation would be a sign of psychopathy.'

If that view is correct, Peter Manuel was psychopathic from late childhood onwards and would have been unable to fit in with any society at any time in human history.

Once established, his psychopathy was continually built upon and strengthened to the point where he saw no wrong in slaying Sydney Dunn (if in fact he did), Isabelle Cooke and the Smart family in the space of just over three weeks.

A motive for killing Dunn is not clear; with Isabelle Cooke it seems it was sexual gratification. The slaughter of the Smarts, like the murder of the Watts and Mrs Brown, was probably a source of satisfaction and indulgence, but with the Smarts he combined his murderous lust with a spot of theft. Had he not, he might not have provided the investigation into their murders with valuable evidence.

Peter Smart lived with his wife and son in Sheepburn Road, Uddingston in a bungalow they had built in 1954. Mr Smart was the manager of a firm of civil engineering contractors in Glasgow and on 31 December 1957 he was paid his monthly salary of £187 15s. 11d. He went to the Commercial Bank of Scotland at Parkhead Cross in Glasgow and withdrew £35, £10 of which he paid to his office in new blue sequential Commercial Bank pound notes. From that date he was on holiday until 6 January 1958 and the holiday plan was to possibly visit his parents, who lived at Ancrum near Jedburgh in the Scottish Borders, and to visit friends who were hoteliers at the Dumbuck Hotel at Dumbarton.

The office closed early as it was New Year's Eve, and Mr Smart, having decided to stock up with whisky for the visit of friends to his house or to take with him on his travels, went to a pub in Uddingston to buy a few bottles and have a drink. He came back into the bar later that night and from what he told the publican, his intention was to get up early and drive, probably to the Borders. He left at closing time at ten o' clock and made his way home.

Mrs Doris Smart had spoken to neighbours, who came over for half an hour in the evening and left well before 'The Bells' at midnight. Fifty years ago, bringing in the New Year was anticipated far more keenly than it is today. Families saved up to buy a 'Ne'erday' bottle which often sat for a couple of months in a cupboard awaiting the big day, when it was, and still is, customary to visit neighbours and relations to 'first foot' them and celebrate the onset of a new year and another year's passing. To signify willingness to receive guests it is customary to leave the lights on, otherwise darkness denotes the option of an early night without visitors.

The Smarts compromised, their lights going off at about 2.30am after they had toasted each other before going to bed, young Michael having been dispatched to his room much earlier.

At Manuel's subsequent trial, Lord Cameron asked a planning

officer who had prepared a map of the area after the murder of Isabelle Cooke, what the distance was between the Smarts' house in Sheepburn Road and the Manuels' house at 32 Fourth Street, Birkenshaw.

The answer was just under a mile by road and about a fifteen-minute walk.

When Mary McLachlan was attacked in 1955, she had been coming up the Lucy Brae from the direction of Uddingston, which is the quickest route on foot to and from Uddingston. That short distance was the gap between the lives of Peter Manuel and Peter Smart and hard-working respectability was no firewall to a most unwelcome first foot.

It's still difficult to accept that the Smart family could have lain undiscovered from about 6am on New Year's Day until the morning of 6 January 1958, but that is what happened.

A combination of tentative arrangements and frugal use of the telephone meant that Mr Smart's parents and brothers in the Borders and the McManus family in the Dumbuck Hotel in Dumbarton both assumed that Peter Smart and his family had visited the other. The neighbours in Sheepburn Road noticed nothing amiss either.

Indeed, they later talked of apparent normality in circumstances which were akin to a plot in a horror story.

Mr Jackman, who lived across the road, had gone over to close the garage doors, which he had first noticed were lying open about 10am on 1 January; both he and the postman, who delivered mail on 2 January, noticed all curtains closed except for those of the lounge to the left of the front door. A dustman that afternoon noticed that all the curtains were now open. One of Michael's pals had looked in at the house at about 2pm on 3 January and all the curtains were now closed. Then later that day a close friend and neighbour noticed that the lounge curtains were now drawn but the window was open. She considered that to be most unlike Doris, who was a proud house-keeper, but when her husband saw a light on through the curtains later that night, they simply assumed that the Smarts must have come home.

Again, the postman and Mr Jackman noticed that the curtains

which had been closed in the dining room were open on Saturday 4 January, something also noticed by the next-door neighbour, Mrs Duncan. Later that day a neighbour noticed they were closed, but again most un-Doris like, they were drawn unevenly with a gap at the top and overlapping at the bottom; later that day they were open again.

When Mr Smart failed to turn up for work at 8am on 6 January 1958, the whole unbelievable story started to unfold.

First, the police phoned the office to find out why his company car, an Austin A35, had been abandoned in Florence Street in the then notorious Gorbals area of Glasgow on 2 January. Some local kids had attracted police attention when they were seen playing in it.

Colleagues from work actually went to 38 Sheepburn Road and walked round the house, but all seemed secure. After a while, they went to the police and when they made enquiries with neighbours, the decision was made to force entry. The living room was festooned with Christmas decorations and all appeared normal. Then a sergeant went into the bedrooms and found the bodies, all shot in the head whilst lying in their beds, which were now saturated with blood, the unmistakable smell of death pervading the house.

When the news of the slaughter of the Smarts spread, the local populace frenziedly bought up all the security chains and bolts they could lay their hands on; to the police, who were fully engaged on the Cooke murder enquiry, it sounded at first like a sick joke, but it was all too real.

Only one person would have been capable of explaining why Manuel did what he did between 1 and 6 January 1958, and that was Manuel himself.

What satisfaction he achieved by continually returning to the death scene is hard to fathom. His pleasure could only have come from being in temporary charge of a solid respectable house whose inhabitants he had executed. By returning, he reaffirmed his power of life and death over them and his contempt for their lifestyle.

He might even have returned for one reason alone: to make sure that the family cat was fed.

25

PARTY TIME

Student nurse Mary McDonald, on duty at Glasgow's Southern General Hospital in the early hours of the morning of 1 January 1958, was treated to two phone calls from her friend and fellow nurse, Teresa Manuel, the first interrupted when the nursing sister suddenly appeared in the ward and Mary quickly hung up.

In the course of both calls, Teresa's brother Peter was in such good spirits that he sang down the phone to her. The first song was 'Come Back to Sorrento' and he sang it in Italian. Then he sang Al Martino's hit from 1952 'Here in My Heart', the first line of which is 'Here in my heart I'm alone and so lonely'.

The contrast is poignant; at about the time of Manuel's serenade, the Smarts were wishing each other a 'Happy New Year' serenely and mercifully unaware that for them 1958 was going to last approximately six hours.

And the exuberant romantic on the phone was coldly setting up an alibi before he crept out into the chill of a New Year's morning, ghosted down the Lucy Brae and casually shot the Smart family as they slept, ten-year-old Michael included. His classic round National Health glasses were still lying on his bedside table where he had placed them the night before, when the police found him on the morning of 6 January.

On New Year's Eve, Manuel had been stony broke. He had bought a bottle of wine with money his brother James had given him and they had gone drinking with their father in the Stag in Viewpark, Uddingston. To his mother's great joy, Peter had been at confession at Christmas for the first time in many years – a fact which later sparked off a debate about the extent of a priest's duty of confidentiality. She had given him five shillings after church. When the father and sons left the Stag and had gone on to a different pub, Peter kept the change from a pound note his father had given him to buy a round of drinks.

Joe Brannan had met them and had seen it happen. He reported that Peter had taken the change and said, 'That's a pound I owe you,' to his father. In Manuel's mind was that something that had to be honoured? And was that enough to cause him to repay his debt as quickly as he could and by any means?

By tradition at New Year, the family gathers together at home before midnight, and the Manuels, together with cousin Ronald Faubert, on leave from the US Army, assembled at 32 Fourth Street. They saw in the New Year, stayed up drinking, phoning Mary and singing until they eventually started drifting off to bed. Mrs Manuel made porridge for her husband, who was working as usual that day, before she went to bed at about 5am, leaving her two sons clearing up and washing dishes.

It probably gets no more surreal than that.

A cold-hearted serial killer aged thirty-one, still living with his parents, doing the washing up and biding his time for his family to go to bed so he could sneak out and kill, hopefully for profit.

The house was busy and Peter had managed to ensure that he was the only one downstairs, as he slept in a fold-up bed in the living room; James had seemingly gone to bed at six and Samuel had got up at seven.

If his father's testimony could be trusted – and there is no obvious reason why it should – he later said that Peter was sound asleep on the fold-up bed when he got up.

Could he have committed the crimes and been back home in an hour?

The police reckoned he could have.

In an informal re-enactment, they showed he could have travelled to and from Sheepburn Road in about twenty minutes, then given himself half an hour to break in, murder all the occupants, steal whatever he wanted then get back before his father got up.

Even if Samuel was up to his old trick of saying anything to 'assist' his errant son – something he was to do to the bitter end – the testimony of John Buchanan was noteworthy. He was the owner of the store near the Lucy Brae who had heard the screams of Mary McLachlan in July 1955 and he knew the Manuel family well. He recalled that his first customer and 'first foot' at about 10 o'clock on 1 January 1958, was a well-groomed, high-spirited Peter Manuel who bought cigarettes and chatted sociably.

After buying the cigarettes, he went to Joe Brannan's house, and they resumed drinking, going to the Woodend Hotel in Mossend.

Brannan recalled that Manuel had gone from total penury to complete carelessness with money, to the extent that he handed over a £5 note thinking it was £1, then bought staff a drink for bringing the mistake to his attention.

In expansive mood, Manuel was now rewarding people for their honesty.

He bought whisky and wine for the Brannan house and gave a florin to each of the two Brannan children. At his trial, there was evidence that he had been seen on a bus returning from Glasgow that morning, but he explained to Brannan that he had gone to the Gordon Club in Glasgow and been given some money 'in connection with the Watt murders'.

Later he went to a family party where he sang again, this time 'Auld Scotch Mither of Mine' and spent nearly £10 on drink and cigarettes he brought with him. When his parents decided to go home from the party, he paid a pound for a taxi for them and afterwards paid the remnants of the party into a dance at the local miner's club, near the family home.

At his trial, there was evidence that he had received three payments from the National Assistance Board in December 1957 and January 1958 and had a bank account with 2s. 2d. in it.

Not exactly the springboard for extravagance.

So even if Samuel Manuel was lying about the time, John Buchanan was not. And Peter simply did not appear to be different that morning when he came into the shop.

If anything, he looked relaxed and in good form.

Why?

He could only have had a couple of hours' sleep and had clearly spent time on personal grooming by the time Buchanan saw him at ten o'clock.

Was he in such obvious high spirits because he had 'come into' some money? There can be no suggestion that he had not killed the unfortunate Smarts, so it can be assumed that rather than suffering any ill effects after killing two defenceless adults and a young boy, he was positively buoyant.

Mrs Manuel in particular seems to have misread the signs and been jubilant that her son, so recently released from prison, was showing genuine indications of mending his ways.

And such generosity to his nearest and dearest!

As they rode back to Birkenshaw in a taxi on New Year's night, the Manuels must have basked in a successful twenty-four hours of family togetherness, with Peter being particularly attentive to his parents and cousins.

Over the next few days, to ask him where he was going as he left the house at odd hours would have been churlish, given his age and the difficulties he appeared to have overcome.

But leave he did, to return repeatedly to the scene of the crime at Sheepburn Road to open and close the curtains, to put the lights on and off, and to gloat at the bodies of people who had been misguided enough to have conformed to all the rules.

And to feed the cat with salmon.

A neighbour had noticed it and fed it when she saw it out, but Manuel had obviously let it into the house, as a half-empty tin was later found in the kitchen.

He was concerned about the animal's welfare now that its owners were obviously not going to be around to feed it.

The risk of being found on the premises was clearly outweighed by the thrill of being there. Why even think of taking the car from the garage, given the likelihood of neighbours seeing it being driven away in the narrow confines of Sheepburn Road? A bigger thrill could be had by using it, even if just to exhibit total mastery and control.

The best was yet to come, though.

Constable Robert Smith left his house on the morning of 2 January 1958 to take part in the search for the clothing and possessions of the missing Isabelle Cooke in the River Calder. He lived near Sheepburn Road and was in uniform when he approached a grey two-door Austin A35 stopped at a junction at 8.10am. He said he spoke to the driver about where he was going. They were going in the same direction, so he got a lift and they chatted as they travelled the two and a half miles to the search site.

He later attended an identification parade and picked the driver out.

It just had to be Peter Manuel.

26

INVESTIGATION AND ARRESTS

In November 1953, a sixteen-year-old youth called John Chalmers was tried for the murder and robbery of a workmate. The court sat at the historic town of Stirling with Lord Strachan – in those days, pronounced 'Straw-an' – presiding. The jury found Chalmers guilty and he was sentenced to be 'detained during Her Majesty's pleasure'. He appealed against the conviction and it was heard by a 'Full Bench' of five judges, who allowed the appeal and quashed the conviction.

Despite the fact that Chalmers had confessed and then led detectives to where the victim's 'purse' was found in a cornfield, the Appeal Court decided that what had happened in the course of the trial was unfair.

In those days, the court jealously guarded the rights of those 'under suspicion' and it's fair to say that many aspects of the criminal justice system were fairer in Scotland then, as compared to the so-called 'Human Rights' culture which pertains now.

After police started their investigations into the assault on Chalmers' victim, they questioned everybody in the foundry where the deceased worked, and in the course of that, spoke to Chalmers. They later spoke to him again and in the light of what was said this time, they decided to interview him further and he was taken to a police station. He then made a further statement and took them to the cornfield shortly afterwards.

At his trial, the prosecution made no mention of the first statement which caused police to take him to the police station, but led evidence of him taking them to the cornfield and recovering the purse. The Appeal Court judges held that the discovery of the purse was part of the same process as the giving of the statement and was unfair and should be disregarded, and that all that then remained in terms of evidence was the statement made after the purse was recovered and accordingly there was insufficient evidence to sustain the conviction.

The message was clear: when a person has become a suspect, any confession has to be 'spontaneous' and cannot be allowed in evidence if, for instance, it appears to have been elicited by 'cross-examination' or other 'pressure' by the police.

There seems little doubt that Manuel knew of the Chalmers case. He had studied criminal law during his sentence in Peterhead Prison, and avidly read newspapers and current affairs. A momentous decision like Chalmers was obviously well publicised, and it undoubtedly influenced his behaviour after his arrest and during his trial in 1958.

The importance of ensuring a suspect's rights also seems to have affected the police approach to the investigation, and they did so carefully, indeed too carefully for some critics.

Matters, however, were in hand.

First, they had Joe Brannan on the team, and when he reported that Manuel had miraculously come into money at the very start of 1958, they investigated further. Staff at the Commercial Bank of Scotland were interviewed and the same ethereal force which caused Mrs Platt to find out what was in the lumpy mattress interceded again. The morning that Mr Smart had gone to the bank to withdraw £35, a block of brand-new blue pound notes had been issued, some of which were traced to the customer who had followed Mr Smart in the banking queue on the day in question. A sequence of serial numbers was established and to the joy of the investigation team, some of the notes used by Mr Smart at work to pay his expenses that day followed the pattern.

He had gone home with £25 in new notes in his wallet, cash for the holiday he was looking forward to, and if the notes Manuel had squandered on 1 January 1958 could be traced and matched, Manuel had some explaining to do.

They were and he had.

Secondly – and despite unease at the slowness of the investigation – police made a decision not to rush in.

This proved to be sound judgement.

They were dealing with no ordinary member of the public. Anyway,
they reasoned that if they did the opposite of his expectations, he
might be wrong-footed.

Behind the scenes, of course, no chances were being taken, in case
he struck again, and given what he had done up till now, the next
outrage would have to be pretty spectacular. A squad of twenty officers now watched his every move, and because it was Manuel they
were observing, a warning was added to their orders, lest the next
victim was one of them.

If any of the team was more than fifteen minutes late in reporting
back from duty, that fact was to be communicated to senior officers,
who now believed he was capable of anything. Some of the police
involved started checking all doors and windows of their houses
before entering, in case he was hiding inside.

The public were in panic. In the phrase of the time, the killer had
achieved what only Hitler had previously done and caused families
to 'evacuate' their children, particularly their daughters, from
Lanarkshire and Glasgow to relatives elsewhere. Scout packs and vigi-
lante groups patrolled the streets and offered escorts to women at
night, and women who lived alone armed themselves with knives, sat
by the phone and imagined that the slightest sound after dark signalled
their final moments. Security equipment sales broke all previous records.

What of Manuel?

He made the remark about 'the bastards digging up his garden
again' to Brannan when the Smart murders were discussed, so it
seems he was expecting police to charge in as usual.

He was definitely rattled this time, though.

Previously he had dictated strategy and the police, then unaware
of the studied criminal calibre of their suspect, had rushed in and
failed to secure any residual evidence. He never left fingerprints.
And they would have to assume there would be no incriminating
evidence at 32 Fourth Street either.

On the face of it, therefore, they were apparently doing nothing.

Brannan reported that Manuel was getting edgy and wanted both of them to take off to London. Joe had not unreasonably pointed out that he had a family to look after, so declined the suggestion.

But it was significant and encouraging that Manuel's steely nerve was wavering.

Timing was now the key.

At 6.45am on 14 January 1958, the murder squad went to his house with a search warrant. Samuel was just leaving for work. He was quickly disabused of any notion of work for that day and persuaded to come back indoors, where he began his usual rant about police oppression and the remedies that would inevitably follow once lawyers, councillors and Members of Parliament got to hear of this latest outrage. Brother James too was about to go to work, but Peter was asleep in the same fold-up bed he had used thirteen days before.

Peter demanded sight of the search warrant, then started to swear and challenge the officers. He behaved as they expected and eventually he was told he was being arrested.

Probably just as predictably, Mrs Manuel made him a cup of tea, which he was allowed to drink before he went. Always conscious of his appearance, he selected a red tie to wear before he left 32 Fourth Street, Birkenshaw for the last time.

Contrary to expectations, the police now found the gloves and the camera which were stolen from the Reverend Houston's house on Christmas Day 1957. Members of the Manuel family at that stage had a choice – they could continue the deception about his actions or they could accept that the time had come.

Teresa chose the latter.

She informed the police that Peter had given her the camera as a Christmas present.

Samuel, however, stuck to the script. He told them the sheepskin gloves were a Christmas present but as to who the donor had been he couldn't quite remember, possibly someone from America.

Being in possession of recently stolen goods in criminative circumstances raises a presumption of theft in Scots law. Armed with the gloves and the camera, the police went to see the Reverend Houston and he identified them as the items recently stolen from his house.

Whom would members of a jury believe – Samuel Manuel or the Reverend Alexander Houston?

In a move then regarded as bordering on 'sharp practice', the police took Samuel Manuel to Bellshill Police Station to 'continue with their enquiries'. This led to him being charged with breaking into 66 Wester Road and stealing money, the camera and the gloves whilst acting with Peter Manuel.

No-one seriously could have believed that Samuel Manuel had one night turned his back on a lifetime of crime-free behaviour to team up with his wayward son and embark on a housebreaking expedition. In truth, Samuel's real crime was not the sort recorded at the Criminal Records Office, the crime of unthinkingly supporting whatever his son had said, even if it was transparent gibberish solely designed to stave off impending criminal charges. How could he even start to explain or justify why he unquestioningly and stoically backed Peter at all times? Did he never speak to him in private to find out what was really going on? Was he too afraid to know the truth or was he just frightened of his son, knowing what he was capable of doing? In this instance, he didn't even know what Peter had said or was going to say about the gloves, as he had been arrested and removed prior to the identification by the Reverend Houston of his own possessions.

Detective Chief Superintendent (later Assistant Chief Constable) William Muncie afterwards wrote his memoirs and included his involvement in the Manuel story. He had arrested him for housebreaking as a youngster, been involved in the various murder enquiries and ultimately delivered the warrant for his execution to the Governor of HM Prison Barlinnie, Glasgow in July 1958.

He also collaborated with the author, John Bingham, who wrote *The Hunting Down of Peter Manuel*. It is worth quoting what Bingham wrote about this delicate stage of the investigation: 'It is the author's opinion that although the police may have had cause to suspect Samuel Manuel of illegally receiving the gloves, they were also aware of mutual family affection, and apart from the question of pure justice in the matter of the gloves there may have been some secret hope that the arrest of the father would spark off at least something of interest from the son.'

In a footnote, he recorded, 'Questioned on this point, Detective Chief Superintendent Muncie would only reply that the author had "a nasty suspicious mind".'

Anyway, it had the desired effect and 'something of interest' was indeed 'sparked off'. Manuel not only confessed to some of the murders he had committed, but he also incriminated himself by taking the police to various significant locations.

At the appeal hearing following Manuel's convictions, Lord Cameron's reasons were given for repelling the objection to the admissibility of statements Manuel made following his and his father's arrest. Referring to Samuel's arrest, he observed: 'I see no reason to think that the arrest was not fully justified in the existing circumstances, and none to infer that it was part of a manoeuvre to bring police pressure to bear upon the accused to furnish a confession or incriminating information in relation to the unsolved murders which had taken place in Lanarkshire and were still the subject of anxious police inquiry.'

To this day, there are those who disagree and clearly see the move for what it was – a rare opportunity to exert emotional pressure on a spree-killing psychopath in the one area in which he was decidedly vulnerable.

27

FIRST CONFESSIONS

The son was taken to Hamilton police office and the father to Barlinnie Prison. A series of identification parades led to a procession of witnesses picking Peter Manuel out as having either paid for items, mostly alcohol, with the stolen notes or having given them out as presents. Included in the latter were relations from the party on New Year's Day.

His confidence returned to the point where he decided to dispense with the services of a solicitor, probably imagining he could, yet again, bamboozle slow-witted 'busies', as he called the police. He also quickly mobilised his blame-deflection technique and implicated a character called Samuel 'Dandy' McKay from the Gordon Club. For an impromptu reaction to his possession of the new banknotes, Manuel came up with a characteristic odyssey of fantasy and fool-hardiness in equal proportions.

His story was almost childlike, something often observed in those with psychopathic tendencies. He claimed McKay had paid him for a guided tour of the area round Sheepburn Road as he was at the planning stage of a hold-up, and required local knowledge.

Yet again, Manuel was attempting to persuade the rest of the world that other people made themselves vulnerable to betrayal by bringing him into their nefarious schemes. They seemingly sought his expertise and advice on matters which they could easily have reconnoitred themselves, and then brainlessly pursued their plans, unaware that they had left themselves open to betrayal, detection and arrest.

It also illustrates the low opinion he had of the intellect of fellow criminals.

Blaming another person often happens when a person is charged with a crime; blaming someone who could easily demonstrate total non-involvement and turn up the heat in return simply illustrates either desperation or a growing realisation that the suspect, surprisingly, never really understood the basic rules of the game and was actually naive.

The first rule, of course, is to say nothing. Manuel, for no patently good reason, had elected to speak up and had thus given the authorities something to work on.

The Manuel murder team had considered their approach, and they knew McKay well. When he was told about Manuel's assertion, not only was McKay angry, the police allowed him to face Manuel and tell him so. He also accurately predicted that Manuel 'would swing for it'. Then he went to a different part of the police station and told the enquiry team that on 19 December 1957 he had been involved in getting a Beretta automatic for Manuel.

That incident, together with the psychological pressure of his father's arrest, began to gnaw at him.

Deliberately, no member of the enquiry team said anything to him about his father, but significantly, Manuel asked. The effect of hearing that his father was in Barlinnie Prison on a charge of housebreaking was instantaneous.

Just after midnight on 15 January he asked to see Inspector Robert McNeill. That he then waited two and a half hours for the meeting to take place was the subject of approving comment at the forthcoming trial from Manuel himself. He said that he would have done the same if roles had been reversed.

The knowledge that Samuel was in jail tipped the scales and he said that if he could see his parents, he would 'clear up' some 'unsolved crimes in Lanarkshire'. The police had called the psychology correctly; it was clear that the father-son relationship was not all one-way devotion by the father.

He continued by saying that once his parents were present he would 'make a clean breast' of things, and then take McNeill to where Isabelle Cooke was buried.

The police later insisted that he had been properly cautioned at all appropriate times and that he had eschewed the services of a solicitor. Manuel was to provide an alternative version of events at the trial, but what is beyond dispute is that he wrote, in his usual layman's legalese:

15 January 1958.

To Detective Inspector McNeill, I hereby promise you personally that I am prepared to give information to you that will enable you to clear up a number of unsolved crimes which occurred in the County of Lanarkshire in the past two years.

This promise is given that I might release my father and my family from any obligations or loyalties they may feel on my behalf. I wish to see my parents and make a clean breast with them first.

The crimes I refer to above are crimes of Homicide. I further wish to stress that I volunteer this statement of my own freewill, without duress or pressure of any description being brought to bear on me.

(signed) Peter T. Manuel

Some psychologists argue that the key to the personality of the psychopath is his childlike failure to comprehend that he has actually done something wrong. He also sometimes believes that his behaviour is only truly assessed by those originally tasked to judge him, in this case, his parents. The above note seems to bear some of that theory out; it also is redolent of Manuel's style, for example, 'hereby promise you', 'enable you to clear up' crimes which 'occurred', the promise is given in order to 'release' his father and family from 'obligations or loyalties they may feel'; the crimes are 'Homicide' and no 'duress or pressure' had been 'brought to bear' on him.

Then he suddenly decided that the note 'would not do' and he wrote another one.

Why?

Was it a ploy to be exploited in court? He certainly tried to make something of it in the trial itself, even pointing out that the first note and the second note had different signatures, one reading 'Peter T. Manuel' and the next one being devoid of the middle initial. Like others with a smattering of knowledge, he seems to have believed that legal procedure was full of technical pitfalls which could be exploited by those clever enough to spot them.

The second statement read:

15th January 1958
To Detective Inspector McNeill, I hereby freely and voluntarily give the following promise. I will lead information about the following specified crimes:
1. Anne Kneilands
2. The Watt murders
3. Isabelle Cooke
4. The Smart murders
On condition that my father is released and allowed to see me and my mother.

The information I refer to concerns me, Peter Thomas Manuel, and my part in the above mentioned crimes. I will give complete and precise information on these crimes that will clear them up completely.

(signed) Peter Manuel

At the very least, he was trying to manoeuvre himself into a controlling situation with the police, trading off knowledge and getting something in return. The Inspector and the rest of the squad knew that if they did the unexpected it would keep him performing, so McNeill played it cool, explaining that he would need to check with the prosecutor – the Procurator Fiscal – before he could give any assurances.

Manuel, however, was desperately keen to continue – partly at least in order that he could later allege unfairness via police pressure and promises – and he gave more information about the Smart murders.

Despite being cautioned, according to the Inspector, he said:

I did it about six o' clock in the morning of New Year's Day. I got in the kitchen window. I went into a bedroom and got eighteen or twenty pounds in new notes and four or five ten shilling notes in a wallet. It was in a jacket hanging on a chair in the man's room. I shot the man first then the woman and I then shot the boy, but at first I thought it was a man in the bed.

I then went into the living-room and ate a handful of wee biscuits from a tray on a chiffonier and I got about eighteen shillings from a red purse in the woman's hand-bag. I took the man's keys and then took the car. The car key was on a bunch on a ring.

I put it in the Ranco car park and took it to Florence Street the next day. I left it there about eight o clock the next morning. I gave a policeman a lift on the way. He is a young fellow who lives in Powburn, but I never took these cigarettes I saw in the papers.

I threw the gun in the Clyde and the keys in the Calder at the bridge. I think I threw the purse there too.

Few homicidal housebreakers would let the police know that they ate biscuits from a tray on a 'chiffonier' – a chest of drawers – and he somehow tried to portray the shooting of the child as a mistake, a fine distinction for a man about to confess to killing two young girls and shooting three sleeping women.

Permission was given for the meeting. His father was brought from prison and his mother from the family home. She was about to learn the awful truth that she must have suspected and her husband must already have known.

How did he break the news to his parents that he was the serial killer who had been spreading terror for years? He started by asking after their welfare, then his sister's then his brother's and in return they enquired of his.

It was awkward.

Then he turned to one of the policemen and asked about his father and if he was to be freed from prison. Despite being told the answer was no, he turned and faced his father. He asked why he had not simply told the truth and told the police that he had given the gloves to him.

Samuel didn't or couldn't answer.

Hunting and killing a terrified young girl was easy for Manuel – talking frankly to his parents took great courage on his part. He spoke softly and told them that he always had difficulty speaking to them and could never tell them all the truth.

His mother recognised her son's difficulty and tried to make it easier for him. She said that she already knew he couldn't tell them everything and that he sometimes kept things to himself. She had always hoped he would return to the religious fold that both she and her husband inhabited, and she thought it significant he had recently attended confession. She was now about to hear a confession that would ruin what was left of her life.

He looked at the only two people who had always supported him against a hostile world, and said, 'There's no future for me. I have done some terrible things. I killed the girl Kneilands at East Kilbride and I shot the three women in the house at Burnside.'

His parents were devastated, but he went on to tell them that he had also shot the Smart family on New Year's Day.

Perhaps Samuel was shocked by the sheer volume of the crimes, but Bridget had never really wanted to believe any of it. Pitifully, she was later to unsuccessfully try to petition to stop the execution.

After the harrowing meeting, she was returned to her home courtesy of a police car whilst Samuel went back to prison. The warm memory of their son's generosity in paying their taxi fare home from the party a fortnight before was now bitter.

Shortly after that, Samuel was liberated from prison.

Physically at least.

28

ISABELLE FOUND AND MORE CONFESSIONS

During the twelve years since Detective Chief Superintendent Muncie had first arrested Manuel for housebreaking, they had met 'professionally' on several occasions. As Manuel's outrages increased in degree and volume, Muncie developed what colleagues termed 'Manuelitis', whereby he suspected him in every major incident.

Manuel and his father called it victimisation.

Muncie experienced the frustration of a police officer sure of his case but playing by the rules, whilst Manuel let it be generally known that he had settled his differences with him in an encounter in a lane during which Muncie came off worse, sustaining a broken nose.

The usual fantasy, but Muncie conceded that he was concerned about the possibility of Manuel perpetrating some personal attack on his house, particularly as he had the misfortune to stay within 'Manuel country'. As other officers were later to confess to doing, Muncie was in the habit of checking his house before going in.

The Smart murders had also had a bad personal effect. Mrs Muncie was still haunted by her memory of six-year-old Michael Smart pushing a toy wheelbarrow 'helping' his father as he built the house in Sheepburn Road in 1954.

After his arrest, Muncie took the opportunity of going into Manuel's cell, unsure of how the encounter was going to go. To his surprise, he found Manuel reflective and reasonable. When they discussed the Kneilands murder, Muncie claimed that Manuel expressed a wish that he had been stopped at that stage, but that he had been 'fighting these things in his head for years'. Again he protested that he would not have shot Michael Smart had he known it was 'a wee boy' in the bed.

This information was 'off the record' and not used in court; anyway, normal relations resumed as he left the cell, with Manuel stretching his arms out and complaining that the prison garb he had been issued with was not fit for a scarecrow, his appearance as ever being crucial to his self-esteem.

Before that, though, police had cracked the case.

They had judged correctly that Manuel would be anxious to portray himself as their equal in all respects, and that once the 'deal' was done to take the heat off his father, he would then honour his side of the bargain.

Having offered to show where Isabelle Cooke was interred, he was given his chance as officers temporarily liberated him from Barlinnie Prison. According to them, he took the lead and led them to the spot. At the trial, Manuel naturally made out that he had been led by them.

Once given his chance, Manuel set off like a bloodhound, in an unexpected direction. As officers struggled to peer through a coal-black night, Manuel was perfectly at home and sure-footedly made his way over fields and fences. On the way, he stopped to explain that he had first tried to bury her at a certain spot, but had been disturbed by a man taking a shortcut, so he had carried her a further two hundred yards on.

Further on, he stopped to pull one of Isabelle's dancing shoes from under some bricks and then a second from underneath some ashes. Then he went to a farm road, stopped and paced out a distance from a tree, noticing the field had been ploughed since he had been there, and stopped again. He looked back at the tree again, stood his ground and casually announced that he 'was standing on her'.

Isabelle had not been far from home all the time.

She had been gagged with her headscarf to stop her screaming as he had done what he had to do. Afterwards he strangled her with her bra which was still tied tightly round her neck, before he went on his characteristic 'scattering' spree with her possessions.

An excited young girl had walked out of her family's home and into her worst nightmare.

At the grave, Manuel was impassive.

Businesslike, he then suggested he would write out a full confession when he got back to the police station, which he did.

It started at 4.15am, he wrote five pages and it lasted two hours. At the instigation of the police, the initial part of the statement was formal and he wrote:

4.15am

Thursday, 16th January, 1958.

I am at present in custody in County Police Headquarters, Hamilton, on a charge of murder. I have been informed that I am not obliged to say anything unless I wish to do so, but whatever I say will be taken down in writing and may be given in evidence. I have been informed that I am entitled to have the benefit of legal advice before making this statement. I wish to make a statement.

Signed: Peter Manuel

Date: 16.1.1958

Witnessed: Matthew Cleland

Inspector

After that, he continued:

I hereby confess that on the 1st of January, 1956, I was the person responsible for killing Anne Kneilands.

On the 17th of September, 1956, I was responsible for killing Mrs Marion Watt and her sister, Mrs George Brown. Also her daughter Vivienne.

On the 28th December, 1957, I was responsible for killing Isabelle Cooke.

On January the first, 1958, I was responsible for killing Mr Peter Smart, his wife Doris and their son.

I freely admit and acknowledge my guilt in the above

mentioned crimes, and wish to write a statement concerning them.

The first part of the statement concerned Anne Kneilands and his peculiar story of her seemingly pestering him then virtually inviting her own end.

Then, dealing with the Watt murders, he went back, changed the date from the 17th to the 16th of September, and continued:

I left the Woodend Hotel, Mossend, at 10.00pm in the evening. I took two women into Glasgow, one named Jessie Findlay I dropped from a taxi at 283 High Street, Glasgow. The other one who I only know as Babs I took to Merchiston Street in North Carntyne. I left her there and took the taxi to Parkhead Cross. At the Cross I caught the bus to Birkenshaw. When I arrived home I met a man I knew and he took me in a car up to Burnside.

He had another man and a woman with him, we broke into a house in Fennsbank Avenue, number eighteen. We were there some time and somebody went to bed, I do not remember much about this house. The car was left in a lane in a small wood bordering the East Kilbride Road.

After a while I went scouting about looking at other houses. I found a house that looked empty and went back to number eighteen. Someone had brought the car round and put it in beside the house in front of the garage. I told them and they drove me up and I got out at the other house. The others did not like the look of it, so they went back to the house a(t) number eighteen. I broke into the house by breaking the front door panel, which was made of glass. I then went in and opened a bedroom door. There were two people in the bed. I went into the other room and there was a girl in the bed. She woke up and sat up. I hit her on the chin and knocked her out. I tied her hands and went back into the other room.

I shot the two people in this room, and then heard someone

making a noise in the other room. I went back in and the girl had got loose. We struggled around for a while and then I flung her on the bed and shot her too. I then went back to number eighteen and found them all asleep. We then took the car and they dropped me at Birkenshaw, and they went on to Motherwell, at about 5am on the 17th of September. I did not steal anything from the house at 5 Fennsbank Avenue. That same day I went into Glasgow and flung the gun in the Clyde at the Suspension Bridge. I got the gun in a public house in Glasgow called the Mercat Bar, which is at Glasgow Cross. I do not remember the date I got the gun. I got the gun as one of a pair I bought. The man who fixed it for me told me the two men who came into the pub were policemen. The other gun was taken from Burnbank. I never found out what became of it.

His account of the murders in the Watt house appears to be reasonably close to the truth, and this time he does not pretend that the real culprit later told him what had happened in great detail, as he alleged to Watt himself. At the trial he was to revert back to the other man, named as Tallis, as being responsible and then to change tack altogether and blame Watt for the whole episode.

His account of the break-in at number eighteen, the house belonging to the Misses Martin, was imaginative. He has the members of the gang seemingly breaking into a house in order to find somewhere comfortable to go to sleep.

Perhaps that is because that's exactly what he often did when he broke into houses. The attribution of this odd behaviour to three other persons who were not even there hints that at least he regarded it as perfectly normal behaviour and something that a jury would accept as likely.

His story as to how he got the gun seems pretty factual, except that it was later shown that the Webley transaction took place in a lane in Hamilton.

His statement had then gone on to the murder of Isabelle Cooke:

On the 28 December, 1957, I went to Mount Vernon about 7pm.

Going by bus from Birkenshaw to Mount Vernon, I walked up a road leading to the railway bridge that runs from Bothwell to Shettleston.

Just over the bridge I met a girl walking, I grabbed her and dragged her into a field on the same side as Rylands Riding School. I took her along the field following the line going in the Bothwell direction. I took her handbag and filled it with stones from the railway. Before going any further I flung it in a pond in the middle of field. I then made her go with me along towards the dog track. When we got near the dog track she started to scream. I tore off her clothes and tied something round her neck and choked her. I then carried her up a lane into a field and dug a hole with a shovel. While I was digging, a man passed along the lane on a bike. So I carried her again over a path beside a brick work into another field. I dug a hole next to a part of a field that was ploughed and put her in it. I covered her up and went back the way I came. I went back to the road and got her shoes which had come off at the outset. I took these and her clothes and scattered them about. The clothes I flung in the River Calder at Broomhouse. The shoe I hid on the railway bank at the dog track. I went up the path and came out at Baillieston. I walked along the Edinburgh Road and up Aitkenhead Road to Birkenshaw, getting there about 12.30am.

The first hole I dug I left as it was.

The 'first hole' had indeed been a puzzle to the police, but now they had seen and heard his explanation, it appeared he was probably being about as truthful as he could get. If that was so, and the sequence was correct, what a dreadful ordeal for Isabelle, with him taking her handbag, filling it with stones and throwing it away as she wondered what was going to happen to her after she had been dragged away from the path.

Like Anne Kneilands, he had offhandedly 'met' Isabelle Cooke, but in this case, at least he made no effort to suggest that she had tried to befriend him. The puzzling feature of the story was how he was able to lay his hands on a shovel so easily. Was it lying handily nearby, and did he take it then put it back? If it was, it seems mightily convenient and should perhaps have been something the enquiry officers would have noticed or heard about. And, of course, he could not bring himself to tell the real truth about the sequence of events. When she started to scream, he obviously became aroused enough to tear her clothes off, strangle her and bring himself to a homicidal sexual climax.

Manuel then turned to the Smart murders:

On the morning of the first of January I left my home about 5.30am. I went down a parkpath to the foot of the Lucy Brae. Crossing the road I went into Sheepburn Road and broke into a bungalow.

I went through the house and took a quantity of bank notes from a wallet I found in a jacket in a front bedroom. There was about twenty to twenty-five pounds in the wallet. I then shot the man in the bed, and next the woman. I then went into the next room and shot the boy. I did not take anything from the house except money. I got the gun from a man in Glasgow in a club. The Gordon Club. I took a car from the garage and drove it up to the car park at Ranco Works. Later that day I took the gun into Glasgow and threw it into the Clyde at Glasgow Green.

The next day, Thursday the 2nd I saw the car was still in the car park, so I drove it into Glasgow, at about eight o' clock in the morning and left it in Florence Street, in the South Side. Then I caught a bus back home.

I got into the house through a window, and left by the back door.

Signed. Peter Manuel

This statement was completed at 6.15am on 16.1.58

Matthew Cleland Inspector Witnessed by me

Donald Macleod Constable 137 Witnessed by me

Samuel Mather Constable 15

Again, this seems to be a reasonably cold, unvarnished and relatively factual account of what actually happened and could be bolstered at the trial by other known facts. Even so, his choice of Florence Street was interesting, as this was where one of the employees of the Gordon Club, an Andrew Thomson, lived and, tactically he may have been sowing the seeds of an incrimination of Thomson or McKay, which did not, however, materialise. He also falsely claimed that the Beretta had been given to him in the Gordon Club, instead of the truth, which was that he had got it in Thomson's house, so in that respect he was possibly still trying to keep his options open.

And yet, he had provided his life's enemies with enough information for them to feel reasonably confident about a conviction on any of the capital charges. He had even appeared anxious to help clear things up, as he had promised.

Perhaps the simple truth is that he felt important and self-empowered when he relived his exploits and he may even have imagined that the police had a secret admiration for him.

29

FISHING FOR GUNS

It had been an incredible few hours.

Apparently because Samuel had been held on what on any view was a minor matter, his son had willingly filled in all the gaps in the knowledge of the investigating officers. If, as he was to do, he later alleged duress and pressure had been exerted on him by the police, he would still have to explain how the nocturnal journey across the fields had landed the expedition at the exact spot where Isabelle Cooke had been interred in a makeshift grave.

He would also have to get round his 'special knowledge' of where the guns were disposed of.

If they could be found.

Not only had he taken the police to the banks of Glasgow's major river, he had shown them the exact spots where he had dropped the weapons into the murky waters. The Clyde is still tidal at both search areas, and almost all river traffic and industry is downstream of them. Despite that, the water was thick with muck and visibility was, and still is, very poor.

An operation to recover the Beretta attracted thousands of inquisitive onlookers and went on for over two weeks. It involved magnets and a small barge trawling the area. Apart from the usual detritus, there was no result.

The police must have firmly believed that Manuel was telling the truth about dumping the weapons at the specified locations, and they persevered. They brought in a larger magnet and incorporated a crane, but again to no avail. Finally, they decided that a new approach was needed and they employed a professional diver from the Clyde

Navigation Trust. His grid method was logical and effective and by groping about in the mud and silt, he found the Webley after half an hour and the Beretta a couple of days later. The Beretta was inside a makeshift parcel with two pairs of ladies' gloves, one pair of which was identified as having belonged to Mrs Smart of Sheepburn Road.

To the layman, the Chalmers case was probably illogical. Here was a self-confessed murderer who led police to property stolen from the victim, and yet the Appeal Court held that the conviction could not stand because of the unfair treatment meted out to the suspect. The major misconception surrounding the case is that unfair treatment by the police was the overriding factor in the appeal. Rather, their Lordships particularly disliked the way the evidence was seemingly screened by the Crown at the trial to effectively portray a distorted sequence of events.

If Manuel was gambling on convincing a judge that he had been treated unfairly by the investigating officers, he was definitely not helping himself when he offered to take police to the spot where he had thrown a piece of iron used to murder Anne Kneilands, together with her underwear, into the River Calder. At that stage of proceedings, the police were allowed to carry out further enquiries before an accused is 'fully committed until liberated in due course of law'. His request was granted on 18 January 1958 and a search of the river at the spot suggested revealed several pieces of metal, one of which could have been the weapon used.

The guns were examined by ballistics experts and the striation marks on spent cartridges matched those recovered from the respective murder sites. By that time, Mr Platt had brought in the bullet from the mattress and the link was made with the break-in at his house and the theft of the prototype electric razor. The case was strengthening, and it was boosted further when the keys for both the Smart house and the car stolen from there were found in the River Calder at the spot where Manuel said he had thrown them.

His actions in leading police to the body of Isabelle Cooke, then to the correct location of the guns and then to the General's Bridge to find the Smarts' keys would today be regarded by a Scottish court as exhibiting 'special knowledge' of the crime. It is one of those tiresome phrases in vogue for a while and purportedly much beloved of policemen clearing their backlog of crimes whenever a compliant car thief or rattling drug addict is arrested for a crime. Courts have accepted 'special knowledge' in alleged responses to charges of car theft such as 'the car was blue and X registered', on the basis that the perpetrator alone would know such gripping information. The logical link, of course, disappears where the particular 'special knowledge' can be shown to be common knowledge to all the inhabitants in a particular area, or, as is often alleged, the relevant crime reports are placed before the suspect and the details are discussed prior to interview.

Indeed, there have been instances of 'special knowledge' confessions from two and sometimes three different culprits for crimes committed by a single accused, and there have also been occasions when a confession does undoubtedly have the hallmarks of genuine 'special knowledge'.

For instance, there have been cases where a housebreaker confesses to stealing something which the householder was not aware had been taken and only discovers its disappearance when asked to check.

The concept had not been fully elevated to self-corroboration in 1958 and, perhaps more sensibly, was regarded as just another piece of evidence for the jury's consideration.

The guns had been recovered from the Clyde in early February. By 15 February, Manuel had been charged with nine murders, including the murder of Sydney Dunn in County Durham, England, for which the Scottish courts had no jurisdiction to try him. On 4 April 1958, he appeared at Glasgow Sheriff Court to answer the indictment and at that stage a simple plea of 'not guilty' was intimated and trial was fixed for the High Court at Glasgow for 14 April 1958. The special defences of alibi and incrimination were intimated but not made public, and speculation was rife, particularly in relation to any allegations about William Watt.

The trial was adjourned to 12 May 1958 after the case was called in the High Court at Edinburgh and more time was sought to prepare the defence, the 110-day committal to prison being extended to 30 June. The trial was set for Glasgow despite suggestions of unfairness due to pre-trial publicity and understandably strong public feeling in Lanarkshire. The pragmatic view was that Manuel's crimes were so notorious and well publicised that no court in the land could guarantee jurors who had not heard of him.

Sometimes there's no point in pretending.

There was widespread morbid fascination in what was to come.

30

THE INDICTMENT

Before the 'Trial of the Century' began in Glasgow High Court on Monday 12 May 1958, members of the public had been queuing up all night to take up the sixty seats allocated to them. The beat police had been told to make sure that the queue did not exceed that number, and they kept an eye on the situation.

The first in the queue was a Mr Perryman from Motherwell, who took his place at 7.40pm on the Sunday evening, settling down in his overcoat and silk scarf with a piece of toast in his pocket to sustain him through the night. He claimed to know Manuel quite well and said he was going to attend every day. Mr Perryman was said to live at 97 Dalriada Crescent, Motherwell and Mary Bowes, who was one of the persons incriminated by Manuel for the break-in at 18 Fennsbank Avenue, lived at number 103 in the same street, so perhaps Mr Perryman knew more than just the accused.

A luckless sixteen-year-old joined the queue at 11pm on the Sunday, spent the night on the street and was dispatched home at 8.30 on the Monday morning, as the police on duty deemed him too young!

An exiled and excited Glaswegian – now resident in Edinburgh – and her friend settled down for the night with a flask of tea, and biscuits and sandwiches, having earlier dropped her two children off at her mother's house in Castlemilk, Glasgow.

Many were turned away before the 'lucky' sixty were ushered in to the court building at 10.10am.

Inevitably, some of them fell asleep during the day's evidence and were warned about snoring by police officers in court. It was said that some girls had smuggled opera glasses into court in order to study the accused up close and at leisure.

Press interest was intense and special passes were printed to ensure no impersonators managed to sneak in. Sixty-eight seats were reserved for reporters and they travelled from all over Britain and abroad. For the first time in Scotland, a television crew stood outside and reported at the end of every day's proceedings. This was then regarded as the cutting edge of media coverage, and it was fronted by Bill Knox, who went on to make a career out of crime reporting and writing crime fiction.

The judge was Lord Cameron.

Unlike today, in 1958 the press treated judges reverentially and His Lordship was described as a former Dean of Faculty and one of Scotland's leading pleaders before his elevation to the Bench. He had been in the Naval Reserve in both World Wars and had been awarded the Distinguished Service Cross for gallantry at the Normandy landings.

Surprisingly, for such a high-profile case, it was his first criminal trial on the bench, but as an experienced King's Counsel, he had defended the infamous Patrick Carraher in his first murder trial. The Notable British Trials series, which features both of Carraher's murder trials in volume 74, includes a photograph of a young Cameron perilously close to a smile.

He was described as having 'a deep love of all that is Scottish', his hobbies ranging from yachting to painting, and – according to the *Bulletin & Scots Pictorial* – he had the ability to 'speak with authority on almost any subject..

The *Bulletin*'s back page reported the evangelist Dr Billy Graham's view that God would let Communists destroy America as a judgement, his argument being that American sins were necessarily greater, having been committed 'in a great light', whilst Russian sins were done in a 'vast ignorance'.

The western world was coming to terms with the aftermath of the Second World War, but the West of Scotland was about to deal with the repercussions of Manuel's killing spree.

The prosecution was not conducted by a 'Law Officer' but by Mr Gordon Gillies, Advocate Depute. The tradition at the time was that neither the Lord Advocate nor the Solicitor General would go 'on circuit' furth of Edinburgh, and, as we have seen, neither prosecution nor defence saw any practical value in having the trial moved there. Mr Gillies was junior counsel – that is, someone who has not taken 'Silk'. He was assisted by the Crown junior, twenty-six-year-old Ranald Iain Sutherland, of whom more later.

In Scotland, a solicitor is engaged by an accused to represent his interests and, if need be and depending on the gravity of the case, the solicitor engages an advocate, known in England as a barrister. Manuel's solicitor was John Ferns from Hamilton who had 'gained' Manuel as a client in the course of duty as an 'agent to the poor'; it had been sheer chance, as a spell on 'poor duty' usually involved representing drunks and thieves.

Instead, he found himself propelled into the glare of Manuel's limelight.

Defence counsel were Harald Leslie QC, an Orcadian who later took the judicial title Lord Birsay, and Malcolm Morison. Ferns was to remain with Manuel throughout the entire trial, but counsel were to have a rocky ride.

In those days, both defence counsel undertook their brief gratuitously. They undertook instructions but no payment was sought, a practice dating to an Act of the Scottish Parliament of 1424, which decreed: 'Ande gif thar be ony pur creatur that for defalt of cunying or dispense cannot or may not follow his cause the King for the lufe of God sall ordane that the Judge before quha the cause suld be determined purvey and get a lele and wys advocate to follow sic pur creatures cause.'

From then on, every murder accused in Scotland was entitled to have the services of a 'true and wise' senior counsel, the Faculty of Advocates drawing up a list of junior counsel to defend poor persons appearing in the High Court and senior counsel, including the Dean of Faculty, to appear in murder cases.

Before the trial commenced, a tricky situation arose which the

Dean of Faculty had to adjudicate on. At consultation in Barlinnie Prison, Manuel predictably instructed a special defence of incrimination of the doubly unfortunate William Watt in respect of the murder of his family. Harald Leslie, however, had been instructed to act for Watt should the authorities have been misguided enough to take the case to trial, and accordingly a conflict of interest had arisen. In effect, Leslie was barred from acting.

Not only was all that had passed between him and Watt strictly confidential, but he was obviously excluded from using his knowledge of Watt's proposed defence to assist Manuel, particularly as he was now being instructed to suggest that Watt had committed the murders instead of Manuel.

Watt must have wondered what else could go wrong in his life, and of course, something did. Before Manuel's trial, he was in a road traffic accident and when he eventually testified, it was from a stretcher.

Eventually, the Dean of Faculty appointed a second Senior Counsel, W. R. Grieve QC, known as 'Bertie', to act for Manuel specifically in those chapters of the case dealing with the Watt murders, and Leslie then continued to act, albeit temporarily, in all other aspects of the case.

The press had wind of the special defence as early as the pleading diet of 3 April, the trial, of course, having been originally set down for 14 April but adjourned on defence motion. The *Bulletin* headline boldly proclaimed: 'World kept guessing about Manuel's special defence' on the day the trial started.

Whether the world noticed or not, when the special defences were read out after the indictment, the packed court gasped in astonishment. High drama was guaranteed, particularly when Watt gave his evidence, as he was now being officially blamed for the murders of his own family by the defence.

There was a second special defence of incrimination of the two Crown witnesses, Charles Tallis and Mary Bowes, in relation to the third charge, the break-in at the Martin house in Fennsbank Avenue and a special defence of alibi for the murder of the Smart family on 1 January 1958, to the effect that he was at home between the hours of 1am and 10am during which time the crimes were believed to have been committed.

In the modern system, special defences are commonplace. In 1958, Manuel's incrimination of Watt was nothing less than sensational, and such a defence had not been used in a murder trial in Scotland since 1862 by Jessie McLachlan. That case was immortalised by William Roughead as 'the Sandyford Mystery' and was handily sandwiched between two other famous 'Glasgow' trials, Madeleine Smith in 1857 and Dr Pritchard in 1865. The major difficulty with incrimination, or impeachment, is that the accused is, in effect, saying to the jury that the authorities have got it wrong and that the accused, with virtually no resources, has uncovered the true culprit.

An onerous task.

In the case of Jessie McLachlan, she undoubtedly was correct in blaming James Fleming for the murder of Jess McPherson, although paradoxically she was actually convicted of the crime, mainly due to her legal advisers.

Similarly, Timothy Evans justifiably impeached Reginald Christie at the Old Bailey in 1950, and although Christie was able to defer his guilt until he too was charged in 1953, both were hanged.

Since neither Jessie McLachlan nor Timothy Evans had succeeded with their incriminations – and they were correct in their accusations – Manuel clearly had little justification in blaming Watt.

The indictment read as follows:

1. On 2nd January 1956, in Capelrig Plantation, East Kilbride, Lanarkshire, near the fifth teeing ground of the East Kilbride Golf Course assault Anne Kneilands aged seventeen years, daughter of and residing with John Patrick Kneilands at The Stables, Calderwood Estate, East Kilbride, and did strike her repeatedly on the head with a piece of iron or other similar instrument, take off her knickers, rob her of a watch, a pair of ear-rings, a French coin, a belt and a handbag, the contents of which is to the Prosecutor unknown, and you did murder her, and such is capital murder within the meaning of the

THE INDICTMENT

Homicide Act 1957 Section 5(1)(a) as applied by Section 16 of said Act.

2. Between 12th and 15th September 1956, both dates inclusive, break into the house then occupied by Henry James Platt at 14 Douglas Drive, Bothwell, Lanarkshire, and there (a) steal an electric razor, a chronograph, a micro-meter, a slide gauge, two calipers, a punch, two cutters, a box of drills, a wrench, a scribing block, a set of blocks, two lenses, a ring, a watch chain, a broken signet ring, a pair of cuff links, a watch and £2 and six and a half pence of money and (b) maliciously discharge a loaded firearm and damage a mattress.

3. Between 15th and 17th September 1956, both dates inclusive, break into the house then occupied by Mary Ann Hargrave Martin and Margaret Martin at 18 Fennsbank Avenue, High Burnside, Rutherglen, Lanarkshire and there steal two finger rings, four pairs of nylon stockings and 6s. of money.

4. On 17th September 1956, break into the house then occupied by William Watt at 5 Fennsbank Avenue, High Burnside, Rutherglen, Lanarkshire and there (a) assault Marion Hunter McDonald Reid or Watt, residing there, and did discharge at her a loaded firearm and shoot her in the head, and you did murder her, and (b) assault Margaret Hunter Reid or Brown, 461 King Street, Stenhousemuir, Stirlingshire, and did discharge at her a loaded firearm and did shoot her in the head, and you did murder her, and (c) assault Vivienne Isabella Reid Watt, aged sixteen years, residing there, and did strike her with your fist, struggle with her, discharge at her a loaded firearm and shoot her in the head, and you did murder her, and such are capital murders within the meaning of the Homicide Act 1957 Section 5(1)(b) as applied by Section 16 of said Act.

5. On 25th December 1957, break into the manse occupied by the Reverend Alexander McCrae Houston at 66 Wester Road, North Mount Vernon, Lanarkshire and there steal a camera, a pair of gloves, a sock and £2 of money.

6. On 28th December 1957, on the footpath between Mount

Vernon Avenue and Kenmuir Avenue, Mount Vernon, Lanarkshire assault Isabelle Wallace Cooke, aged seventeen years, daughter of and residing with William Clifford Cooke at 5 Carrick Drive, Mount Vernon, and did seize her, struggle with her, drag her into a field, tear off her clothing, tie a brassiere round her neck and a headsquare round her face and mouth, rob her of a pair of shoes, a brush, a fan, a stole, a pouchette of cosmetics and a handbag the contents of which are to the Prosecutor unknown, and you did murder her, and such is capital murder within the meaning of the Homicide Act 1957, Section 5(1)(a) as applied by Section 16 of said Act.

7. On 1st January 1958 break into the house occupied by Peter James Smart at 38 Sheepburn Road, Uddingston, Parish of Bothwell, Lanarkshire and there (a) assault said Peter James Smart and did discharge at him a loaded firearm and shoot him in the head, rob him of a number of keys and £30 of money and you did murder him, and (b) assault Doris Hall or Smart, residing there, and did discharge at her a loaded firearm and shoot her in the head, rob her of a pair of gloves, a purse and 18s. of money, and you did murder her, and (c) assault Michael Smart aged ten years, residing there, discharge at him a loaded firearm and shoot him in the head, and you did murder him, and such are capital murders within the meaning of the Homicide Act 1957, Section 5(1)(b) as applied by Section 16 of said Act, and

8. On 1 January 1958, in the garage at said house at 38 Sheepburn Road, Uddingston, aforesaid, steal a motor car.

M. G. Gillies, Advocate Depute

The charges made British legal history, as Manuel was the first person to be tried on eight murder charges at the same time.

It might seem puzzling that break-ins and thefts were listed beside murder charges, but in 1958 murder charges were categorised into 'capital' and 'non-capital' offences, as provided by the Homicide Act

1957, 'capital' obviously leading to the death penalty.

Two examples of capital murder are in the indictment, namely murder committed in furtherance of theft – hence the allegation of robbery of Anne Kneilands and Isabelle Cooke and surely nowhere close to the real motive – and the murder by shooting of the unfortunate occupants of the Watt and Smart households. Lord Cameron expressed the view that there was little logic in the distinction; in the course of the trial, the Advocate Depute called the distinction 'a creature of Parliament'.

A befogged reporter later quoted him as saying that 'murder was a feature of Parliament'.

The Homicide Act was enacted following the huge public disquiet about the outcome of the Craig and Bentley case in England.

Bentley was hanged aged nineteen in 1953. He was illiterate and said to have a mental age of eleven. In the course of a break-in, Bentley is famously said to have uttered the ambivalent 'Let him have it, Chris' to Craig, who promptly shot and wounded a policeman. Craig went on to shoot and kill another policeman. Bentley stood beside the wounded officer for half an hour whilst Craig fired at the police, but it was he who was hanged and not Craig, who was only sixteen at the time. The whole question of execution was debated and the 1957 Act restricted the death penalty to certain types of murder.

In Manuel's case, the jury were obliged to work out if he set out to rob the girls and their murders were 'in furtherance' of that plan, which is patently ridiculous. Anything taken by him was often more in the manner of a keepsake, or followed the serial killer behaviour of 'scattering' victim's possessions in a wide range of places round the murder scene.

That said, his possession of the money from the Smart house was to prove highly significant.

Moreover, there was evidence that he had interfered with his female victims' clothing in all the murders except that of Mrs Smart, so, in a sense, the jury had to overlook that as it would suggest indecency rather than theft.

When the 1957 Act was proposed, Parliamentary draftsmen probably had difficulty envisaging murders 'in furtherance' of sexual gratification.

That both the Kneilands and the Cooke murder were 'in furtherance of theft' and a contravention of section 5(1)(a) is, on one view, understandable, as was 5(1)(b) – the shootings – for the 'Watt' murders.

However, would a jury understand why the Smart murders were a straight 5(1)(b) when the charge also alleged theft?

The dilemma as to who should and who should not hang was continually debated at the time, as was the wider question of the morality of state execution, but there do not appear to be any genuine concerns or moral issues in Manuel's case.

The Craig and Bentley case and the Manuel case were united in one respect. Manuel and his ilk and Craig more than Bentley were viewed with alarm by those in judicial authority, representing what appeared to be a genuine social threat to a society having to deal with teddy-boys and wannabe gangsters.

Craig in particular epitomised the threat, wearing a long trench coat and trilby as he fired at and challenged police officers to try to capture him before plunging head-first into a neighbouring greenhouse in an effort to escape. Such behaviour represented anarchy in 1950s society, and although Manuel was trilbyless and much older than Craig and Bentley, it was obvious that all three were affected by the same Hollywood-inspired malaise that led to certain misguided individuals actually believing they were fighting a just, if vague and unspecified, cause.

Derek William Bentley has the words 'A victim of British justice' written on his gravestone, and in 1998 his conviction was deemed unsafe.

No such sentiments or misgivings have been expressed in the case of Peter Thomas Anthony Manuel.

31

THE TRIAL

The courtroom itself has two tiers, with the upper section for the public who braved the overnight elements and the ground floor for the press and those 'with priority'. Included in the latter category were witnesses who had given evidence and wished to remain to watch proceedings. The jury box that the fifteen jurors were to inhabit to listen to the gory details of Manuel's nocturnal activities was situated to the right of the judge's bench in 1958 and the witness box was to the left. The layout was changed in later years. Behind that there are seats, now redundant, but then used for the magistrates and sheriffs of the city to watch proceedings whenever they, presumably, found themselves with time on their hands.

That first morning, the Lord Provost of Glasgow, Sir Myer Galpern, wearing his Chain of Office, attended and took his seat, as did several Glasgow Baillies.

The Crown productions were laid out in the court before the trial started and curious inhabitants of the public benches peered over the balcony to make out the outline of bloodstained bedding, clothing, pieces of iron and guns.

At 10.37am a hush descended as Manuel came up the stairs from the white-tiled cell corridor below and took his seat in the dock between two policemen wearing white gloves and carrying truncheons.

He was immaculate.

His hair was dampened and swept back and he was wearing slate grey slacks and a navy blue blazer which he continually groomed. He had a large notebook with him and in the course of the evidence he was seen to take extensive notes. Throughout the trial, he remained smartly dressed and at lunch he refused to partake of the bread and cheese the authorities provided for accused persons in those days. Instead he elected to pay for the same menu that counsel were offered, one newspaper disapprovingly reporting that he was allowed to enjoy the likes of salmon salad followed by ice cream and pineapple.

The sitting was constituted when trumpeters broke the uneasy silence and the Macer entered ahead of a procession consisting of Lord Cameron, Lord Migdale, who presided over cases in the South Court, and the Reverend Robert Morris. The minister and the Macer were black gowned and the Their Lordships were in the traditional scarlet and white robes worn by Senators of the College of Justice when presiding over criminal matters.

The court, Manuel included, stood as the Reverend Morris prayed for divine assistance in achieving earthly justice, and then both he and Lord Migdale retired, leaving Lord Cameron in charge of that onerous task in the North Court.

The clerk called the diet and Manuel calmly confirmed his name, then his counsel, Harald Leslie, intimated a plea of 'Not guilty' to all charges, together with the special defences already lodged with the clerk.

He then drew the judge's attention to a copy of the *News of the World* for Sunday 11 May 1958 which ran a story about the trial and also printed a purported photograph of Manuel. Mr Leslie described it as 'an impropriety' and went on to allege unfairness to his client as 'the likeness' might well affect identification.

He had a point.

Although the prosecution case largely depended on Manuel's 'confessions' and the recovery of incriminating items, identification was still an issue. To this day in Scottish criminal trials, a witness speaking to actions by an accused is asked if he or she 'can identify that person' and if so, whether they can see him in court. A large hint to most, but not all, is that the accused is more than likely to be the person sitting in the dock between two police officers, although these days the dock escort consists of civilian security staff. Not all

166

witnesses know that, of course, and there have been many mis-identifications, deliberate or not, of court personnel, members of the public and even the occasional presiding judge.

In the light of that requirement, and even though the perception of contempt of court by a newspaper has changed radically since 1958, the publication of a photograph of an accused would still be frowned upon today. Why a newspaper editor considers that a pre- or mid-trial picture of an accused is a necessary adjunct to a factual account of the case has never really been satisfactorily explained in any case.

At the start of the Manuel trial it was completely inexplicable, and Lord Cameron retired to consider the matter. Before doing so, he directed remarks to the press representatives present in court, telling them that nothing should be done which could jeopardise a fair trial. He then rose until 11 o'clock and the 'Trial of the Century' briefly faltered, particularly for those such as Mr Perryman and others who had slept overnight in the queue.

The article itself was hardly controversial, simply pointing out that one hundred citizens had been summoned for jury service for the trial. It pointed out that whilst eighty-five were likely to go home, the fifteen selected would be 'exiled' for a month and would be clos-eted in a hotel with no contact with the outside world and be driven in a 'motor coach' to the Saltmarket six days a week until the end of the trial. The headline was carried in an edition of the *News of the World* subtitled the 'Late London Edition'. Intriguingly, the contentious photograph does not actually appear to be of Manuel!

The editorial decision to print the photograph was either based on false information or was a calculated risk. Either way, it was an ill-judged move and if a photograph of a person other than Manuel was published deliberately, that would have been equally reprehen-sible as it still potentially could have had an impact on the question of identification.

When the trial resumed, the judge intimated that he was going to refer the matter to the Lord Advocate for the consideration of crim-inal proceedings against the newspaper, although no action appears to have been taken by him.

The jury of nine men and six women was then empanelled, with one name being objected to. In 1958, both the defence and the prosecution had three peremptory objections and further objections 'on cause shown' to jurors who had been selected. Their occupations were also disclosed and a generally held view by certain defence counsel was that teachers should always be objected to, on the basis that they dominated proceedings in the jury room and were unfailingly reactionary. That may or may not have been true in 1958, but by the time peremptory objections were abolished forty years later, occupations were not disclosed and teachers were probably far more difficult to stereotype.

At 11.02am, the first Crown witness, Police Constable Thomas Rae of Hamilton Police, was called. He was almost the last on the list of the 280 cited by the prosecution. His evidence was formal and related to his preparing a plan of the area where the Kneilands murder had occurred in 1956 and to doing the same in relation to the Cooke murder in 1958.

John Kneilands then gave evidence about the last time he had seen his daughter Anne and about eventually reporting her missing. He only glanced at Manuel once as he recounted identifying her body in the City morgue, next door to the High Court building. He identified a pair of shoes, an earring, a watch and a French centime as all having belonged to his late daughter. Mrs Martha Kneilands followed and spoke of her anxiety about Anne not having returned home on the night of 2 January, but Anne's twenty-year-old sister Alice struggled to keep her composure as she recounted seeing her sister leaving the house 'for the last time' on the night of 2 January 1956.

Andrew Murnin, now an ambulance driver, told the court how he and a friend had escorted Anne and Alice home after a dance on 30 December. A date was made for the Monday for 6 o'clock at Capelrig Farm where the bus terminus was, but Murnin had failed to make the meeting as he had gone to a party and 'met some friends', a euphemism for having too much to drink.

For the defence, Mr Leslie asked if others were dancing with Anne and he confirmed she had danced with 'quite a number'.

168

Mrs Jean Simpson then told of Anne coming to her house at about 6.20pm and leaving to catch the 6.40pm service a short distance away.

Then Hugh Marshall spoke to hearing the scream or yell from the golf course at about 8.40pm or 8.50pm that night. He raised his arm as if he was defending himself and explained that it was 'as if someone was hitting you and you cried 'Oh!' Maybe the noise he heard was Anne Kneilands, but he was unable to say if the voice was male or female.

George Gribbon then told of his discovery of the body. Her right arm was over her face and her head was 'split open'. The court then heard from a police Inspector that she lay near trees beyond a gully and a barbed wire fence. Her clothing had been dragged up as if it had been pulled up as her body was dragged along the ground, and a stocking and some underwear were missing. She had probably been killed at one place and then the body had been dragged to another spot, as there was an area where the grass was flattened and saturated with blood some distance from the final resting place. A belt from a coat and a watch lay nearby.

It looked as if she had been moved to a better place of concealment. She had scratches which he associated with her struggling over the barbed wire fence, and other items such as a headscarf, the French coin, an earring and some beads were found about 340 yards from where her shoes were found, one of which appeared to have been sucked off by the mud.

The Inspector identified a tree branch in court which he had taken from the scene as it had possibly been used as the murder weapon.

After lunch, 'Bertie' Grieve cross-examined the Inspector. Sometimes the art of 'crossing' a witness can lead to an unexpected breakthrough and other times it leads to an unwitting strengthening of the Crown case.

Grieve had little to work on and he tested the Inspector as to his recollection of which stocking was missing from the body; he had said it was the left one but the photographs of the body showed in fact it was the other one which was gone, and the witness accepted he had been mistaken.

Lord Cameron asked how far apart the shoes were and he was told twenty yards, the closest being 110 yards from the saturated area.

The first mention of Manuel came with the evidence of Constable James Marr. He said he had been looking to speak to Mr Gribbon about the finding of the body when he met and talked to a man who was part of a squad of Gas Board workers waiting for a lift home. One of them had recent scratches to his nose and right cheek and he identified Manuel as being the person he had seen. Constable Jardine then told of the alleged theft of the wellingtons from the hut which caused him to speak to the foreman, Richard Corrins, and at that point he had also seen the scratches on Manuel's face.

The Crown made no effort to lead the evidence of either episode of Manuel's attention-seeking behaviour, when he asked Marr if 'they could hit the man back' and when he claimed that both he and Corrins had chased a shady character from the site. It would have been competent to lead these chapters of evidence, but presumably a decision was made that it might only complicate matters.

Corrins then gave evidence about seeing the marks on Manuel's face when work resumed on 4 January and he told him he had got them in a fight, and the work colleague John Lennan spoke to the scratches looking as if they were made by fingernails. When he was asked if he could identify him in court, Lennan and Manuel exchanged smiles before he confirmed it was the man in the dock he was referring to.

Manuel was to continue with this attitude and later in the trial when a relative looked about the court for him, he leaned forward and said 'Psssst!' to attract his attention. Considering the charges he faced, it has to be doubted that the jury would have been impressed with such chutzpah.

The court sat until 5 o'clock on the first day and wasted no time in getting on to the other charges. When evidence was led from the photographer at the scene of the Kneilands murder, and his evidence included the Watt murder scene, the newspapers reported 'Watt Triple Murders Given Early Mention', even though no further evidence was led at that stage, apart from the finding of a bullet in Mrs Watt's hair and the test firing of bullets inside 5 Fennsbank Avenue.

Instead, the Advocate Depute moved on to the Platt housebreaking and the strange tale of the recovery of the .38 bullet. Mr Platt testified that it was 'so fantastic' that a bullet could be fired into the mattress that they just forgot all about it. Indeed, when Mrs Platt gave evidence, she informed the court that her husband had actually 'carried it about with him for a while' then it lay in a drawer in the kitchen before the 'penny dropped'. After Mr Platt measured it he quickly handed it in to the police.

The son of the house, Geoffrey Platt, identified his electric razor, which now had 'TL' scratched on the case, something which is still lacking an explanation, unless it was another of Manuel's false leads, such as an abandoned attempt to implicate Tallis.

The day finished with the break-in at the Martin house at 18 Fennsbank Avenue and the evidence of the stolen stockings and rings. Miss Margaret Martin also spoke of the tomato soup ruining her carpet, and someone eating a tin of spaghetti and scattering orange peel and pips about.

Lord Cameron then admonished the jury not to speak to outsiders about the case, and he also advised them to take their minds off their work as much as possible when they were not actually in court. This would prove to be sound advice in view of the harrowing evidence which was still to be heard over the next couple of weeks.

The papers reported that a crowd of several hundred, mostly women, was gathered outside the court building that evening. Curiously, the report added that 'most of them waited to see Lord Cameron and counsel leave.'

Really?

Were they waiting to see them?

32

THE WATT CRIME SCENE

The 'Trial of the Century' was given due prominence in the media. For Scotland, and to a slightly lesser extent, Britain, it was the O. J. Simpson or the Michael Jackson trial of its time.

Newspaper and radio coverage held sway over a television exposure in its infancy. As witnesses came and went, photographers patiently requested images – trial reports abound with them posing carefully and giving full details of their occupations, marital status and even their addresses. On one page, you see Deanna Valente and her mother glamorously dressed for the occasion and looking improperly cheery. On another, you have Laurence Dowdall posing with hands in the pockets of his smart suit, a camel hair overcoat casually open and surrounded by gawping onlookers studying his every detail. 'Scout' O'Neil, Manuel's parents and siblings, a young Douglas Bryden and almost all who spoke at the trial are captured forever in fading 1958 vintage.

And of course, the star of the Crown witnesses, William Watt, is seen in a variety of situations, hobbling into the court building with the aid of walking sticks in one picture and being transported by ambulance personnel on a stretcher on his way in to testify in another.

Reporting on the second day's proceedings, the *Bulletin & Scots Pictorial* was fully caught up in the frenzy. 'Gun Drama at Manuel Trial' is the headline for Wednesday 14 May 1958 and goes on to relate the story of 'Scout' O'Neil selling the gun to Manuel for £5, and the tale of the shot cow.

At the foot of the same page, there appears a story of a man sent to jail for eighteen months for stealing three pairs of socks. According to the junior reporter concerned, forty-six-year-old James Cullen admitted the offence at the High Court in Glasgow. Was there really a case of sock theft being heard by Lord Migdale in the South Court at the same time as the Manuel trial in the North, or was the correspondent excitedly caught up in the main story and actually meant to say the Sheriff Court?

Day two started with Manuel pleasantly smiling and saying 'Good Morning' to his legal team before trumpets sounded and Lord Cameron came on the bench at 10.14am.

It continued with details of the Martin housebreaking but then moved on to the main event, the Watt murders.

The Watts' housekeeper, Helen Collison, gave evidence about arriving at the house at 8.45am on Monday 17 September 1956 and going to the back door, which was always left open for her, except on that day she found it locked. Vivienne usually left it unlocked after she went to college, so Mrs Collison reasoned that she had decided not to go that day, or that she had a cold.

She rapped on the window after trying the door, but to no avail. As Mrs Watt did not keep the best of health, she tried to avoid disturbing her, and she managed to prise Vivienne's bedroom window open a couple of inches and looked in to see what she thought was somebody lying at the foot of the bed. She then knocked on Mrs Watt's bedroom window, and got no reply before noticing a glass panel at the door was smashed.

Mrs Valente from next door appeared and finally the postman, Peter Collier, put his hand through the smashed panel and opened the door and went in.

Mrs Collison had followed him and when they went into Mrs Watt's bedroom they immediately saw both women in the bed were dead. They were lying on their sides both facing the window and sunlight was streaming in through the curtains over the bodies. When she went out and told Mrs Valente they were dead, she ran back to her house screaming, but Mr Collier asked if there was a phone in the house so he could contact the police.

She then went into Vivienne's room and saw blood all over the pillow and the girl covered up by the bedclothes. As soon as she heard two or three 'big snores' from the dying teenager she told the postman to phone an ambulance as well, in case her life could be saved, but he said the police would be there soon and they should wait for them to arrive before doing anything else. In court, she was shown and identified Vivienne's torn pyjamas.

Grieve now had the task of cross-examining Mrs Collison within the framework of Manuel's instructions, namely that William Watt had carried out the killings. He carefully went about his assignment, first probing the state of relations between Watt and his wife. In her evidence-in-chief, Mrs Collison had mentioned that when she couldn't get into the house she thought perhaps Mr Watt had come home and he asked her why she had considered that possibility. She answered that she thought that maybe a row had started and that everyone had left the house, but then she added that she had never actually seen a row take place in the house.

She agreed with the suggestion that she had seen very little of Mr Watt after the family had moved to Burnside in July 1956. She had later spoken to Watt about what had happened and had asked him if he thought it had started as a robbery and Watt replied 'No' as only Mrs Watt's watch was missing. She then asked him if he had any idea who had done it, and he answered mysteriously that 'if it was who he thought it was, he knew them'.

Watt had also asked her if she knew where the keys for the bureau in the dining room were, and when Grieve asked if she knew why he wanted them, she said he wanted the 'society books'. Grieve pursued the point, asking what she thought he meant by that and she answered, 'Insurances'.

So soon after the deaths?

A motive?

A further motive?

The court then heard from Dr Arthur Nelson that Vivienne had a bullet wound to the left of her left eye, and both Mrs Watt and Mrs Brown had been shot close to their right eyes, though Mrs Brown had a second wound to the side of her head.

Deanna Valente, described, as newspapers could do in 1958, as 'a nineteen-year-old attractive brunette', told the court about spending the Sunday afternoon with Vivienne. They had gone into town, eaten at a cafe and bought rolls at Denholms bakery, owned by Mr Watt. In the evening, Mrs Watt and her sister had listened to records and she and Vivienne had tuned in to the 'Hit Parade' on Radio Luxembourg.

She had gone home at about 11.40pm and heard music from the radio in the Watt house for a good while after that. Although she mentioned the phone call from Mr Watt, she could only remember what Vivienne had said about her father forgetting her weekly money but promising to double it the following week.

As a cigarette end and a spent match had been found beside a burn mark on the carpet in Vivienne's room, she was asked if they had smoked in the room that night, and she said they had not.

Gillies probed as to the state of the relationship between Watt and his daughter, but Deanna thought they seemed to get on well. As Mrs Watt's health was an issue, he asked her how she appeared that night. Deanna said that Mrs Watt had never looked so well and she looked very happy.

In the general disarray of the room, a bra had been found on the floor. Probably in an effort to find out if Manuel had removed it from her at some stage, Gillies asked if Vivienne ever told her she wore a brassiere in bed. In polite 1950s Scotland such an enquiry was risqué, and Deanna reprovingly answered, 'That is not a nice thing to say to anyone!'

Lord Cameron – with an eye to the evidence to come – asked her if she could recall how Mrs Watt had addressed her husband on the phone. A blazing row might have been significant, but Deanna disappointed the 'overnight mission' theorists, when she simply answered, 'Bill'.

Mrs Valente then related her testimony about the finding of the bodies before the Advocate Depute asked about her domestic arrangements for keeping large sums of cash. She explained that her husband owned a confectioner's business but that he did not keep cash at home and there was no safe in the house.

Manuel, of course, had alleged that there was cash in the house next to the Watts, but was Mrs Valente going to reveal such facts to what seemed like the world's press?

Superintendent Andrew McClure provided details of the state of the Watt house. Vivienne's bedroom was in a mess, and apart from the cigarette burn on the carpet, the bedside lamp was smashed and lying on the ground, as were items of clothing and buttons torn from them. The packed court gasped when he was handed pyjamas and a nightdress which were totally covered in dried blood. It was also reported that the pyjama bottoms were torn 'from the waist to the crutch'. Perhaps the word 'crotch' was deemed impolite by a sub-editor.

Day two was concluded with a visit to Glasgow's seamy side.

First up was 'Scout' O'Neil who told of Manuel's request to get him a gun; he had put him in touch with Peter Hamilton who came up with the goods after a furtive meeting, just a few days before the Watt murders. 'Scout' said Manuel told him he wanted the gun for a hold-up in Liverpool.

When Hamilton gave evidence, he confirmed the story, but was keen not to be seen as having profited from the sale. In his mind, he maybe thought that he would be seen to be less culpable if he appeared nonchalant about the whole question of remuneration. He insisted that no price was mentioned, no doubt thinking that that might distance him from the murders, but Gillies pressed the point and asked him if that was the case, was he not interested in the price?

Hamilton said 'No'.

'Why did you accept the £5?'

Temporarily forgetting where he was, Hamilton replied, 'Well, would you no' have took it?'

Lord Cameron had heard enough.

He ordered him to answer the question and reminded him that, according to the witness, the gun was to be used in a hold-up. Hamilton mumbled that Manuel had been looking for a gun and he'd given it to him.

'How did you come to get £5?'

'Well, he just gave it to me,' Hamilton explained, feebly.

'Bertie' Grieve cross-examined Hamilton and made further inroads into what was left of his credibility. The court was to understand that 'bookmaker's clerk' actually meant 'bookie's runner', and he further clarified that that involved making a living taking street bets.

The final witnesses of the day were two of Manuel's drinking friends.

Joseph Liddell had met him in the eponymous Crook Inn in Uddingston and at one stage Manuel showed him a gun, which he pulled from his waistband. Manuel told him he came across it when he was helping a secondhand dealer clear a house. He took it, he said, so he could take it to Glasgow to sell to 'some poor bastard who would blow his brains out'.

The truth – that he had bought it – was obviously too mundane.

That conversation had been on Friday 14 September 1956, three days before the Watt murders.

John Lafferty had met Manuel on Sunday 9 September 1956, a week before the killings.

A 1950s Scottish Sabbath was a serious matter. The licensing laws were strict, bordering on medieval, and the only way an alcoholic drink could be lawfully purchased in a hotel by a non-resident was if the customer was able to demonstrate he was a bona fide traveller. That was achieved by the licence holder keeping a register that the drouthy itinerant had to complete with details of his name, address and his journey. That Manuel and Lafferty were drinking in the Woodend Hotel for five hours before he boasted that he had shot a cow, demonstrates the efficacy of the legislation.

An early indication of defence tactics emerged when, dealing with the tale of the shot cow, Harald Leslie – who had resumed the lead – suggested to Lafferty that his client 'was given to being a bit fanciful'.

Lafferty agreed.

Warts and all, the likes of O'Neil and Hamilton testifying as Crown witnesses probably helped rather than hindered the prosecution case, giving the jury a flavour of the way Manuel lived his life and the character of his acquaintances.

Had it not been halted in its tracks by the accused man himself, the 'bit fanciful' approach adopted by Leslie stood as good a chance as any of demonstrating to the jury that Manuel was a dreamer – not, it has to be conceded, anything resembling a defence – but merely the first step into a tactical minefield for the defence team.

33

THE CROWN JUNIOR STEPS IN

A stranger to the trial buying the *Bulletin & Scots Pictorial* for Thursday 15 May 1958 would suppose that William Watt had been on trial.

The headline proclaimed,

'WILLIAM WATT IS INNOCENT'

Described as 'the most electrifying evidence to be heard in a British court for many years', the paper related the evidence of Laurence Dowdall as he recounted his meetings with Manuel and their discussions about the Watt murders.

As he did so, it was reported that Manuel 'did not flicker an eyelash' and 'remained nonchalant'.

At the end of the trial, though, Manuel vowed to kill certain people and Dowdall was close to top of the list. When he heard that Dowdall had gone to Bermuda on holiday he remarked that he 'hoped the sharks would get him.'

What the *Bulletin* called a 'thrill packed day' began an hour late. Initially, impatient spectators thought the delay was due to the accident-prone William Watt falling on the steps of the court. He was already using crutches to get about after being injured in the car crash, and now was preparing to face up to whatever forensic insult was to be added to his physical and emotional injury. He was not to be called that day, though.

The real reason for the delay, however, was that the Advocate Depute, Mr Gillies, suddenly felt unwell – 'giddy' to employ the term used at the time – and a decision had to be made about progress for that day. Lord Cameron was told of the situation in chambers and he was anxious to press on with the trial. Traditionally, the main prosecutor is assisted by a 'junior' and that role is usually performed by someone recently called to the bar. On that day, twenty-six-year-old Ranald Sutherland fulfilled that function and when he heard that an experienced Advocate Depute, Victor Skae, was on his way to take over from Gillies, he must have been relieved.

It was to be short-lived.

Lord Cameron decreed that the Crown junior should take over in the meantime, and the trial resumed with the inexperienced Sutherland promoted to leading rather than noting evidence in the highest-profile murder case in the country for many years. When Skae arrived after the start of proceedings, he was content to let the junior continue in the main prosecutor's role for the morning's evidence.

Sutherland dealt with the chapter of evidence which involved the peculiar events surrounding Tallis and Bowes. The prosecution would have been expected to lead Tallis in any event to speak to Manuel's possession of a gun, but given Manuel's special defence that he and Mrs Bowes had broken into 18 Fennsbank Avenue, an extra dimension had been added to their testimony.

The whole purpose of a notice of special defence is to give some prior warning to the prosecution of the line being taken, so that, in theory, they can investigate the veracity of the claim. Nowadays, if no notice is given, the whole line can be objected to by the prosecution, with the inevitable result that the man in the dock is less than understanding with his legal team, if he has given clear and timeous instructions that a notice be lodged.

High-profile as the trial might be, there was a problem with Manuel's special defences which the Crown seemed surprisingly relaxed about.

Judicially, he had given notice that Tallis and Bowes had broken into the Martin house; he had also alleged that William Watt had murdered his own family. There was no notice, however, that Tallis had crept out of 18 Fennsbank Avenue to cross over to number five to carry out the Watt murders. The court was about to hear what he had told Dowdall about the mystery man who had been 'in the horrors' after the shootings, but in terms of pre-trial preparation, he had obviously given no instructions to formalise that assertion into a full-blown special defence naming Tallis.

Similarly, his story to Watt about how a bullet had got into a mattress in a house in Bothwell again implicated Tallis and Bowes, but no special defence to the effect that they had broken into the Platt house had been lodged.

It must be assumed that as these aspects of the case were being led by the Crown, and that as it was thought that Manuel was not actually going to follow those lines of evidence, a relaxed approach to the formalities was taken. As the trial progressed, however, the jury might have formed the impression that Manuel was not quite as smart as he thought he was, and that he had been so criminally active that he simply got mixed up as to what happened and where. That said, his previous forensic experience had shown that a party defender was given generous latitude, something that might have influenced his decision later in the trial to sack counsel.

Tallis was the first to testify that day.

He was brought from Peterhead Prison and he had a history of housebreaking. Sutherland asked him if Manuel had spoken to him about guns and Tallis agreed that he had. No charge had been libelled to cover the evidence, but it seems that in 1956 Manuel had possession of a gun for which he had difficulty getting bullets. He complained to Tallis that when he placed a bullet in the gun it simply fell out of the chamber.

Hardly the stuff of Capone or Dillinger.

Tallis advised him how to solve the problem, because, he claimed, he was an engineer but not a firearms expert.

The prosecution moved on to cover Manuel's assertion that he and Mrs Bowes had broken into the Misses Martin's house. Tallis stoutly denied it, and gave a detailed account of their activities for the weekend of 15 to 17 September 1956, which involved the wedding of Mary Bowes' son, Allan, visits to relatives, and a drink – just hours before Manuel and Lafferty were to arrive – in the Woodend Hotel.

The hotel was used by many thirsty 'travellers' but few bona fide citizens, it would seem.

Tallis accepted that on Monday 17 September he had gone to the Crook Inn with Manuel, where they discussed many things, including the Suez Crisis. Once that had been done, however, they went to Manuel's home in Birkenshaw, then on to Glasgow.

Manuel showed him two rings which he described as 'the two hottest rings you ever saw in your life.' If the jury were unaware of Tallis's larcenous propensities before, they were left in no doubt when he said he told him that he had seen hundreds of hot rings and didn't see why these two were any hotter than the others.

They were in a different bar in Glasgow when Tallis read about the Watt murders and the break-in at number eighteen, a mere sixty yards from number five. He quizzed Manuel about the 'hot' rings and was told that he had already put them down a drain under Central Station bridge, known still as 'The Heilanman's Umbrella' in honour of the fact that during the Depression unemployed Highlanders met and sheltered there when it rained.

Tallis finished the first part of his evidence by denying he had ever been in William Watt's company.

Harald Leslie cross-examined. The arrangement had been that Grieve would deal with that chapter of evidence covering the Watt murders, and it might seem surprising that he did not cross-examine Tallis, as his evidence impinged on events in Fennsbank Avenue.

Tallis denied knowing about guns; he also denied being in Burnside at any time or arranging to get a gun for Watt. He also denied that he had told Manuel he had been paid to 'wreck a house in Burnside' and that he had tried to enlist Manuel's help to do so.

Presumably on Manuel's instructions, Leslie then asked him if he had ever owned an electric razor, to which he answered he had not. Was he following instructions that Tallis had something to do with the break-in to the Platt house, and does that question suggest that Manuel had scratched 'T' and 'L' on it – 'Tallis' being too obvious – hoping

Scottish Criminal Records Office photographs of a dapper, 19-year-old Manuel taken at Barlinnie prison Glasgow in April 1946.

Right: Anne Kneilands who was murdered in January 1956. Despite confessing to the crime, Manuel was acquitted of her murder in 1958.

The road to Capelrig Plantation, East Kilbride, January 1956.

Margaret Brown, Mrs Watt's sister, who was spending a couple of nights at the Watt house while William Watt was away fishing.

Vivienne Watt, murdered by Manuel in September 1956 aged 16. Manuel knocked her out before shooting her.

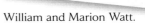

William and Marion Watt.

Police activity at the Watt bungalow in Fennsbank Avenue, Burnside, Glasgow, September 1956.

The Cairnbaan Hotel near Lochgilphead, Argyllshire. The police tried to show that William Watt had driven from here to his home in Glasgow, murdered his wife, daughter and sister-in-law and then returned to the hotel, all during the early hours and dawn of 17 September 1956.

© MIRRORPIX.COM

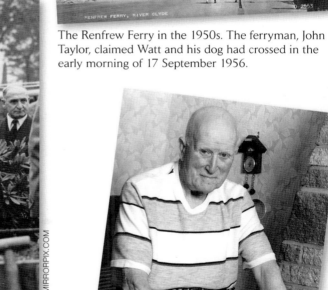

© ALISON CUMMING

The Renfrew Ferry in the 1950s. The ferryman, John Taylor, claimed Watt and his dog had crossed in the early morning of 17 September 1956.

© MIRRORPIX.COM

Watt at his family's funeral a few days before his arrest for their murders.

Watt aged 87, photographed in 1994.

© MIRRORPIX.COM

A police tarpaulin covers the site where Manuel buried Isabelle Cooke's body. He led police to this spot in darkness o the morning of 16 January 1958 a announced he 'wa standing on her.'

© MIRRORPIX.COM

© THE HERALD AND EVENING TIMES PICTURE ARCHIVE

Isabelle Cooke, murdered by Manuel on 28 December 1957.

© THE HERALD AND EVENING TIMES PICTURE ARCHIVE

© MIRRORPIX.COM

Bespectacled Michael Smart seated, front row, at Cub camp. The youngest of Manuel's victims, he was shot in the head whilst sleeping.

© MIRRORPIX.COM

Peter and Doris Smart, murdered by Manuel on 1 January 1958.

The Smart house in Sheepburn Road, Uddingston, Lanarkshire, built by Peter Smart in 1954.

The Webley revolver used in the murders in the Watt house, freshly recovered from the River Clyde (January 1958).

Right: Part of the crowd outside Glasgow High Court, straining to catch sight of Manuel being transferred to a police vehicle for transport to Barlinnie prison at the end of a day's evidence.

John Cameron KC in 1938. The Manuel trial in 1958 was his first criminal case following his judicial appointment. (See page 157)

Police bundle items recovered from a search of Manuel's house into the back of a (rather dirty) police van. (See page 114)

© MIRRORPIX.COM

Below: Defence witness Robert McQuade arriving to give evidence about someone resembling Pete Smart buying 'a shooter' from Manuel in a pub on Hogmanay 1957.

19-year-old Deanna Valente and her mother in the afternoon sunshine outside the court on 13 May 1958.

Some of Manuel's surviving sketches; 'The Lady and The Lion', 'Amy Johnson' and a self portrait.

The Lady and The Lion

Right: Some of Manuel's hand-written notes from the 1958 trial. Note the reference to his role 'in obtaining (Watt's) release' and to his 'deliberately trying to create a suspicion of murder in (the) Smart affair.'

Below: The great and the good all tried to put in an appearance at the 1958 trial. Apart from Sir Compton MacKenzie writing his observations, the famous caricaturist Emilio Coia attended and observed Manuel in the dock before producing the sketch below.

TRIAL'S CLOSING STAGES
JUDGE DIRECTS JURY ON ANNE CHARGE
THE COLDEST EYES I'VE EVER SEEN

MANUEL TRIAL 16th DAY

EMILIO COIA GIVES AN ARTIST'S IMPRESSION

Crowds await the verdict outside Glasgow High Court, 29 May 1958.

The different faces of Manuel. (See pages 3-4)

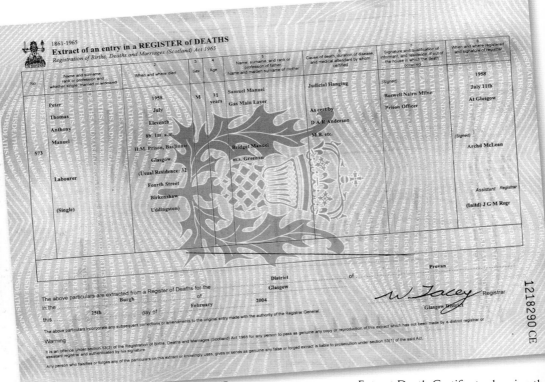

Extract Death Certificate showing the
cause of death as 'Judicial Hanging' at
8.01 hours on 11 July 1958.

that it might lead a trail in that direction? And had Manuel done that after he realised he had said too much about the bullet in the mattress?

Leslie then turned to the break-in at number eighteen, asking about details of footprints in the back garden, the theft of stockings from the house, and being disturbed by a car coming to number nineteen, all details designed to bolster the theory of Tallis's involvement.

Tallis stood his ground, and went on to deny that he had 'a gun to dispose of after the Watt murders', a question implying that he had helped someone else cover up after the murders and a line of evidence lying more in Grieve's specific province, it might be thought.

The true test of the efficacy of Leslie's questioning, of course, would have been if he had been allowed to finish the job and build upon these, and no doubt other, points to the jury.

But it was not to be.

Mrs Bowes and her sons followed Tallis into the witness box.

She said the same as Tallis in all major respects. The nature of the cross-examination was based on Manuel's natural embellishment and it no doubt worked against him. No matter how reprobate Tallis was, the jury were being asked to accept that a forty-one-year-old widow with two sons had suddenly decided to go housebreaking with her lover. She was described in the press as 'tastefully dressed in black and grey' and 'gave an indignant denial to the suggestion that she had been concerned in a housebreaking'.

However, Leslie made one decent point.

It was known that distinctive footprints had been found at the rear of 18 Fennsbank Avenue and although she firmly denied they were hers, she had to agree that she did have a pair of wedge-heeled sandals.

The trial then moved on to the evidence of the owners of the Cairnbaan Hotel.

Mrs Leitch said that when she was told of the killings and Watt came back to the hotel as she had asked him to do, to begin with he could not grasp what she was telling him. At first he seemed to think she was talking about her own daughter Marion, rather than Mrs Watt, but when it dawned on him, he immediately became distraught.

He made a phone call then said she was right, they were dead.

As Watt had originally been charged with the murders, the Crown were duty bound to go into this chapter of evidence in detail.

Gillies had sufficiently recovered to resume leading evidence in the afternoon, and he established that not only were the Watts friends of the Leitch family, but as a family the Watts were 'happy and on good terms'.

Two significant points were covered.

She recalled a journey one evening during the week in question in the Vauxhall with Watt when the car's lights flickered. She became anxious, but Watt fiddled with the switch and they came back on again.

Secondly, he had previously come to the hotel about four times with his wife, but there had been times when lady guests were staying at the hotel at the same time as he was when Mrs Watt was not there, a point Grieve pursued in cross-examination. It seemed that he and a male friend had occupied a twin room at the same time as a Mrs Milligan and her sister had inhabited a similar room. The point seems to have been left hanging there in the nature of an insinuation, nowhere close to making a link with motivation for murder.

Grieve also established that the back door of the hotel could be left unlocked at night, a fact known to Watt, so that it would be possible to go out, leave it unlocked and return the same way.

Others spoke of Watt behaving perfectly normally that week and acting 'appropriately' – whatever that suggests – when news of the tragedy arrived.

The local postman and his father were in the hotel when Watt received confirmation of the deaths.

They said he broke down and cried.

Then Laurence Dowdall electrified the packed court with the fantastic tale of his meetings with Manuel. Normally in criminal courts in

Scotland, there is a bar to hearsay evidence being admitted. That, however, is relaxed when it comes to statements made by an accused, so, with the exception of one technical point raised by Grieve, Dowdall was free to relate the full story of how Manuel had asked him to 'come to see him' – the jury were not to know that entailed a visit to prison – to discuss proposals to their 'mutual advantage'.

A very rare moment of levity occurred when after Dowdall had asked Manuel why he did not take his information to the police, he said that Manuel 'indicated in a few sentences that he regarded the police with some disapproval'.

The public gallery started to laugh.

The accused man did not.

He went on to tell of Manuel saying that he knew Watt was innocent as he knew the man who had done it and he had told him all the details. He also told him of the Platt break-in and the shooting of the mattress after 'some sort of quarrel'. Dowdall then told of the tense first meeting at the Whitehall Restaurant in Glasgow, where Watt came face to face with his family's assassin. He had eventually left the unlikely pair talking together.

Shown Crown production number 41, he identified it as the sketch that Manuel had made of a Webley Mark IV; he was aware that he could not say he had 'slipped it into his papers' after meeting Manuel in Barlinnie Prison.

Grieve had a difficult task. How best to approach the evidence of a respected lawyer recounting something which bore heavily on his client?

He began by questioning whether Dowdall should be telling anyone about what had transpired between him and Manuel. The basis for that assertion was that if he was acting as Manuel's solicitor, he was bound by confidentiality. Dowdall considered the point then replied that he was not actually acting for Manuel, but for Watt.

He had to be careful.

Should he have let it slip that Manuel had written to Dowdall under the guise of seeking advice about an appeal, it could have revealed a previous conviction and have led to the trial being deserted.

Dowdall circumspectly replied that during the 'preliminaries' Manuel had sought his advice, and at that stage he had a dual capacity, acting for Manuel and also Watt. When he asked Manuel what he would do if he passed the information to the police, Manuel said he would simply deny it.

It was put to him that he had seen the interior of the Watt house before he spoke to Manuel, but Dowdall dismissed that point.

By the end of the third day of the trial, a partial picture of Manuel was emerging in the jury's mind.

Here was a man, by his own admission – given the nature of his counsel's questioning – constantly on the fringes of housebreaking and murder; moreover, he was seemingly and unreasonably framed by a couple who spent their leisure time together violating local houses.

On top of that, the most prominent criminal solicitor in Scotland had apparently volunteered to join the conspiracy by going on a guided tour of the Watt house at 5 Fennsbank Avenue prior to meeting with Manuel.

Much was going to hinge on William Watt's performance on day four.

Given his injuries, he was going to find it difficult enough to make himself comfortable on the Wednesday night but the prospect of the outrageous suggestions that awaited him on the Thursday morning probably meant he got little or no sleep that night.

34

WATT GIVES EVIDENCE

In his factual account of the proceedings, *The Trial of Peter Manuel: The Man Who Talked Too Much*, John Gray Wilson sums up the situation that faced Watt that morning:

'Witness No. 40 on the Crown list was William Watt. It is probably safe to say that no witness has ever been more eagerly awaited by spectators at any trial in Scotland. Husband, father and brother-in-law of three murder victims, he had himself been detained for over two months in connection with their deaths and then been released. He was now charged with the murders by the man in the dock.'

Watt had been wheeled into the building on a hospital trolley then carried into the North Court on a stretcher.

After formalities, he gave evidence for two hours.

He told of his wife's ill health and his fishing holiday to the Crinan Canal, and how it was cut short when he was summoned to the hotel to hear the dreadful news. That morning he had intended to get up at 5.30am to fish one of the pools but had slept on after the alarm had gone off. When he awoke, he misread the time as 6.40am when it was actually 7.35am, so he got up and drove to look at the level of the water in the pool before breakfast.

The windscreen of the car had been covered with frost.

The 'misreading' of the time, and other factors that were to emerge, still leads to the intriguing question whether, if Manuel had been charged with the Watt murders on their own, the jury would have been so definite in their verdict.

As he told the court of the call to his brother-in-law's secretary, who confirmed the deaths, Watt broke down in tears and covered his face with his hand.

Manuel 'averted his eyes' until Watt recovered his composure and partook of the traditional court panacea, a glass of water. He then spoke about being 'identified' by two witnesses, after which he spent sixty-seven days in prison. He said that Laurence Dowdall had been retained to act for him, and in one of their meetings, Dowdall had asked him about the layout of his house and mentioned a man called Peter Manuel. After his release, he confirmed he met Manuel in the Whitehall Restaurant, after which they went on to a pub.

In the pub, Manuel had spoken about Vivienne and said he knew who had murdered her. He had then taken a newspaper photograph of Anne Kneilands from his pocket and showed it to him. She was at the seaside and was holding her skirts above her knees; Watt had looked at it, handed it back, and Manuel tore it up and put the pieces into an ashtray.

Manuel had gone on to tell him about the break-in at Watt's house being a mistake and about Tallis, Bowes and Martin Hart being involved. He had claimed that a mistake had been made as 'the Valente girl' had been seen at number five, and that had led to the wrong house being broken into.

Had Manuel actually seen her there that night after he had used number eighteen as a base camp, or was he using knowledge gained from the newspapers?

Manuel had gone on to say that the plan was to shoot all the occupants of the house except one, who would then be terrified into revealing the whereabouts of the safe. Tallis had broken the glass panel and after he had gained entry, Mrs Watt had been shot first.

Watt started to shake and sob at this point in his evidence, and the Macer came forward with a glass of water, and a doctor, specially stationed in court, stepped forward and took his pulse, before Watt composed himself and carried on. He continued by saying that Manuel had told him that Tallis had struck Vivienne, tied her hands then shot her.

Manuel had been able to describe every item of furniture in the house, and when Watt had challenged him about it, he said that Tallis had told him.

Watt said he had then asked Manuel about a rumour he had heard that he had had the gun from the 'Burnside job'.

Manuel had denied it.

Watt had then revealed that he had actually taken 'Scout' O'Neil to the police and he had told them that he had arranged to get the gun for Manuel. Faced with that information, Manuel had lamely replied, 'Oh, that gun. I had several guns.'

In another version of the bullet in the mattress yarn, he said that Manuel had told him that Hart had fired a gun at Tallis in the Platt house and the bullet had gone into the mattress and it was the same gun that had been used in Watt's house. Tallis had then, for some illogical reason, asked Manuel to throw the gun into the Clyde.

When Grieve cross-examined Watt, he went straight to the heart of the theory that Watt had killed his wife in order to pursue a care-free, sybaritic lifestyle, a hypothesis which then, as now, sits clumsily with the facts.

'Were you always faithful to your wife?' was the start of the attack. Watt admitted 'several' lapses.

The scenario of filling the car with fuel and driving to Burnside via the Renfrew Ferry and killing his family was put to him, all of which he denied.

Grieve, however, made two points which might have been telling.

Watt conceded that he might have asked Sergeant Mitchell if he thought he had done it, although he could not remember saying that. He also conceded that he may have also suggested that someone called Ferrier might have been responsible, as one of those who 'hung around Burnside'.

If Manuel had allowed his legal team to finish the job, presumably the jury would have been addressed by both Leslie and Grieve, and it seems likely that Grieve would have been able to capitalise on the general unease surrounding Watt's position.

In the aftermath of the murders, his well-publicised activities might not have appeared as those of a man seeking the truth, but as those of a desperate man trying to offload the blame; he agreed that he had told Mrs Collison that he thought he knew who had really done it.

On the basis that it was someone 'in the family', he said he suspected his brother-in-law had committed the murders – a theory, it has to be said, as ill-fitting as the one implicating Watt himself.

As for Watt agreeing with Sergeant Mitchell's view that he was a man 'with a smirk and without a tear', Watt replied that that was 'an absolute invention and quite like Mitchell too'.

What prompted the famous retort of 'What a profession!' was Grieve's proposition that he was able to inform the brother-in-law he had suspected of being the culprit, that his wife Margaret had 'got it first', the suggestion being that Watt knew this as the murderer. Watt said it was a lie that he had ever said that 'Margaret had got it first.'

It would be fair to say that, overall, he appears to have been able to offer a reasonable if not fully convincing explanation for meeting the man who had murdered his family. Amongst other things, he said that when he was in prison, he had heard what sort of madman Manuel was and that when he heard that Manuel had asked to meet him, he had done so only because he had been told he wanted to see him.

He described Manuel as the man responsible for all his troubles and that all the police – apart from one – were not listening to him when he said that Manuel was definitely the murderer.

He scoffed at suggestions that he had admitted to Manuel that he had been the murderer, or that he had tried to persuade Manuel to help him manufacture evidence to clear him of the crimes, or that he had given Manuel £150 to try to get him to ensure that someone else was arrested for the murders.

He said he was 'not in the least surprised' that Manuel was saying things like that.

Re-examination was brief and covered the fact that there was only a small amount of life insurance on Mrs Watt's life, so weakening one strand of suspicion. He was also asked about Ferrier and he explained that he was someone he had sacked and who might therefore have had a grudge against him and his family.

William Watt was then free to leave the building to try to get on with his troubled existence. The backdrop of lingering suspicion and the whispering onlookers would, however, plague him to the end.

As he left that day, though, he was not to know that Manuel planned one more cruel surprise for him.

35

EVIDENCE FROM THE STREET

Other news took second place to the coverage of the trial, but life went on.

On 18 May 1958, Paisley-born racing driver, Archie Scott-Brown was killed at the Belgian Grand Prix when his Lister Jaguar overturned on the sixth lap and burst into flames. What made his choice of career remarkable was that he had only one arm.

It was reported that Glasgow's rock'n'roll fans were disappointed with the news that Tommy Steele had cancelled a date at the Empire due to exhaustion.

Anthony Greenwood MP claimed that Britain was going to 'grind to a standstill' unless something was done about coping with the level of traffic on the roads.

Group Captain Peter Townsend was said to have had a meeting with Princess Margaret for six hours at Clarence House as press speculation raged that they were about to announce their engagement; they never did and that in itself led to further conjecture that despite being a decorated war-time pilot, he was still a commoner and therefore unsuitable for admission to the Royal Family.

The retired Moderator of the General Assembly of the Church of Scotland was criticised for taking the church 'down the road to Rome' for expressing liberal views about observance of the Sabbath, and a minister from the Free Presbyterian Church was quoted as saying, 'We deeply deplore that the Moderator of the Assembly of the Church of Scotland shall take advantage of his exalted office to sow the tares of Popery in this Covenanting land of the Reformation.'

'Tares', incidentally, are crop-ruining weeds referred to in the Bible.

A Harley Street doctor was sentenced to five years' imprisonment after he was convicted of trying to procure the miscarriage of a thirty-five-year-old nursing sister who died as a result of the attempt.

The law reports for 1958 included a case which debated whether an accused was entitled to plead provocation after he had seriously assaulted two women, one of them his wife, with a bottle. He had returned to his home in Dundee to find the pair engaged in 'those unnatural practices between females to which the name Lesbianism has been given' and the question for the court was whether such behaviour amounted to adultery and therefore provocation. Lord Guthrie had directed the jury that 'Lesbianism is not adultery but I do not think that anyone would hold that it is a less serious infringement of the duty of a wife than adultery is.'

June 1958 produced a news report entitled, 'Sex equality? Not likely', the story being that five thousand women had listened to a debate on equal rights about home ownership on separation or divorce at the Albert Hall in London. The conclusion was that they voted down the idea of equality 'with a bang' and the report ended confidently, 'Of course they did. No woman in this country wants sex equality. No woman ever did or ever will.'

July brought news of a hotel in Coventry where the price of a half-pint of beer cost eight pence if the buyer was white and a shilling if he was black. The owner, a Mr Herbert, explained that he was trying to discourage 'coloured folk' from using the premises as the white patrons didn't like drinking with them. A shilling-paying customer from Jamaica, curiously described as 'opal-black', told the reporter he felt insulted.

Day four of Manuel's trial had ended with the agonies of Isabelle Cooke's parents, grandmother and uncle all telling of their vigil turning to nightmare. Her lonely suitor, Douglas Bryden, spoke to waiting forty-five minutes in vain for her to arrive at their meeting place; the neighbour Mrs Gardner told of hearing the noise 'as if someone had got a fright' near to the path Isabelle had gone down.

Thomas Docherty said he had caught a bus from Viewpark to

Glasgow at about 6 o'clock the night she had disappeared. Manuel, smartly dressed of course, had come upstairs, acknowledged Docherty, then gone back downstairs as there had been no seats upstairs. Asked to identify Manuel in court, Docherty picked him out, at which point Manuel smiled back at him. Manuel had got on the bus at Birkenshaw but was not on board when it arrived at the Glasgow terminus, suggesting that he could have got off in the North Mount Vernon area.

Special Constable Donald McFarlane was out with his dog on the night of 28 December 1957 when he saw someone he later identified as Manuel climb through a broken fence from the railway there and make his way to the road. As he did so, the man lifted his arm and covered his face, but McFarlane claimed he had got a good look at him as there was a 'brilliantly lit' full moon that night together with street lights there.

In his evidence, Bryden had described a 'dark dry windy night' which clashed with McFarlane's version of night-time conditions. In cross-examination, therefore, Leslie pointed this out and suggested the full moon occurred a week after that date, but McFarlane maintained he could clearly see and identify the man.

Lord Cameron established that he had been as close as fifteen feet to the man, whom he saw for a few seconds only.

The final charges on the indictment, the Smart murders, were dealt with on day five.

Neighbours spoke to the curious goings-on at the house, with the lights being turned on and off and curtains continually opening and closing.

The cashier at Mr Smart's work spoke to the new blue notes which he had been given and the licensee of the Noggin Inn in Uddingston told of Mr Smart leaving the pub at 9.40pm on Hogmanay and saying he 'would probably see him after midnight', a proposition unlikely to meet with sanction from Mrs Smart.

Dapper as ever, it was noted Manuel had managed to change into a new checked shirt and red tie for that day's evidence.

194

Victor Smart gave evidence about his brother and his family failing to arrive at their parents' house in Jedburgh in the New Year. Given the weather conditions, he said, he was not too surprised and was not worried until he received a call from his brother's work on 6 January 1958, after which the awful truth emerged. Following the call, he travelled to the city mortuary in Glasgow and identified the slain family.

The chapter dealing with the discovery of the bodies after several days led to the youngest witness in the trial, eleven-year-old David Pirrett, describing the last time he had met his school friend Michael Smart. He had been in the same class as him at Muirend Primary School in Glasgow and they had been playmates.

He is reported to have said, 'On the day before Hogmanay I was playing with him in his house. There was an illuminated Christmas tree in the living room and I was going back to play with Michael in the afternoon but didn't go as I had to go to the dentist instead.'

Michael had told him he was going to see his grandmother in Jedburgh.

Another neighbour said that Doris Smart had told her she had wanted to come back from Jedburgh in time to go to the Dumbuck Hotel at Dumbarton for her wedding anniversary early in the New Year. Knowing that the Smarts were intending to be away at that time, the neighbours were not particularly concerned, but they were a bit puzzled when they saw the curtains alternately opened and closed.

A part-time taxi driver, George Gibson, from Old Mill Road in Uddingston, said he remembered seeing a small Austin saloon coming towards him on Sheepburn Road at about 5am on 1 January 1958. The driver did not have his lights on and even after he had flashed his lights to alert him, he paid no attention. They were only yards from the Smarts' house and the car resembled what he now knew was theirs. There was a heavy white vapour from the exhaust as if the choke was out, suggesting that the engine had just been started. He thought there were two people in it.

Even if Gibson's timing could be accepted, his observation of two people on board probably diminishes the likelihood of this sighting being genuine, although it might be expected that two people on board a different car at that time would have realised their importance to the enquiry.

Then the court heard the curious episode where Manuel had apparently given PC Robert Smith a lift in an Austin A35 – the car was described as an A30 by others but they looked the same – at 8.10am on 2 January. If that evidence was accepted by the jury, here was Manuel impudently flaunting his new acquisition a few hours and a day after the murders and within a very short distance of the locus. In those days, police constables frequently 'asked' members of the public for lifts, and if Manuel had refused he would have immediately drawn attention to himself. Of course, he co-operated and, according to Smith, he drove him the two and a half miles to the River Calder, where he was assisting in the search for Isabelle Cooke's belongings. Smith claimed that on the way, the unlikely duo chatted about the weather and the state of the roads. If Smith was right, Manuel had successfully hidden the car for twenty-four hours.

Where?

In cross-examination, it was suggested that Smith had only been able to pick Manuel out as a result of 'discussions' with colleagues and by using photographs but, not surprisingly, Smith disagreed.

A Mrs McMillan then told the court that she had seen Manuel coming off a bus from Glasgow at about 9.05am on 2 January and that he was not as smartly dressed as he usually was. Another witness had said she had seen the Austin at about 8.40 that morning parked near 267 Florence Street, Glasgow and that it had not been there the night before.

The evidence appeared to tie in quite neatly to the effect that he had dumped the car after being forced to give a policeman a lift in it.

The shopkeeper who had featured in one of Manuel's earlier trials, Mr Buchanan, said that Manuel had been his first customer at 10am and that he was very smartly dressed. An unusual occurrence in Lord Cameron's court – laughter – accompanied his recollection that he could well remember him because it was unusual that anyone should be 'so well groomed' on New Year's morning.

The implication, then, was that Manuel realised he could be linked with the vehicle and must have rushed home to freshen up after getting off the bus, then gone out to make sure he was being noticed.

Manuel's apparent generosity at the engagement party and the dance on 1 January was described by relations and friends. A Mary McCamley gave evidence about Manuel being in possession of new-looking blue notes in her house that night. She described how he had taken them out of his pocket and read out the numbers, which were consecutive. Even by Manuel's outlandish standards, there could be no clearer way of attracting attention to his sudden wealth.

When evidence emerged that he only had the sum of 2s. 2d. in his bank account, he ostentatiously turned to the dock escort and in a loud stage whisper said, 'I'd forgotten about that! I wonder if I could withdraw it!'

The papers reported that tension was heightened when Joseph Brannan gave his evidence. They unwittingly described him as 'an intimate friend' of Manuel's, but Brannan's real role in the story was, of course, not revealed at the trial. He spoke rapidly in a low voice and required little prompting from the Advocate Depute as he recounted the times he spent in Manuel's company. He had gone with him to the Labour Exchange to draw benefit every Wednesday and Friday and apart from that, they spent most of their time together drinking or going to cafes. The Crown also led – without defence objection – a chapter about the two of them going out to carry out a bag-snatch, which Brannan said he refused to do, and for which there was no libel in the indictment.

He said he had met Manuel on 27 December and Manuel had mentioned he had broken into a minister's house in Mount Vernon and got a small amount of money and a camera. Four days later he had gone drinking with Peter and Samuel Manuel in the Royal Oak. That was the occasion when Peter had picked up a pound belonging to Samuel and said he would owe him it.

Clearly, he had been short of cash.

The next day, however, Manuel had come to Brannan's house and given his daughter and son two shillings each. After that they had gone to the Woodend Hotel and Manuel had rewarded the honesty of the waiter who had pointed out that Manuel had given him a five pound note and not a pound note, as Manuel had thought, by buying drinks for the hotel owner and a friend. He had come into money, he explained to Brannan, after going into the Gordon Club and been given it 'through the Watt business'. Manuel had also made a comment about being surprised that Austin A30s could go so fast.

The effect of Brannan's testimony on the jury is hard to gauge. He had been friendly with Manuel and, in their eyes, was probably from the same mould. He had accepted he had spent thirty shillings drinking with Manuel in one night, a lot of money in 1957 and suggestive of a lifestyle incompatible with being unemployed with two children to look after – unless he had access to other sources of finance.

Intriguingly, Leslie touched upon Brannan's one vulnerable area in his cross-examination. Whether he did so knowingly or not, his reference to their 'friendship' must have caused Brannan some uneasy moments. He asked him if giving evidence against Manuel gave him 'pain' or not, and at that point, Brannan must surely have thought that the court was about to discover his true role. He answered 'I don't think so' and said he had been friendly with him.

No doubt to Brannan's relief, it was left at that.

Lord Cameron pursued the Austin A30 point and it emerged that Manuel told Brannan he was driving it on 1 January, something the prosecution had failed to elicit.

Day five ended with another sojourn into street life in 1950s Glasgow.

This chapter was to lead to the recovered Beretta being traced from owner to owner and ending up in Florence Street, Glasgow, oddly enough the street where the Austin A35 was found.

The starting point, evidentially, was no less than the infamous William Fullerton. Former Glasgow gang leader and no stranger to violence, he was said to have been the inspiration for the song

'The Billy Boys'. He explained that sometime before May 1952, a John Totten had asked him to get him a weapon 'for his protection' as he had heard that a rival gang had designs on his 'pitch-and-toss school', which ran on the banks of the River Clyde at Cambuslang and sometimes attracted between 200 and 300 people. Obviously, a crowd of those proportions must have been difficult to hide, so it has to be assumed that the authorities' remit either didn't stretch to policing the area or it was simply known about and tolerated. The game involved gambling that a thrown coin would settle closer to a marked line than all the others that were thrown, with the winner taking the lot, although the 'school' owner took his cut in the process.

Totten seemingly kept the gun in a hut near the venue and he had fired it into the ground a couple of times. The anticipated takeover attempt had happened and – whether the gun was needed or not, we are not told – the anxious 'school' owner was sentenced to four years' imprisonment.

Fullerton explained that Totten had approached him to get a gun because, 'Years ago, I was a wee bit notorious for my ability to . . .'

Leslie butted in 'To get guns?'

'No, for my ability to fight, but not with guns!' Fullerton enlightened him.

Logically, of course, Fullerton might not then have been the best citizen to source such an item but, nevertheless, he did just happen to procure the Beretta plus ammunition from the ubiquitous 'soldier in a Glasgow pub' for £5, Totten giving him an extra £1 for his acquisitive talents.

He identified the Beretta in court as identical to the one he had got for Totten.

When his turn came, Totten naturally gave a different version.

He claimed Fullerton had offered the gun to him and due to the anticipated trouble, he had succumbed to the notion. After the trouble occurred, he had taken the gun home and put it on top of a wardrobe but then became concerned that such an item was in his house after he was imprisoned, so he arranged for a prisoner called 'Tony', who was being released in December 1952, to deal with it.

In cross-examination, Totten admitted that he also had a Luger. That item was seemingly needed for the same reason as the Beretta, namely protection.

Mary Totten, his wife, explained that a man – later identified as Robert Joseph Lowe, and now a prisoner in Wandsworth Prison, London – had called at her door and asked for 'the message', which she understood was the brown paper bag on top of the wardrobe, which she duly handed over.

For his part, Lowe said she gave him a Luger, a Beretta, a spare magazine with about nine rounds in it and a box with twenty-five to thirty rounds in it for the Beretta. There were definitely two guns and neither was in a brown paper bag. He had left them in a drawer at 118 Florence Street, but they disappeared between prison sentences and he had last seen the Beretta in 1953.

The Crown did not attempt to make a link with Manuel and the Beretta at that stage. Perhaps the point of that last chapter of evidence was to reassure the fascinated denizens of the city that the police were still in control and that they could trace illegal weapons, even from years earlier.

And anarchy, whether in the shape of the likes of Fullerton, Totten or Peter Manuel, would not prevail.

36

DANDY, THE PROFESSOR
AND A TRIAL WITHIN A TRIAL

The jury consisted of nine men and six women. All were married and the trial must have been a strain both personally and domestically. Unlike the system today, they were not allowed home each night of the trial, but were closeted in a 'West End' hotel, and after the first week of the trial it was reported that special bus trips were organised to entertain them on the Saturday and Sunday. Their mail was passed to them but censored, as were newspapers where there was reference to the trial. There could not have been much left of the papers to read that first weekend.

Each evening, they played cards or read books, but were expected to retire to bed at ten o'clock. They were allowed to take or make urgent phone calls, but when doing so were accompanied by the court clerk who listened in on the call to ensure no direct or clandestine reference to the evidence was made.

To all intents and purposes, the jury was almost as much in captivity as Manuel was.

There's a story from the 1980s, when juries were still obliged to retire to hotels for the night when considering their verdict, that a male and female juror approached the straight-laced clerk and asked if it was alright if they both occupied the same room that night. After running the rules through in his head, the clerk eventually gave his verdict; as adults, they were entitled to behave in any fashion they so wished, but as jurors they must not discuss the evidence.

He was quickly reassured that that was not their intention.

Another aspect of modern criminal trials is that they run from

10am until 4pm on weekdays only. Reports of trials from previous centuries reveal that they ran without breaks, so that the judge would eat and drink – and perform other functions as a consequence – on the bench, and jurors could leave the courtroom to stretch their legs even during the hearing of evidence. The evidence itself could start at 8am and run all day and night every day except the Sabbath, after which the jury would deliver a verdict. The jealous closeting and the long hours in the Manuel trial were vestiges of antiquated procedure, and although the consumption of food and drink in court did not happen in 1958, it seems to be making something of a comeback in modern times.

The Manuel trial sat each day until about 5.30pm and also until about lunchtime on a Saturday.

That first Saturday there was further evidence about the Beretta. The licensee of the Mail Coach public house told of all the customers talking about the Smart murders and one person in particular drawing attention to himself. He was telling others about the propensities of automatic weapons and claimed that Berettas were very treacherous because of their recoil.

It just had to be Manuel, and he was duly identified in court.

Brannan and another drinking crony had been his immediate audience in the Mail Coach.

The link with the actual gun was made when employees of the Gordon Club told of Manuel going to Andrew Thomson's house in Florence Street and taking 'the parcel' away. Before being dropped off in the city centre, Manuel had opened it up and in it were the gun and a matchbox with small bullets inside.

Not only had the Gordon Club's Samuel McKay identified the gun as the same, he spoke about Manuel trying to borrow £150 from him sometime between 6 and 10 January 1958 so he could flee to England.

Lord Cameron had intervened during Thomson's evidence; by that time the real truth about the club had emerged, and instead of it being a 'bridge club', it was eventually conceded by witnesses that it was actually a gambling club. What particularly irked His

Lordship was that Thomson was sullen in his demeanour and spoke very softly. He also denied knowledge of the gun, which had been in his house for over four years, saying its existence had 'slipped his mind'.

His Lordship had heard enough.

He warned him he was there to do two things; to tell the truth and to tell it clearly and that he 'was not doing the second' and he had 'grave doubts if he was doing the first'.

Despite that admonition, when it came to identifying Manuel, Thomson peered round the courtroom and pretended he could not see him, notwithstanding the fact that they obviously knew each other.

Twelve days later, the Gordon Club was raided and McKay and Thomson were fined for helping to run a betting establishment.

It was reported that Manuel paid particularly close attention to the first of the Crown expert witnesses, Professor Andrew Allison, who had carried out the autopsies on the murder victims. As the gory details unfolded, it was noted that Manuel had begun to grip his seat and crane forward to listen carefully.

Was he enjoying the gruesome particulars?

If so, he must have relished the fact that the witness was handed the top of Anne Kneiland's skull to illustrate that a piece of metal found at the scene fitted into one of the grooves smashed into it using 'very extreme violence' and that blood, bone and brain matter were spattered for a distance of eight feet from it at the scene.

The witness gave evidence-in-chief for four hours but was cross-examined for only ten minutes. One of the points raised was that the professor could not say that the times of death of any of the victims could be gauged with certainty.

That, of course, could have implications for the Watt and Smart killings.

When suicide was suggested as a possibility in these cases, he offered the view that with six individual suicides you might reasonably expect to find six guns lying beside six bodies, as 'the person who shoots himself . . . leaves the weapon behind'.

In the case of Vivienne Watt, he suggested that her bedroom appeared to have been rearranged in some way and that she might have been moved after she had struggled and been shot. He said he had the impression that there had been an attempt to cover up the fact that a struggle had occurred.

If that was the case, why would Manuel have gone to that trouble?

Vivienne had an area of bruising at the entrance to her vagina. Had there been some failed attempt at raping her, which he later tried to conceal?

After the medical evidence, Detective Inspector Robert McNeill was called by the Crown on the Monday of the second week of the trial. He told the court about Manuel's last moments of freedom, as nine police officers invaded 32 Fourth Street, Birkenshaw at 6.45am on 14 January 1958, with the search warrant for money or keys stolen from the Smart household. He also recalled the contrasting reactions of Manuel's parents, with Samuel complaining bitterly about harassment and Bridget making Peter a cup of tea.

In fictional gangster mode, Manuel read the search warrant and then told his mother to phone a reporter called Jimmy Bell and the lawyer Laurence Dowdall. McNeill had explained that they were intending to take him to Bellshill police office for an identification parade, and at that point Manuel uttered the phrase that His Lordship later commented on as being possibly significant, 'You can't take me, you haven't found anything yet.'

McNeill described the house search and the items found, and then the fact that father and son had been taken to different police stations.

After an identification parade, Manuel was told of his father's situation and at that point he decided to talk about the money, foolishly implicating 'Dandy' McKay. Enquiries were made to check the information and after a second parade, Manuel was charged initially with the break-in and theft from the Reverend Houston's house in Mount Vernon, the break-in at the McMunns' house in Uddingston and the Smart murders.

The following day he was taken to court and remanded in custody and later that day Manuel asked to speak to McNeill. It was at that point that McNeill held back for over two hours before granting his request and when he and Detective Inspector Goodall eventually spoke to him, it was clear that Manuel wanted to 'clear things up'.

Manuel had said, 'It's important and it concerns unsolved crimes in Lanarkshire.' After being cautioned he asked about his father. When told he had been remanded in custody charged with theft by housebreaking or alternatively reset, Manuel suggested that if his parents were brought to the police office, he would make a clean breast of things and take the police to where the girl Cooke was buried.

At that point, Harald Leslie sprang to his feet and intimated an objection to the line of evidence. The witness and the jury were asked to retire at 4.16pm that afternoon and the point was developed further in legal debate. Leslie invited the court to hear evidence in chambers and not in open court, which illustrates that the proposed 'trial within a trial' was a new and fairly untried procedure, having been decided upon only four years before and having been embarked upon on only one previous occasion.

The objection was that the evidence to be led was incompetent, as it was based on statements by the accused which were not voluntary or spontaneous; moreover, the accused had been detained from 7am on 14 January until 3pm on 15 January without access to a legal adviser. The end result – and the really contentious issue – was the six-page statement which was 'not that of the accused, but that of a police officer' according to the submission.

Lord Cameron decided to hear the evidence before ruling on the matter.

He then turned to the press benches and 'suggested' they exercise very wise discretion in their reporting of the issue.

Although the jury were cut off from the outside world, and had their phone calls listened to and their newspapers strictly censored, His Lordship's concern was that some of the facts to be heard at that stage might 'by some mischance' reach the ears of the jury and prejudice a fair trial.

The 'new' procedure was then followed.

It was Manuel's first tactical throw of the dice and his life was at stake.

37

OBJECTION REPELLED
AND McNEILL'S EVIDENCE

The trial had started with a rebuke to the *News of the World*, whose decision to print what ostensibly was a photograph of Manuel led to the newspaper being reported to the Lord Advocate for possible prosecution. Editors were now particularly careful to heed the court's advice about being circumspect about 'the trial within the trial'.

By that stage, however, the mere mention of the case made it possible to sell newspapers that didn't report actual evidence but instead simply notified news-hungry readers of the fact that several CID officers had said something about some unspecified aspect of the case.

Most announced that Manuel himself had testified, and subsequent narrative concentrated on commenting on the height difference between the large policeman on dock escort duty and the accused man, who had been dwarfed as they made their way to the witness box from the dock.

Manuel had given evidence for about an hour and it was said he gave his answers in a clear confident voice.

Looked at again and in the light of the case law of the time, his legal team probably had moderately high hopes of the judge being persuaded that the confession was not purely voluntary. However, Lord Cameron listened to what both sides had to say then swiftly dealt with the issue, saying, 'I have come to the conclusion that no ground has been established for excluding the statements, to which objection has been taken, from the consideration of the jury. It will be for them to assess and determine what weight or value, if any, is to be ascribed to those productions and to any verbal statement which the accused may be proved to have made.'

Ultimately, laypersons probably have less understanding of yet more faith in the legal process than most lawyers do, and for good reason. A certain professional cynicism matures hand-in-hand with experience – case-winning technicalities and stonewall appeals being relatively rare creatures in practice.

The layman fails to take the surreptitious shadow of public policy into account in the whole process. Chalmers, whose conviction was quashed on appeal, was not only much younger, he was also much less of a social danger despite clearly being involved in the death of another.

The theory that Manuel had relied heavily on the success of the line that undue pressure had been exerted on him and that the 'confession' had been unfairly obtained, was borne out soon after the court's decision. The court's approach in the Chalmers case does appear to have been a factor in his decision to volunteer the confession, and when that went against him, he genuinely had to rethink his new, more perilous situation.

Lord Cameron having adjudicated, the trial resumed where it had left off.

Inspector McNeill simply carried on with his evidence where he had been interrupted, except that this time the jury now heard it for the first time.

He was asked about production 142, the main confession, and what led to its creation. Thereafter, he described what had happened after it had been given, including the night-time journey across fields to retrieve Isabelle Cooke's body and the daytime expedition to the suspension bridge across the Clyde to the spot where one of the guns was dropped and then on to the 'white bridge' where the other was thrown.

Before that, McNeill gave an account of Manuel's meeting with his parents during which he told them he had been responsible for the murders of 'the girl Kneilands', the three women in the house at

Burnside and the people in the house at Sheepburn Road. He also said to his parents that he was going to show the police where he had buried 'the girl Cooke'.

That was duly done, with Manuel manacled between two officers. At his behest, they had started at Baillieston House, where he said he could get his bearings. They eventually stopped walking at about 2am, when Manuel stopped, took his bearings and suddenly announced that he thought he 'was standing on her'. By 2.15am, digging had uncovered her wretched remains and Manuel had recovered her dancing shoes, which had been secreted in different places. Before she had been found, he also led police to where one of her walking shoes was hidden, and when he was told they were then going directly back to police headquarters, he demanded to know that her body had definitely been retrieved.

He was said to be anxious to ensure she was found that night.

Given that the evidence had already been aired, a point about the second statement, production 141, arose, relating to the section that read that he would 'freely and voluntarily' give information about the murders 'on condition that my father is released and allowed to see me with my mother'.

Clearly, that was the crux of the matter; when questioned on the point by the Advocate Depute, McNeill claimed that he had understood its importance and had explained to Manuel that he was not in a position to give him any undertakings.

If what McNeill said was true, the police held the initiative and knew it.

In effect, a suspect had offered to clear up several murders, conditional mainly on one thing – his father's release. The police refused to accede to it yet the suspect kept his side of the bargain, so they must have been confident that by holding out they were not jeopardising the subsequent confession.

Leslie had a mountain to climb. He had to cross-examine on the following points: (a) incriminating items had been found at Manuel's home address; (b) his client had asked for the meeting with the police; (c) at the meeting he had made three statements which could be described as detailed confessions; (d) when his parents arrived he not only confessed in their presence to all the murders but intimated that after that he intended taking the police to where Isabelle Cooke was buried; (e) he had then actually taken the police to her makeshift grave; (f) he had shown the police where her shoes had been hidden; (g) he had taken the police to two separate locations where guns were said to have been thrown, and evidence was going to be led which confirmed they were found at those spots. And finally (h) he took police to a bridge where he said he had thrown Anne Kneilands' bag and underwear, and then retraced his route from the Willow Cafe to the golf course, where he identified an area where her body had been left.

Where to start?

Leslie pointed out the stark inconsistency in Manuel seemingly assisting the police in the Kneilands murder but when asked if he had anything to say when charged with it, replying, 'No, nothing.'

McNeill said he did not think it inconsistent because of what he knew of the accused's character, and that 'he had known him.'

Leslie suggested that Manuel had been charged 'essentially because of admissions coming from himself', but McNeill pointed out there was also other evidence supporting the admissions.

McNeill also explained that if Manuel had requested to see his parents alone, he would not have allowed it because of the nature of the charges and the fact that it was his parents and he had 'previous dealings' with them.

All of this was really just a smokescreen, it seems.

With the 'unfairness' point lost in the legal debate, there was a strict limit to what could be achieved.

The suggestion to McNeill that the position of the body and the other items found had been 'indicated' to Manuel amounted to no more than going through the motions.

Lord Cameron underlined that it was Manuel who had sought the meeting with McNeill, that there was 'no possible room for mistake' in recollecting the words he used and that he had led police 'to the precise place where the body of that girl was discovered in the dark'.

He then complimented McNeill, saying he had given his evidence 'very clearly indeed'.

The defence team were understandably concerned about what the jury had heard on what was the ninth day of the trial.

They need not have been.

Their participation in the fray would soon be at an end.

38

MANUEL TAKES OVER

The papers recounted how Harald Leslie's three-year-old son Robert had run forward to greet his father at their home in Queensferry Road, Edinburgh with 'I'll take your hat, Daddy' as his father had returned unexpectedly early that day. Coincidentally, a press photographer happened to be on hand to capture the moment, and it has to be said that the sacked counsel looked relieved.

The *Bulletin* reported that Manuel sacked his counsel at the start of proceedings on the tenth day of the trial, and, 'A few hours later, just before 3pm, Mr Leslie, carrying valise and briefcase, was driven up to his bungalow home in Queensferry Road.'

And there he told a reporter, 'Mr Manuel decided to conduct his own defence – and that's that,' adding, 'For the next day or two Mr Leslie will relax with his family, his first break in weeks of – in his own words – living with the case.'

The way it had happened indicates that the development came as a complete surprise to his legal team. Normally if a conflict or a difficulty with a client's instructions arises, counsel will inform the clerk of court in order to let the judge know before he comes on the bench.

Just after 10 o'clock on 22 May 1958, after Lord Cameron had sworn in the next Crown witness, Manuel stood up in the dock and said, 'My Lord, before the examination of this witness begins, I would like to have an opportunity to confer with my counsel.'

The judge glowered at a perplexed Leslie, who agreed that an adjournment was appropriate.

Forty-five minutes later, Leslie informed the court that he and his colleagues were no longer able to act, 'Manuel being desirous of conducting the remainder of the trial.' After being thanked by the judge, Leslie, Grieve and the junior, Morison, bowed and left the courtroom.

The communings between a client and his legal representatives are necessarily confidential.

In his book of the trial, John Gray Wilson appears to be privy to quite a lot of the exchanges in this delicate area. He had travelled through with all three of the soon-to-be-dispensed-with counsel from Edinburgh that morning and, not surprisingly, the main topic was the trial and the strength of the previous day's evidence. In his book he suggests that Manuel had been disgruntled with the questioning of some of the witnesses. He goes on to say that counsel's task was made far more difficult 'by the way their client's story had changed and was still changing'.

He describes Leslie and Grieve's approach as putting 'the bare minimum of general questions to foreshadow the defence evidence without becoming too much involved in dangerous detail.'

He rightly observes that the unskilled advocate damages his case by failing to distinguish between favourable and unfavourable points, and often underlines the 'bad' points by repeatedly asking questions where the experienced cross-examiner desists. The end result, of course, is that the witness often recalls details that were previously unspoken. It's what is called 'the question too far' and there are numerous examples cited by court practitioners, often against themselves.

Some years ago, one high-profile counsel, who should have remained firmly in his seat as his client had not been identified, stood up and stated that he observed the witness had failed to mention his client and could the court therefore assume he was not there?

The witness specifically focused on the third accused, apologised for his omission, pointed at him and proceeded to list the catalogue of violent behaviour he had indulged in on the night in question.

Manuel had surprised his legal team and was clearly calling the shots. He had written: 'I hereby signify that having considered the case at this stage, I wish counsel to withdraw from case. P. Manuel' in Leslie's notebook.

The submission having failed, Manuel had decided to go for broke and place all his faith in the naive hope that his natural and undisputed eloquence and charm would secure an unlikely acquittal.

After all, it had worked before.

That there were eight murder charges and very strong evidence seems to have eluded his calculations, and it represents further insight into his inability to grasp the realities of his situation. Mr Ferns continued to act as his solicitor, although he had no rights of audience, so the client was asking the questions, and was now exactly where he wanted to be – in the limelight. He confided in other prisoners that as he was 'the little guy' he would get all the jury's sympathy.

Before proceeding, Lord Cameron addressed Manuel as follows: 'Manuel, do you now wish to conduct your own defence for the remainder of the case, or would you like an adjournment of the case to enable you to instruct other counsel to proceed?'

In a firm voice, Manuel intimated he was going to conduct his own case.

From that point on, he revelled in being the centre of attention.

Observers remarked on his reflective manner and his attention to detail when studying Crown productions. He developed a routine of whispered discussions with his solicitor and sucked on a pencil whilst fixing the witnesses with a studious air.

More recent television footage of Ted Bundy defending himself shows a similar performance.

Detective Inspector Thomas Goodall was the first whose evidence was to be the subject of cross-examination by the accused man. He spoke to much of what McNeill had done and when it came his turn to question him, Manuel was described as 'peppering' him with questions to such an extent that some reporters complained of being unable to keep up with the evidence.

Wilson noted, 'His questions were fluent and well-phrased, with only one or two grammatical errors of the "I seen" sort. His voice had the unfortunate glottal stop of the urban Scot. His forensic manners were good.'

Put another way, he showed remarkable composure for someone depending on his own wits to escape death.

Manuel called the witness 'Mr Goodall'.

His main contention was that the police already knew not only about the existence of the gloves and camera in the house at 32 Fourth Street but also of the location of the body of Isabelle Cooke. In what Wilson describes as a 'maladroit' series of questions, Goodall initially described him as 'a perfect nuisance' during the search, but with repeated prompting he eventually disclosed that he was cursing and swearing at the police just before the search of his house began.

The major initial effect of Manuel taking the helm was that the jury's task was quickly simplified; there could be little room for doubt now and either the police were irretrievably obsessed with blaming an innocent man or Manuel was involved to the point where the prosecution evidence could hardly be bettered.

A glimpse, perhaps, of Manuel's thinking emerged when, as he accused Goodall of pressurising him into confessing, he asked him if he had said that if Manuel confessed to eight murders he 'would go down in history'.

The policeman denied he had said that or that he was 'impressed' that Manuel had shown 'a real regard' for his father.

It was entirely possible, of course, that the police could have said these things in order to play to Manuel's ego, but it is hard to see how this line helped the defence, even if the witness agreed to the proposition.

When it came to finding the first of Isabelle Cooke's shoes, Manuel pointed out that a large squad of policemen had already painstakingly searched the area, yet Goodall maintained that Manuel had gone straight to the exact location in the dark, had shoved a brick aside and picked it up all whilst handcuffed to two officers.

215

The detective insisted that he had done so and what's more had used the hand which was handcuffed to him.

Time and again, Manuel formulated reasonable points that a seasoned practitioner would have handled properly.

Manuel to Goodall: Is it your evidence that having approximately ten hours notice that you were going to search for a body, you arrived at the suspected locus without a shovel?

Goodall: That is correct. We had grave doubts as to whether or not you were telling the truth. We didn't realise you were telling the truth until you found the first shoe.

To the jury, that exchange could have been significant.

He had a point.

According to police evidence, he had made a full confession and as he carried out his promise to locate the victim's body, they had somehow contrived not to bring a shovel!

When doubt is cast on one section of a body of evidence, it can spread.

The trouble for Manuel was that he either failed to follow a good point up, or he framed his 'good' points in such a way that he invited a barbed response, which, to be fair, is sometimes difficult to avoid.

A further example relates to his questions about Brannan.

Manuel was obviously unaware of the nature of his relationship with the police, and he must have caused some apprehension when he asked the police questions about him at the trial.

As he had been with Manuel during the 'spending spree' episode, Brannan had been 'detained' by police to protect his cover.

Manuel to Goodall: Why was Brannan placed on an identification parade?

Goodall: Just in case there was a mix up between you and Brannan.

Of course, it's now known that Brannan's status needed to be protected and one way of ensuring confusion was to make it look like Brannan was also a potential suspect.

The evidence that there were two persons in the Smarts' car in the early hours of 1 January had been given earlier, and Manuel knew it was wrong.

Manuel to Goodall: Was Brannan informed by you that a car had been seen leaving the Smarts' house on the morning of January 1st with two men in it?

Goodall: No – a witness said he had seen a car coming up Sheepburn Road with, he thought, two men in it.

Manuel to Goodall: Did you consider that there had been two men, two possible suspects, in that car, and that one of them might have been Brannan?

Goodall: We had to consider the question of two men or three men or five men.

In that exchange, neither man could afford to reveal the full truth.

Manuel knew he was unaccompanied when committing the Smart murders and Goodall knew he had to shield Brannan and so maintain some semblance of not discounting his involvement.

Detective Superintendent Alexander Brown gave evidence next. He spoke to much of what had already been given by McNeill and Goodall.

Again, Manuel's questions were a curious mixture.

He elicited the fact that the spring clip on the magazine of the recovered Beretta was missing and questioned whether the gun could be loaded.

Brown said he could not answer that as he was not a ballistics expert.

Surely the only effect of that line would be that the jury now had a properly held belief that Manuel regarded himself as something of an expert on guns? His father Samuel used to boast to workmates of his son's technical knowledge in that field.

Manuel was also clearly feeding his ego in the course of the trial.

At one point, Brown said he had doubts about Manuel's motives in taking them to where the body was found as it could easily have been an escape attempt.

Brown said he had warned other officers about that possibility.

Manuel, at five feet four inches tall had been handcuffed to two large officers at all times.

Manuel to Brown: They were warned about what?

Brown: About any escape attempt by yourself.

Manuel to Brown: And they were warned they must take the chance of being alone with me?

Brown: Yes.

Perhaps Manuel's self-importance received a boost, but it's doubtful if that exchange edged the jury towards reasonable doubt about his guilt.

Cross-examining in a trial for only the second time, however, Manuel exhibited a genuine subtlety on some occasions.

Returning to the proposition that the police already knew the location of Isabelle Cooke's corpse, he wondered why the police had not acted on the evidence of Special Constable McFarlane, who had apparently seen him at a fence at the railway that night.

Brown claimed that he had to be absolutely sure before acting.

Manuel to Brown: When you say you wanted to be absolutely sure, you mean that you wanted to be absolutely sure of where the body was?

Brown: I had no idea where the body was. A search was being made for it.

Manuel to Brown: I believe a glove was found in the field about thirty feet from where the girl's body was found?

Brown: I know there was a glove found, but the exact location I could not say.

Manuel to Brown: Did you ask for the assistance of tracker dogs?

Brown: Tracker dogs were there before I arrived.

Manuel to Brown: They were used wherever the girl's clothing or part of her clothing were found?

Brown: They were used in every possible way.

Manuel to Brown: Therefore if her glove was found in that field, where her body was found, it follows that these dogs were used in that particular field?

Brown: They probably would cover the field.

Evidentially, in different circumstances it would have been a decent point to make; tracker dogs were within thirty feet of a body, albeit buried, and they failed to detect it?

The main difference that Manuel failed to grasp between his previous forensic triumph in 1955 and his trial in 1958 was that in a case such as this, the Crown were obviously going to double-check all the facts and pre-empt him if possible.

A good example related to a key found in Smart's Austin. It did not appear to fit either of the doors, and after leading up to it with a few questions about McKay and the Gordon Club, Manuel asked Brown if it might be from the locking device on a bookie's clock. Brown could not confirm or deny whether it did or not and the implication arose that perhaps McKay was somehow involved.

A later witness, however, told the court that it fitted a door in Peter Smart's office.

Inexorably, the jury must have considered the prosecution case as watertight, particularly when small but significant adminicles such as that emerged.

By now, the original police conspiracy had grown to include ordinary members of the public; by the end of the evidence, it was to include everyone except close family and a renegade associate, who speedily warranted the contempt of the bench.

39

HIDDEN EVIDENCE

In 1958 a laudable but romantic notion seems to have existed that an accused in a murder trial should not be forced to defend himself. Not only had Manuel's counsel undertaken their task diligently, but they had done so without any definite prospect of remuneration. Even at that, when proceedings resumed on Friday 23 May, both the Dean and Clerk of the Faculty of Advocates were present in court, unbidden by an accused who had no desire for them to intervene in his quest for glory.

The purpose of their appearance, however, was not to offer a second chance to a truculent accused; indeed, seen through modern eyes, their appearance suggests it was a window-dressing exercise designed to ensure no later criticism of counsel's efforts to date. The Bar has indeed changed in the last half century!

The Dean, C. J. D. Shaw QC, informed the judge: 'As Your Lordship is aware, it is a cherished tradition of the Scottish Bar that any person facing capital charges is entitled to call on the Dean of Faculty or any senior member of the Bar for any help they may be able to give. It is only because I am assured in this case that the accused desires to defend himself that the rule cannot be applied. But, for the information of Your Lordship and the Ladies and Gentlemen of the jury, and indeed of the public, I thought it fit to appear before Your Lordship today to explain the position.'

Lord Cameron replied: 'I am grateful to you for coming here to make the position clear and to make it apparent that it is through no lack of available skill and advice – which has been freely available to him – that the present situation has arisen in which the accused is defending himself. I am happy to know that a tradition which has been cherished for so long in this country is still adhered to.'

With that, what John Gray Wilson describes as 'an impressive little ceremony newly devised to meet a novel situation' ended as parties bowed to each other and the office bearers withdrew.

Manuel had a novel idea of his own.

Described as 'impatient' during the Dean's address to the judge, he rose and requested the recall of Inspector McNeill and William Watt and the addition of four new witnesses to the defence list. He explained that he had 'strongly objected' to the way his counsel had cross-examined them and that a lot had been left unsaid. Lord Cameron told him he could not allow him to recall them and examine them 'at large'. Manuel explained that McNeill had investigated him several times in the previous two or three years in connection with certain crimes.

No wonder Leslie avoided that particular minefield.

He also complained that several matters which had a bearing on the charges, and which had been discussed with Watt at their various meetings, had not been covered.

Two prison officers and a David Knox were now also required to speak to what had been said during a visit to him by Brannan at Barlinnie Prison. Superintendent Duncan was also now needed as he had been in charge of the search for Isabelle Cooke's body.

The judge allowed the extra witnesses.

As for the recall of the others, he allowed that too, but on the strict understanding that ground already covered was not to be gone into. They were to be recalled as part of the Crown case.

The Advocate Depute preserved the Crown position by moving to recall Brannan as well, which was also granted. Given Manuel's propensity for inventiveness and ad hoc defence scenarios, it was an understandable precaution.

The first witness that day was Inspector George Watson, who had assisted in the search of the River Calder for Isabelle Cooke's clothing.

He had found a bunch of keys in the area of the river which Inspector McNeill suggested should be searched. Manuel asked if McNeill knew exactly where to look, but was told it was only a general indication of the area that he had given.

Once again, Manuel proved he was sporadically equal to the forensic test he had taken on.

When the farmer in whose field the body of Isabelle Cooke had been found agreed that it had been ploughed around the dates in question, Manuel asked him: If Isabelle Cooke's body was buried in your field on the 28th it must necessarily have been buried in a part of your field that had already been ploughed?

Witness: Yes.

Manuel to witness: And if a body is buried in a part of a field that has been ploughed, I think there would be some indication that the ground had been disturbed?

Witness: Yes there would be more indication the other way.

Manuel to witness: If somebody dug a grave and put a body in it I think he would have extreme difficulty in disguising the fact that the ground had been disturbed?

Witness: I am not an expert.

Manuel to witness: Well, do you think in your experience as a farmer, especially as a farmer familiar with ploughing, that you could bury a body and leave the field looking normal?

Witness: I would not like to say. There should be some disturbance.

In taking this line of questioning, Manuel appears to have been exploiting a discrepancy in the prosecution case. When he took the police to the field he noted that it had been ploughed *since* he had buried the body, but the evidence at the trial was that it had been ploughed by then. His confession had stated that he had dug a hole 'next to a part of a field that was ploughed'.

In other circumstances, it could easily have been a decisive point.

The evidence then moved on to the finding of the Beretta and the Webley in the Clyde. The ballistics expert's opinion was that the

Webley fired all four bullets in the Watt house together with the bullet found in the Platts' mattress.

The Beretta had fired the bullets in the Smart murders.

Manuel's examination centred on how many bullets could be fired from the Beretta in quick succession, given that the magazine platform spring was missing.

The answer was that in ten test firings, the expert was able to fire two shots in quick succession and on only one occasion fire a third straight away.

The point was double-edged.

If that was the case, the perpetrator might have had some difficulty in firing the third shot, but how would a person unfamiliar with the weapon, particularly someone defending himself, know about that?

Whilst technically appropriate and perfectly admissible, surely the question would appear to be the result of personal knowledge and give rise to a nightmarish but probably incorrect vision of Manuel struggling to shoot a cowering Michael Smart, having already killed his parents?

Only one cartridge had been found at the locus and that was found in the Smarts' bed. Manuel now attempted to show that that necessarily meant that the shot had been fired from the bed. The position of the bodies, however, suggested otherwise, together with the obvious fact that no weapon was found at or near the bed.

The bedclothes had been pulled up over Mrs Smart's head and a photograph had been taken to represent how she had been found. Having suggested that the gun could have been fired from within the bed – he would expand on that point in his own evidence – he then finished by getting the expert to agree that 'someone other than the Smarts' had pulled the blanket up over her head before the police came. Given what he had already suggested, it made no sense, and illustrates his lack of judgement. On the other hand, his later outlandish explanation would cover the point.

After lunch, Lord Cameron took the unusual step of asking questions of the witness for twenty-one minutes. The perceived explanation at the time was that His Lordship was trying to assist a party defender by clarifying certain points. That might indeed have been His Lordship's intention, but in so doing, he helped underscore the Crown case, as, it has to be said, Manuel himself had also done.

Judge to witness: Supposing a person acquires that pistol with the magazine in that condition, he would not know until he fired it that it was defective in respect of the lack of the spring?

Witness: If the magazine was fully loaded that would be correct.

As regards who might have taken the two missing cartridges and pulled up the blanket, His Lordship enquired: And that somebody may either have been the person who fired the shots or a third party who may have come to the scene afterwards?

Witness: Yes, that is a possibility.

Judge to witness: That would involve the person who adjusted the bedclothes, if it was a third party, giving no indication to the authorities that he had found these dead bodies?

Witness: Yes.

Manuel himself had manufactured the scenario by his questioning which suggested that he must have fired the gun either before or at the time of the murders, failing which, if he had simply found the bodies why did he do nothing about it?

There was one point, however, where the judge was undoubtedly assisting the accused.

Probably knowing that Manuel's sketch of a gun had been purloined from prison by Dowdall, and having established that the Webley .38 was a fairly common type of weapon with large numbers being in use in the services, he asked: So it would not be surprising that a man could draw with comparative accuracy the outline of the Webley?

Witness: It is not surprising.

The next witness was Superintendent George MacLean, head of the Identification Bureau, who spoke to examining the crime scenes at both murder houses and the break-in at the Misses Martin's house across the road from the Watt house.

Manuel pursued the question of whether a print found on the lintel at 18 Fennsbank Avenue could be a toe print rather than a fingerprint, as MacLean said. As Manuel persisted, Lord Cameron interrupted and curtly informed him that he had had the witness's answer; Manuel lamely pointed out that there had been no check for toe prints.

The point here was that Manuel was to maintain that Bowes and Tallis had been at number eighteen and that she had stood on the lintel in the process of removing her shoes.

MacLean was to observe, however, that to leave a toe print where suggested, the person would have to be an 'acrobat'.

Nevertheless, it may be that the Tallis and Bowes scenario had some resonance with one or two of the jury, who eventually convicted by a majority on that charge.

In the Smart house, MacLean spoke to examining the contents of two glasses. One had whisky in it and the other sherry. Manuel asked him to look at the photographs and to agree that a basin in the kitchen had a beer glass and a whisky glass in it, and he asked: But taken in conjunction with the glasses in the living room, doesn't it tend to suggest that some time during that evening there had been a third person in the house?

MacLean: These are not facts from which you could draw such a conclusion.

Once more, he made a reasonable point which in different circumstances could have been important, and the witness's answer was a little unfair. It would be possible for the jury to infer the presence of a third party; the problem for Manuel was that his bizarre behaviour in the Smart house, where he fed the cat and opened and shut the curtains, made him the main candidate for being the third drinker.

The day's evidence finished in dramatic fashion. The prosecution case concluded with the recall of the witnesses Manuel said he needed, and the first of these was the tortured William Watt.

This time, however, Manuel was asking the questions.

40

WATT VERSUS MANUEL

The *Bulletin & Scots Pictorial* published front-page pictures of Watt as he arrived by ambulance to give evidence for a second time. On crutches, he tried to get in the side door of the court at the Clyde Street entrance, but it was locked and he had to suffer further indignity as he waited until someone inside realised his predicament. As journalists, photographers and curious spectators took in his discomfort, he eventually gained entry when the door opened and two ambulance men helped him into the building, then into a wheelchair brought in specially for the occasion.

In court, he lifted his arm stiffly into the air before taking the oath and was perceptibly calmer than on the first occasion, when he broke down and sobbed.

It had been deeply personal between them from the start, but this was the pinnacle and Manuel enjoyed every second of Watt's situation. For the occasion, he affected a 'legal posture' and pulled his blazer back to allow his hand to rest on his left hip and he allowed a slight smile to play on his lips as he peppered Watt with his 'skilful' questions.

They were twenty feet apart.

Although he glared hatefully at him to begin with, this time Watt chose to answer by referring some of his responses to the judge, rather than have to honour his tormentor by looking directly at him as he answered.

At one point, Manuel suddenly snapped, but then smiled broadly as he said, 'The question was asked by me, not His Lordship!'

The first area he explored was the fact that they had met and gone to a bar where they had a discussion. Note Manuel's flowery language.

Manuel to Watt: Do you recall, Mr Watt, raising the matter wherein you alleged you had been nominated as president of the Merchants Guild of Glasgow?

Watt: No.

Manuel to Watt: Do you recall outlining a plan whereby I would lead information to the Procurator Fiscal with a view to having a man named Charles Tallis and a man named Martin Hart arrested in connection with the murder of your wife?

Watt: That is quite wrong, My Lord.

That was the juncture where Manuel pointed out that he had asked the question. Clearly he disliked Watt not playing the game his way.

The point about the 'Merchants Guild', or Merchants House of Glasgow, as it was properly known, appears to be an attempt to show that Watt had plans and ambitions to change or better his life and could perhaps be seen as a subtle lead-in to more weighty matters. It has to be seriously doubted that Watt would waste time telling Manuel about his professional life, even if only to ingratiate himself with him.

The plan about 'leading' information to the Procurator Fiscal about Tallis and Hart is more puzzling; perhaps he was hoping that some of the jury would simply be bamboozled by the complexity of the web he was trying to weave, or more likely he was reverting to the notion that, for reasons unfathomed, criminals and murderers had an unerring tendency to confide in him. The mystery is why he decided to allege that Watt, whom he had impeached for the murders of his own family, had planned to blame Tallis. Manuel had blamed Tallis for the break-in at number eighteen, and he now jeopardised that assertion if the jury believed Watt and concluded that Tallis had nothing to do with any of this.

It was all or nothing now.

Watt perceptibly gripped his chair when Manuel asked: Do you remember the part of the discussion wherein you described how you had carefully planned for months to kill your wife?

Watt: That is atrocious and a lie!

Manuel to Watt: Do you remember the part of the discussion wherein you stated that so carefully had you laid your plans they had even involved you changing your address?

Watt: That is a lie.

Manuel to Watt: Do you remember offering to give me the biggest boost I had ever if I pulled up my socks and played the game your way?

Watt: That is also a lie.

Manuel to Watt: Do you remember describing to me that you could drive a car better than Stirling Moss?

Watt: That is also a lie.

If Manuel had given such detailed instructions to his counsel, then there might be merit in his assertion that he had not followed them. The strong suspicion, backed by Wilson's comments, is that his 'defence' altered continually. Following a 'minimalist' course might be tactically more effective from counsel's viewpoint, but details such as Watt planning to kill his wife and moving address to facilitate this by keeping her away from her friends in the area, or driving 'better than Stirling Moss' might have had a certain resonance if properly presented to the jury.

If said.

Manuel to Watt: Do you remember that you said to me that when you had shot your little girl Vivienne, it would have required very little for you to turn the gun on yourself?

Watt: No.

Manuel to Watt: Do you remember describing to me the manner in which you killed your wife?

Watt: I never did!

Manuel to Watt: Do you remember informing me that it was your intention at that time not to kill your daughter?

Watt: I never did!

Realistically, Watt must have been fully aware of what Manuel was going to do once he heard the dreaded news that he was to be recalled as a witness.

Whether that made his thirty minutes in the witness box any easier is unlikely.

Manuel then moved on to the meeting at the point where Dowdall was present, and Manuel told them of the bullet in the mattress, found later to have been fired from the weapon that was used in the Watt killings.

Manuel to Watt: Why did you not go to the police with information about this house in Bothwell if you were anxious to prove your innocence?

Watt's intriguing answer was that he had done nothing on Dowdall's instructions, and a further question led to Watt explaining that he understood that Dowdall had passed the details on to the police, as he had also done.

Once more Manuel had uncovered a reasonable line of enquiry only to push it too far.

The same occurred when he alleged that Watt had paid 'Scout' O'Neil for a gun. Watt replied that he had only given him £1 to buy a drink and had given him an old suit as he was 'in tatters'. Had the matter been left at that, the jury might easily have wondered why a seemingly respectable man like Watt was going to such lengths and getting personal with villains. Manuel then took it further and his next question led to Watt justifying his actions as he confirmed that he had actually urged O'Neil to go to the police to tell them what he knew.

Perhaps Manuel surmised that the Crown were going to re-examine those witnesses who had been recalled anyway and he was actively pre-empting points he thought would be made at that stage.

In fact, none of them were.

He asked Watt if it was feasible that, if he, Manuel, had killed his wife, he should take a detailed note of every piece of furniture in his house and then recount it to him, when he should miss out 'the obvious fact' that there was a safe in it?

Watt replied that he had obviously done so. He must have suppressed a temptation to ask Manuel how he knew about the safe.

Manuel's nerve appears to have wavered on only two occasions in the trial, once as he addressed the jury and the other at this juncture. Perhaps it fleetingly dawned on him that adopting a 'legal posture' and having a string of piercing questions is ultimately ineffective where witnesses annoyingly fail to concede all the points in your favour. Worse, sometimes they say things that unexpectedly rattle you.

Manuel to Watt: Did you mention that your only mistake had been using Renfrew Ferry?

Watt: I never crossed Renfrew Ferry and that, I think, is proved now.

Manuel to Watt: You maintain that you never crossed Renfrew Ferry and you can prove it?

Witness: Yes!

That exchange made Manuel stop and think. Was it possible that something had happened that made Watt so certain? Could he actually now prove he had not crossed over on that misty night in 1956?

Even Manuel exercised apparent caution at that point, and he lamely turned to Watt and said: 'Thank you, Mr Watt, that is all.'

Watt was said to give him a 'long piercing look' as he was wheeled out of court.

Ironically, given the gung-ho nature of the rest of Manuel's interrogation, Watt was probably only referring to the discrepancies in the statements of Taylor and Morrison.

Manuel did not seem to know the truth about Brannan's role, and his motive in recalling him appears to have been to get him to deny that he had told the police that Manuel had plotted to snatch a bag or break in to the Reverend Houston's house at Christmas. In the great scheme of things, it's doubtful if any legal representative would have bothered much about these issues. Now Manuel had highlighted them and was making a bigger issue of them than was required.

It also seems that Brannan had visited Manuel at Barlinnie after he gave his evidence. Manuel asked him: At any time during that visit did you deny in any way statements you made during your testimony?

As an attempted exposé of police pressure, it was a disaster.

Brannan replied: I told you that when I appeared in court I would tell the truth, the whole truth and nothing but the truth, as I stand here today and tell the truth.

That Brannan had visited him after giving evidence, and probably said he did deny parts of his testimony, suggests that he was still being used to find out what Manuel's thoughts were. Moreover, neither the police nor Brannan would have expected Manuel to recall him.

The final Crown witness was Inspector McNeill again.

Before he could commence, the judge advised Manuel to be very careful in his questions, and it can only be assumed that he sincerely had a party defender's interests at heart in offering such guidance.

After establishing that the police had studied his clothing for bloodstains and found none, he asked: I understand that in the investigation of a crime there is a process called elimination. Was I fully investigated and eliminated at the time of the Burnside murders?

McNeill: I was not the officer in charge of the whole enquiry. I could only express an opinion.

Manuel to McNeill: What opinion would you express?

The witness said that their enquiries had taken 'another line' before returning in his direction.

Manuel to McNeill: At the time William Watt was arrested, having investigated along other lines, you personally must have thought that you were arresting the man who had shot the three women at 5 Fennsbank Avenue?

McNeill: I was acting under the orders of a superior officer, who, having considered the information supplied by independent witnesses, had no other course than to apprehend the man whom that evidence pointed against.

Manuel to McNeill: But did you believe at the time that you were arresting the man who had shot the three women?

McNeill: It is not part of my duty to give a personal opinion.

Manuel to McNeill: You admit that at the time of the Burnside murders, I was investigated?

McNeill: You were. Most certainly!

He then confirmed that he was not arrested for the Isabelle Cooke murder until arrested for the Smart murders despite there being the evidence of the special constable seeing him at the railway fence on the night of the murder.

He completed his questions by committing the cardinal sin of cross-examination.

Manuel to McNeill: Are you satisfied that you did everything in your power as a policeman to satisfy yourself that you had arrested the correct man in connection with the disappearance of Isabelle Cooke?

McNeill: I have no doubt whatsoever.

Manuel to McNeill: Then there is no doubt in your mind that I killed Isabelle Cooke?

McNeill: I have no doubt at all!

Whatever he was trying to achieve, all he had succeeded in doing was reinforcing the prosecution case by asking questions that would have been inadmissible even for the keenest of prosecutors.

The judge then addressed the accused. It was 4.05pm and the court normally sat until 5pm. He said that as they had come to the end of the Crown case, he wondered if he was in a position to continue that afternoon or whether he wanted to resume the next day.

Manuel answered that he preferred to resume the next day as he wished to go over his witnesses' precognitions.

Lord Cameron turned to the jury and informed them that it was 'in Manuel's own interests' that he should have such reasonable facilities as could be given to him, so he allowed him that extra 55 minutes preparation for the next day.

By the end of the prosecution case, Manuel had successfully pursued some telling lines of evidence; in most instances, however, he had gone on to self-destruct by ignoring the forensic 'stop' signs. In between those, he had committed some classic gaffes, and despite his public demeanour, he must surely have found out by that stage that there was more to the art of cross-examination than he had envisaged.

Brannan probably stopped 'visiting' him in prison after that and Watt must have prayed for a guilty verdict.

That would end the gossip.

Wouldn't it?

Yet even now, Watt's appearances in court were not over.

41

THE CASE FOR THE DEFENCE

It was now Manuel's turn to lead evidence. On top of the defence witnesses already intimated, he also decided to call witnesses on the Crown list who had not been called by the Crown, as he was entitled to do.

The fact of Watt's arrest must surely have caused anxious moments for the investigating police officers and the Advocate Depute. Ultimately, the jury would be faced with the fact that the police were so confident that Watt was the right man for the murders at 5 Fennsbank Avenue that they charged him and he was kept in custody, exactly the same as Manuel's situation.

In a soundbite more in keeping with an inquisitorial rather than an accusatorial system, John Ferns, Manuel's solicitor, said, 'I imagine that all the evidence will finish on Monday. But then there are the summings-up. Before that, I think that Mr Manuel will elect to give evidence himself, and naturally if he does, he will be examined by the judge and Mr Gillies.'

Presumably, he meant assisted by the judge, who undoubtedly came to the prisoner's rescue on more than one occasion during the remainder of the case, and publicly explored the question of his sanity, particularly with his family.

Manuel was said to be studying law books in his cell at Barlinnie in preparation for leading his witnesses and speaking to the jury in an effort to avoid the death penalty.

The convention today is for an accused to give evidence on his own behalf first and before any other defence witnesses, unless there is good reason to do otherwise. That never seemed to be an issue in

Manuel's trial, and although he did give evidence, he did so last. Presumably, Lord Cameron gave his blessing to this arrangement.

Manuel must have been pleased with the arrangement, as it meant he could spin whatever tale he wished without having to bother about the inconvenience of witnesses contradicting him. As with his acquittal in 1955, he was also given generous leeway when putting points to his witnesses or making *ex parte* statements which had not been put to the appropriate Crown witnesses.

William Watt's very public indignity continued.

Manuel called the witnesses from the 'Renfrew Ferry' chapter first, and Watt was wheeled in to the well of the court, this time on a 'hospital couch' for the purpose of identification.

Roderick Morrison identified him as the only member of the identification parade who had crooked his finger when asked to hold a cigarette. When cross-examined, he explained, 'Never in my society have I seen anyone smoking a cigarette in the way that man did.'

He readily accepted that that was the basis of his identification as he had only seen the other driver for a few seconds.

Rather than simply leaving the evidence as a coincidence, the Advocate Depute felt compelled to try to cast doubt on Morrison's credibility and he asked if it was not 'an unusual thing' to waken one's wife whilst driving along Loch Lomondside. In the days before seatbelts, Morrison had an answer for that too. He explained he was being cautious should there be an accident as he had seen the damage to people's faces after they had hit windscreens.

Commentators have remarked that Morrison was a very good witness.

He did not appear to be anxious to be believed and he had a reliable manner.

A very good start to Manuel's case.

When Watt was wheeled in to court for a second time that day, the ferryman, John Taylor, immediately said that he was the man who had crossed over with a black Labrador in the early hours of

17 September 1956. Although he famously got completely mixed up as to the make of the car, his testimony would have been a gift for a skilled jury pleader who could have exploited this chapter to Manuel's probable advantage.

Sergeant Mitchell was then led by Manuel to speak to Watt 'smirking' instead of being brokenhearted. Mitchell said that when he saw Watt and the police officers with him for the first time, Watt had appeared so unconcerned that he assumed they were all Lanarkshire policemen. He had also carried out the experiments to find out if a car could be moved from the Cairnbaan Hotel car park without too much noise and as to whether the journey could be done in the time scale suggested.

He confirmed that both were feasible.

In cross-examination, Mitchell conceded that the 'trial run' had not gone via the Renfrew Ferry, which perhaps undermined the purpose of the test in the first place.

George Brown, Watt's brother-in-law, was called next.

Manuel asked him about a conversation he had had with Watt the weekend after the murders. Having confirmed that he had told Watt his deceased wife had been a light sleeper, Manuel asked him: Did you give it as your opinion that if someone had broken into the house, by smashing the front door, then your wife had most probably woken up?

Before Brown agreed to the proposition, he turned to the judge and explained that Watt had been 'half asleep' with exhaustion at the time.

Manuel continued: Were his words to this effect – 'George, Margaret did get it first'?

Brown: Yes.

This contradicted what Watt had said about that particular discussion, having denied that that had been said.

Brown said he 'thought nothing of the remark until some hours afterwards'.

Another point well made?

Maybe so, or did this line of evidence spring from Manuel's personal recollection of events?

Next, former Chief Superintendent James Hendry and head of Lanarkshire CID found himself in the unlikely position of being called as a witness by Peter Manuel. He had been in charge of both the Kneilands and the Watt enquiries, and Manuel first asked him about the Kneilands case.

In full flight – and probably imagining he had Hendry at his mercy – Manuel proceeded to indulge himself. Hendry agreed he had spoken to Manuel about his movements in early January 1956 and that he had told him he had been at home on 2 January and had gone to the pictures in Glasgow on the 3rd.

Manuel to Hendry: Did I mention that at 7.30pm on 2 January there had been a new series on BBC television called *I Was a Communist for the FBI*?

Hendry: Yes.

Manuel to Hendry: Did you check that and find it to be correct?

Hendry: Yes. That, of course, could be got from the *Radio Times*.

Despite the contradictory title of the programme, it sounds just the sort of topic that Manuel would have used to fuel his notion that he was cut out for international espionage, and as such would have been a 'must see' for him. Obviously, these were the days before video and DVD recorders, but the jury would not have known of the previous meetings between the two when Manuel told childish tales of caricatured criminality as Hendry struggled to keep his face straight.

Hendry agreed that Manuel had been a suspect for the murder but denied that 32 Fourth Street had been under surveillance at that time or when two prisoners had escaped from Saughton Prison in Edinburgh. The latter is a reference to the time Manuel wrote to Hendry to claim the reward for turning them in, and apart from private glorification, his motive in exploring such matters seems obscure.

Previously, the judge had allowed him to ask about an 'opinion' as to whether McNeill had thought Watt was the guilty party, but on this occasion, Lord Cameron decided to disallow him asking the same of Hendry. Manuel did not seem to understand why he was barred from asking it and tried several variations, moving on to asking whether Hendry considered 'Scout' O'Neil's statement about the gun 'truthful or not'.

The judge reminded him that he was again asking for an opinion, and he stopped him from proceeding. Determined not to pass up an opportunity to play-act, Manuel leaned forward with his hands on the dock and with the air of an experienced counsel dealing with an unreasonable adjudicator, said 'Yes, My Lord, I stand corrected.'

Realising that the distinction was lost on Manuel, Lord Cameron then asked Hendry, 'Did you obtain any statement which, on the face of it, appeared to confirm this story or not?'

After Hendry explained that he could not obtain confirmation of what had been said, Manuel's naivety came to the fore again; Manuel to Hendry: Did you ask O'Neill why he made the statement?

Hendry: I believe he said something about wanting to see justice done!

Next, Manuel led prison officers to speak to the visit by Brannan and Knox and the discussion about the break-in at the Reverend Houston's house.

Manuel contended that at that time Brannan had denied making such a statement, and the prison officers recalled that Brannan had denied signing any such statement.

Two issues arise from that.

Clearly in 1958 it was accepted that a prison officer had the right to be present and listen in to any conversation between an inmate and his visitors.

Nowadays – with an untried prisoner – a prison officer would not normally be allowed to be present; whether anything said by an accused and overheard would be admissible evidence is a different matter. Led by the defence, however, the question of admissibility did not arise.

Secondly, David Knox spoke to the same conversation and he alleged that Brannan denied giving the statement let alone signing it. He reported that Brannan had assured Manuel 'he had nothing to worry about' and that he, Brannan, would not acknowledge any statement in court.

Manuel was seemingly perplexed by Brannan's refusal to stick to the game plan in court. Too late, he might have briefly realised what Brannan had been doing all along, and this episode was a vain attempt to retrieve the situation.

However, in spite of that, later references suggest that the penny never quite dropped.

Three weeks before his friend Manuel was executed, Knox too was embroiled in forensic difficulties, albeit of a lesser gravity, but with a familiar witness.

As John Gray Wilson put it, 'It may be of interest to observe that on 16 June 1958, Knox was sentenced to eighteen months imprisonment at Airdrie Sheriff Court for his fourth conviction for housebreaking. One of the witnesses against him was Joseph Brannan.'

42

BRIDGET MANUEL

Day thirteen of the trial was reported in headlines proclaiming that Manuel had now told his story and that he had given ninety minutes' 'fluent oratory from the witness-box' having seemingly transformed from 'a skilled cross-examiner' to 'a persuasive, gifted speaker'. He held the packed court 'enthralled' and, speaking without notes, had kept the court sitting later than it had all the other days of the trial, before the judge had stopped him for the day.

Glasgow's Lord Provost, Sir Myer Galpern, again put in an appearance, and in an observation straight out of the 1950s, the *Bulletin* reported that 'there was a noticeable difference in the appearance of many of the people who filled the public benches' and that 'it was apparent that many professional and business people had sacrificed the day's holiday to get their first look at Manuel.'

The great unwashed who queued outside must have been refused entry; hopefully no-one had slept on the pavement overnight before receiving the bad news.

He began by calling his mother.

Mrs Bridget Manuel was in turmoil. A loving if somewhat detached parent, she was now publicly called upon to bend the truth to support her errant offspring.

No wonder she was a disaster.

He began by asking her name, age and address.

Having established that, he smiled and added, 'I believe you are also my mother?'

She managed to smile back at him before confirming the point.

240

At one stage, she appeared to sway slightly and the court Macer stepped forward to help her before she indicated she was able to carry on.

Manuel went to the events of 14 January 1958, when the family house was searched.

She confirmed he had been sleeping in a chair when the police arrived.

After Manuel's request for her to contact a reporter and Laurence Dowdall, she eventually contacted Dowdall when she heard that her husband had been charged. He said he was prepared to act for Manuel senior rather than junior.

Two days later she had been at home when a policeman came to the door and told her she had to 'come to Uddingston'. Interestingly, Dowdall was in her house at the time, ostensibly there in his capacity as legal adviser to her husband. What Dowdall was doing there is anyone's guess as his client was also in custody.

She was driven to the police station and her handcuffed husband was put in the car beside her. In the dark, he had not recognised her and had simply said 'Good evening' to her. When he realised who she was, he said, 'Good God, have they got you too!'

Neither knew where they were being taken. They eventually ended up in a room with Brown, Goodall and McNeill.

They were told that Manuel was being 'brought to see them' and that he was going to 'read out a statement'. When he came in, she recalled her son had asked his father if he was alright and he said he would not make any statement unless his father was released from custody. Inspector McNeill said he could not do that without Samuel appearing in court again.

Given that Manuel was adamant that he had been pressurised into signing statements, what happened next was, of course, puzzling. Having insisted on Samuel's release before reading the first statement and been informed that that was definitely not going to happen, he simply seems to have accepted the explanation and to have read out a statement which Mrs Manuel described as 'about clearing up a few crimes and a few mysteries about things that had happened in Lanarkshire'. In court, she agreed with the proposition that the statement 'did not mention specific crimes'.

At that stage, Manuel desperately wanted his mother to follow his leading questions, but she plainly failed to catch on in time.

Manuel to Mrs Manuel: Did you hear me making any statement to you?

Mrs Manuel: You asked me if I was alright. You said you didn't know how these things happened or what made you do these things.

Why did Manuel think his own mother would play along with his heavy hints? He was to have better luck with his father, and perhaps he wrongly assumed that his parents had colluded on this point. Too late, the damage was there for all to see and hear. Manuel's inevitable fallback was to ask her if she was absolutely sure about that, and even Mrs Manuel belatedly realised what he wanted her to say, so she opted for a series of 'not being sure' answers.

She did, however, recall one of the policemen, Goodall, saying something like, 'Come on Peter. Speak up. You know what you have to tell. You know what you have to do, Peter.'

Manuel to Mrs Manuel: You heard him in effect urging me?

Mrs Manuel: Oh yes.

Manuel to Mrs Manuel: Did they tell you at any time before that interview that I had been charged with murder?

Mrs Manuel: No.

He went on to ask her about the day of the Watt murders – 17 September 1956 – and she claimed she could recall that neither had he left the house that afternoon nor had there been a visit by Charles Tallis, who of course had said he had been there in relation to the stolen rings.

Without any reference to his alibi for the morning of the Smart murders, Manuel simply sat down at that point.

Had a legal representative committed either that faux pas or the earlier gaffe about 'what made him do these things', there could have been serious repercussions.

As it was, and not for the first time in the case, the judge fulfilled the role of assisting the party defender. Lord Cameron asked him if he was not taking any evidence about the Sheepburn Road charge and Manuel sprang to his feet to confirm that he had been in the family home at 4.45am when his mother had gone to bed and that she had wakened him at 8am.

Coaxing a nervous or unreliable witness through an examination-in-chief is obviously hazardous; often there's worse to come, however, when cross-examination follows.

Gillies, the Advocate Depute, asked her if she had said that Peter made the remark that he 'didn't know how these things happened' and she agreed. She went on to tell him, 'Peter told me he didn't know what made him do these things.'

She maintained that she had not heard her son talk specifically about the present charges but she did hear him say, 'There is no hope for me.' By that time, she was evidently doing her best for her doomed son; her contention that the writing on one of the statements was not that of her son has to be seen in that context.

Untrammelled by professional caution, Manuel then made a bad situation worse.

He re-examined her.

In so doing, he clumsily underlined his earlier blunder lest anyone had failed to spot it first time round.

Manuel to Mrs Manuel: Why do you think I said 'I don't know why I do these things'?

Mrs Manuel: I am sure I heard you say it.

Manuel to Mrs Manuel: Did you hear me saying it plainly and clearly or is it just an instance where you think you heard me saying it?

Mrs Manuel: I heard it, Peter.

Manuel to Mrs Manuel: You heard it?

Mrs Manuel: Yes.

After a series of increasingly calamitous attempts to have her withdraw the suggestion, during which she agreed that she 'couldn't remember' some of the questions asked that night, he eventually decided to go for broke.

Manuel to Mrs Manuel: Then can I put it like this – did you definitely and plainly hear me saying 'I don't know what makes me do these things'?

Mrs Manuel: Well I heard you say it!

Yet again, Lord Cameron appears to have had his duty to ensure a fair trial uppermost in his mind when he clarified matters with Mrs Manuel.

On that last point, the judge asked her if she understood that 'these things' referred to the unsolved crimes they were talking about.

She replied that that did not enter her mind.

Then when he flagged up a possible escape route, she simply failed to realise or take advantage.

Lord Cameron to Mrs Manuel: As a mother, were you very upset and worried?

Mrs Manuel: I had all my faculties.

Lord Cameron to Mrs Manuel: Did Peter appear to be in full possession of his?

Mrs Manuel: I could not answer that, but he was not his usual self. I am talking about his appearance.

She went on to explain his clothes looked dishevelled.

Not a word about his mental state.

Eventually, his Lordship grasped the nettle.

Lord Cameron to Mrs Manuel: When he was living at home with you, did he always appear to be in full possession of his faculties?

Mrs Manuel: Yes.

Her evidence finished, Mrs Manuel could momentarily relax. Although the prosecution case was undoubtedly strong, she had given her testimony in the knowledge that one wrong answer could assist in her son's conviction. The responsibility for her being called at all lies entirely with Manuel. Her burden was almost too much for her to bear, and it showed.

By the end of the trial, and in exchange for their story, the now defunct *Empire News* had paid for her and her husband to stay in a hotel in Ayrshire whilst awaiting the jury's verdict.

It was reported that when they heard of the death sentence, they attended a local church.

Did she pray for her son, or did she pray for his victims?

43

SAMUEL MANUEL

Next up for the defence was Manuel's father.

Unlike his wife, he proved suspiciously compliant with his son's leading questions. In fact, when his evidence is considered, it is tempting to ponder whether Peter's energetic imagination was inherited from him.

Questioned as to whether Manuel said 'he didn't know why he did these things', Samuel was adamant that his son had 'never made a statement'. Moreover, he recalled that his son looked as if he was under the influence of drink or drugs and was not acting of his own free will. Indeed, the police constantly prompted his son, who, he recalled, looked as if he had had 'a lot of pushing around'.

At best, he heard his son mention 'a few crimes and two or three mysteries' but definitely not any specific crimes involving Anne Kneilands, Isabelle Cooke, the Watts or the Smarts.

Blind paternal loyalty had extended an initial police fit-up to the realms of unreality, now including violence and drugging; it has to be wondered why the CID would go to these lengths then spoil it all by letting his parents in to see him in that state.

On the other hand, it's never been fully explained why they were allowed in at all.

As for the day of the Watt murders, he could remember Tallis coming to the house the day before. He wanted to leave four sticks of gelignite there and he took the opportunity to tell Samuel he had a gun in his possession.

As often seemed to happen to his son, aspiring felons obviously felt the need to reveal intricate criminal details to Manuel senior as well.

And there was more.

Tallis had been to the house, he recalled, in August 1956 with an electric razor, which was left there until the police raid in 1958.

On 31 December 1957, the evening before the Smart murders, father and son had gone to the Royal Oak pub. When Brannan appeared, his son had pretended he was short of money so that Brannan would leave their company, which he did. However, they were joined by two other men at that stage. One of them – impliedly the world-weary Mr Smart – who had glasses, a red complexion and was greying at the sides, 'went out' with Peter for a little while.

On 1 January 1958 he could distinctly recall going to bed at 3.30am in an effort to get three hours' sleep, but he could recall actually being awake from 5.45am that morning and he definitely heard no-one leave the house.

At one stage, Samuel said he recalled Detective Inspector McNeill coming to the house the day after the Watt murders. Even though he was ostensibly looking for a gun, he returned looking for Peter's shoes, and he, like Tallis, took the opportunity to unburden his soul of astonishing information. McNeill seemingly confided that not only was he fully aware that Peter was totally innocent of the murders but he let slip that Watt was to be tried on 6 January 1957, which is all the more amazing since Watt had not been charged let alone even fully committed for trial at that stage – a necessary part of the procedure then in fixing a date for the trial.

The next time McNeill came back he had a search warrant in connection with either the Kneilands or the Watt murders but he couldn't recall which.

The judge's patience was dwindling.

Lord Cameron to Manuel senior: How is it that you cannot recollect that? That would be the sort of thing that would stick in your mind!

Manuel senior: I cannot remember.

* * *

247

The Advocate Depute had plenty to ask in cross-examination.

Starting with the stolen gloves, Manuel senior was at a loss to say why he had not told the police that they had been given to him by Peter as a Christmas present.

His Lordship's patience had expired.

Should Samuel Manuel have imagined that he would be able to baffle the court and effortlessly shield his son, he was grossly mistaken.

Lord Cameron to Manuel senior: You say now that Peter gave you the gloves. You must have been aware of that fact when your attention was drawn to them by the police during the visit to your house.

Manuel senior: My Lord, I was excited at the time. I don't know what the reason was.

Lord Cameron to Manuel senior: Well you are not excited now! What was the reason?

Manuel senior: Well, I received a parcel from America.

Lord Cameron to Manuel senior: Is that the best answer you can give?

Manuel senior: I don't know why I said it at the time.

The Advocate Depute asked about the events surrounding the 'family meeting' at Hamilton police office on 15 January 1958. Samuel recalled there being twenty policemen in the room at the time, with a further twenty on the stairs outside. They alleged that Peter and Tallis had been doing a lot of jobs in Uddingston but they couldn't prove it; he knew it could not have been in connection with the murders as 'Peter had not been out of the house', so it must have been housebreakings they were talking about.

By implication, then, Peter was always at home when murders were happening, but possibly furth of the abode when other, lesser, crimes were occurring.

Shown the first two statements, productions 140 and 141, he said his son had read neither of them out at the meeting and he never heard mention of the murders either.

As for the Tallis visit in 1956, he agreed with the Advocate Depute that the request to leave gelignite was 'rather an extraordinary one'.

So was the witness's answer.

Advocate Depute to Manuel senior: Was there any conversation leading up to this matter?

Manuel senior: When we were talking he [Tallis] told me about being out in a car with a lady the week before and the lady sticking a gun into his side. That had happened the Sunday previous. I think he said Peter was with him. He said that this lady stuck a gun into his side, kidding like.

In his book on the trial, John Gray Wilson drily observes, 'One cannot help remarking that, if the Manuels are to be believed, Tallis had a genius for picking dangerous girlfriends.'

Manuel senior appeared to exhibit similar tendencies to Manuel junior when under the spotlight. The most astonishing things occurred but he was oddly impassive to them all.

Apparently knowing that Tallis had a gun in his possession just before the Watt murders, he was asked if he had informed the police of that fact when they visited the house on the day after the murders.

He said he hadn't and couldn't explain why he had failed to tell them.

Lord Cameron re-entered the fray and asked him to clarify that further.

Manuel senior explained he was highly excited at the time, and in any event, he thought the police would have searched Tallis's place.

Manuel re-examined his father, starting with Tallis's possession of the gun. He suggested that when the police questioned him on 18 September 1956 his father might have thought it was not a 'judicial' time to mention guns to them, particularly if he thought Tallis could have passed it on to him.

In short, was he covering up for his son?

Manuel senior readily agreed that that was the case.

That suggestion was reasonable, but dangerous; 'covering up' for one thing might also apply to everything else.

The judge rapidly spotted the flaw in the plan.

Lord Cameron to Manuel senior: Did you inform the police after

18 September 1956 that you had information that Tallis had acknowledged possession of a gun on 16 September?

Manuel senior: No.

Lord Cameron to Manuel senior: So you never came across the appropriate time for telling the police?

Manuel senior: I never told them.

That the judge harboured doubts about the prisoner's sanity is clear.

As with his mother, he asked Manuel's father about noticing anything unusual in his mental capacity over the last two years, and like her, he answered 'no'. Perhaps in the 'deny everything' mode it's perceived as an error to acknowledge any form of weakness, but it could possibly have been a narrow opportunity for a sentence other than hanging.

In that regard, when Manuel called his sister Teresa to confirm the alibi for the Smart murders – she said she went to bed at 4.35am that morning – the judge again took the opportunity to ask about her brother's mental state.

Knowing that behind the scenes she had genuine misgivings about her brother, and the fact that she was a nurse, her answer was interesting.

She said that she had not noticed anything unusual over the last two years. To her it was his usual behaviour and she had always known him to be the same. Was she trying to say publicly that her brother was suffering from a form of mental illness whilst trying not to break ranks with the family?

According to John Gray Wilson, Manuel's legal team did broach the subject of a possible plea on the basis of diminished responsibility, but he literally laughed at the suggestion, saying he wanted to hear no more of the 'insanity business'.

In any event, and unlike her father, she had no qualms about confirming that Peter had given her a present of a camera on the Sunday before Christmas 1957 and that she confirmed that fact during the police raid in January.

*　　*　　*

Manuel's brother James then gave evidence to the effect that he and Peter had volunteered to wash up at 5.45am on New Year's morning. He had noticed the time on the clock on the chiffonier – that word again – so he could not be mistaken.

Manuel's final witness was Robert McQuade.

He probably epitomised all that 'decent' members of society detested and feared most at the time. Post-war western society was now dealing with the Cold War, and from within their own ranks, no less, rebellion was being fomented in the form of rock'n'roll riots and 'Teddy boys'.

McQuade chose to do his duty for truth and justice wearing the uniform of dissent in 1950s Britain. He was pictured entering the High Court with James Dean-style slicked back hair, a large wide-shouldered coat, drainpipe trousers, white socks and the obligatory brothel-creepers. An image of Peter Sellers in some of his classic wide-boy roles comes to mind.

Even before he had uttered a word, any impact he would make would be negative; by the time he had finished his evidence, the jury were probably concerned that they were not at home and in a position to protect their household goods.

Manuel asked him about the night in the Royal Oak and McQuade willingly participated in the obvious fiction that a suicidal Smart had gone there that night desperate to purchase a weapon from Manuel.

He explained that at one stage in the evening, Manuel had asked him to keep an 'edge' for 'busies' – a lookout for policemen – and it had been explained to him that the gentleman in question was buying a 'shooter' from Manuel.

McQuade explained he had obliged by moving nearer to the door and keeping an eye out. Warming to his evidential task, McQuade then turned and addressed the judge personally about Manuel going into the toilet with the man, then emerging after five minutes, after which a drink was sent over to his table.

His Lordship remained composed in the face of impertinent familiarity.

McQuade went on to mention that although he 'could not commit himself to it', he was pretty sure that the man bore a resemblance to the picture he had seen of Mr Smart in the report of his murder.

In cross-examination, he explained he had not gone to the police about the incident because he could have been in trouble for keeping the 'edge for the busies'.

Time for His Lordship to instigate some searching enquiries.

Lord Cameron to McQuade: Did you not think it was important to let the police know that a man unknown to you had acquired a gun on the night of Hogmanay?

McQuade: I wanted to keep out of trouble.

Lord Cameron to McQuade: I didn't ask you that! Answer the question!

McQuade: It wasn't unusual. I didn't think it very important because I didn't think it had any connection with the Sheepburn Road incident.

His Lordship must have pondered that answer; McQuade had just spoken of a likeness between the buyer of the gun and the man in the papers.

Lord Cameron to McQuade: Did you ever inform the police authorities that you had been a witness of this transaction?

McQuade: No.

Lord Cameron to McQuade: Didn't you get a drink as a reward for keeping your eyes open?

McQuade: Yes.

Lord Cameron to McQuade: Didn't you know it was an improper and illegal transaction and you thought it was of no importance?

McQuade: No.

At that, the judge sternly barked, 'You may go!' and McQuade was disapprovingly dismissed from the witness box.

It can only be assumed that McQuade's testimony reinforced – if that was required – any impression that the jury might have had that fantasy played a large part in Manuel's life. The difference between his parents' recollections and the ridiculous content of McQuade's testimony must clearly have smacked of perjury in a desperate attempt to help a guilty man.

If the court had heard some unsavoury and unlikely tales to date, the best – or worst – was yet to come.

Manuel now gave evidence on his own behalf.

44

MANUEL'S EVIDENCE – DAY ONE

At 4 o'clock on the afternoon of the thirteenth day of his trial, Manuel rose in the dock and announced, 'My Lord, I intend to testify on my own behalf.'

The judge invited him to go to the witness box, and Manuel impatiently hurried towards it.

He was to do the same from the condemned cell to the gallows eight weeks later.

A burlesque moment occurred when the much taller white-gloved police escort holding the prisoner's sleeve in token custody, had to jog slightly to keep up with his prisoner as they travelled across the courtroom floor.

Manuel was impatient to tell his tale, and when he spoke, the shorthand writer had difficulty keeping up and the judge had to ask him to slow down.

After administering the oath, Lord Cameron advised him to deal with the charges chronologically, and Manuel generally took that on board. In keeping with his performance to date, he began with a flourish, turning towards the jury and saying, 'Ladies and Gentlemen of the jury . . .' before launching into his story, most of which the court heard for the first time.

Charge 1 – The murder of Anne Kneilands on 2 January 1956.

He said he had been working in East Kilbride on 4 January 1956 when a policeman approached and told him and some workmates that a girl had been found dead in the woods at Capelrig. The policeman asked them to look out for a man.

A week later he was at work when he looked up and 'saw a face with which I was familiar – Superintendent Hendry of Lanarkshire CID'.

Hendry asked him where he had been on the nights of 2 and 3 January, and he had told him. Hendry asked if he had been in East Kilbride and he said he had not, and Hendry then said that a bus conductress had said otherwise.

That night he went home and discovered that the police had taken his clothing and when they returned they asked him why he was so sure that he had not been in East Kilbride and he explained that he had got into a fight at Hogmanay in Glasgow and had gone drinking the following night. He also pointed out that he had watched a certain programme on television.

On returning to work, he found out a workmate had gone to the police and told them about the scratches he had on his face. He had then had 'a few words with the fellow', who then left the job at East Kilbride for another job elsewhere.

This boastful posturing was to punctuate his evidence throughout.

Did he really think that the female jurors were moved by his animal charm and that their male counterparts were impressed by his manliness?

He went on to tell the court about the reporter who proposed he allow his photograph to appear in the *Scottish Daily Express* of 14 January 1956, along with a short article about the murder. The reporter had pointed out that it would show that he had not been in East Kilbride on the night in question.

He had complied and no-one had come forward to identify him.

Behind the scenes, however, someone obviously knew Manuel's character well enough to understand that he could not possibly resist the opportunity of limelight, however brief.

That was all he had to say about that charge.

*   *   *

Charge 2 – The break-in at the Platt house in September 1956.

Manuel claimed he had bought the electric razor from Tallis. Although the break-in took place in September, Manuel maintained that it had come into his possession sometime between June and August of that year. His explanation was that Tallis said he had got it from someone who worked at the Philips factory.

He knew nothing of the other items stolen from the house and the bullet in the mattress was not down to him.

The bullet, of course, linked the break-in with the Watt murders.

How could he explain what he had told Dowdall about it?

He claimed that Dowdall told him the bullet had been fired at a time when Watt was 'covered' – presumably with an alibi – and if Manuel could help find it, it would assist Watt's case. These were the first threads of a soon-to-be-revealed conspiratorial tapestry involving Watt, Dowdall and others who had gone on to entrap Manuel into helping them, thereby pulling him evidentially closer to the Watt murders.

Charges 3 and 4 – The break-ins and murders at Fennsbank Avenue in September 1956.

He had not broken into the Misses Martin's house at 18 Fennsbank Avenue.

In fact, he remembered Tallis boasting about someone paying him to break into a house in that avenue, for which he had been given £1,000.

He had been told to mess the place up to make it look as if someone had spent some time there. Manuel said he told him that for that kind of money, it would have to be Buckingham Palace, but that being offered money to break in somewhere just didn't make sense.

One night in July 1956, he was in Tallis and Bowes' house when Tallis suddenly showed him two .38s, one a Webley. He wondered if Manuel could get him ammunition as he only had .32 bullets? They had broken off the loose lanyard ring on the Webley using a poker and Tallis later told him he had managed to get .38 ammunition himself.

Tallis later met up with him and said he had spoken to 'the man' and he had approved Manuel being in on the £1,000 housebreaking, which, as it turned out, was not to be at the man's house.

He had arranged to meet Tallis at the Woodend Hotel on Sunday 16 September – the day before the Watt murders, and probably the day of the break-in at the Misses Martin's house. Tallis had not turned up, so he went home with a woman before finally returning to his own house at 1am on Monday 17th.

The next day, his father told him that Tallis had come to the house on the 16th anxious to leave a parcel of explosives. However, Tallis had also come to the house about 10am on the 17th and Manuel made him a cup of tea. Tallis then confided he had a couple of rings belonging to Mary Bowes that he wanted rid of, and he asked Manuel to help. Seemingly, Manuel had a contact in that regard, but when he went to see him, he was not in.

Instead, they decided to buy a bottle of whisky and went to the pictures until 4.45pm. After the pictures, they went to the Double Six pub in Glasgow's Broomielaw, then Manuel went out to look for his contact again about 5.30pm. He failed to find him again, but on the way back to the pub had bought an evening paper and for the first time learned that three people had died in a house in Burnside, probably battered to death.

He challenged Tallis about this when he went back into the Double Six.

Not only did he show him the paper's headline, but he then returned the rings to him. Tallis protested that the rings never came from Burnside.

Manuel said he told him, 'You were telling me about some job you were going to do last night up in Burnside, and about a fortnight ago you mentioned a man. You didn't say where he lived, but you mentioned Fennsbank Avenue.'

Tallis said that it wasn't him that shot them.

Manuel replied, 'Charlie, there's no mention in the paper of anybody being shot!'

That night he got home at 10pm.

The police came at 2am. There were eight or nine of them and they searched for a gun, but were not very thorough. McNeill was there and he asked how Manuel was 'getting on with' Tallis, and Manuel said 'Not too bad'.

He also asked if Manuel had a gun and he had said 'No'.

Some time later, he was parcelling up some goods to send to a friend and his mother told him there was a roll of tape in the dining room table drawer. When he opened it, he pushed away some 'knitting things and pins' and noticed an oily rag tied with a piece of belt from 'a girl's frock or dressing gown'. When he opened it, inside was a mark four .38 calibre revolver with five empty shells in it and one live one still in the firing chamber.

He put the gun inside his trousers, put his coat on, went to Glasgow and 'bunged it into the Clyde'.

Meeting Tallis on Sunday 23rd at the Woodend Hotel, he asked him about the gun, but Tallis denied knowledge at first. Later that night he confided that in the house 'things had come unstuck' and after that he admitted he had left the gun in Manuel's house.

Manuel asked him who had shot the three women, but Tallis said he couldn't tell him that.

The *Bulletin*'s court reporter wrote, 'There were gasps as Manuel said Tallis had told him that on Monday 17 September he had met William Watt. Watt's car was parked in a sandpit or quarry behind Fennsbank Avenue.'

Tallis had told him that the planned break-in had been postponed from the first week in September and when they did eventually break in, the house owners had been away that weekend. Mary and Tallis had broken into the house – at number eighteen – and she had been drunk at the time. When a car had come out of the driveway of the house next door, she had panicked and run across a flower bed, but Tallis had managed to bring her back to the house, and she had got into a bed. He had looked out in the street at 3am for the 'other man' but he was late. He had arrived at 3.30am and left at 3.40am, but later returned to number eighteen.

He said Tallis told him that he and Watt had talked for the ten minutes he had spent at number eighteen.

Watt had told Tallis to break the glass panel at the front door of number five when he left.

Watt had returned to number eighteen and offered the two of them a lift into town. He had also given the gun back to Tallis and asked him to get rid of it as he couldn't take the risk of having it in his car.

He later discovered that Mary Bowes had stolen two rings from the house at number eighteen.

Manuel said, 'It was an odd sort of story. It didn't cover his leaving the gun in my house, but I let it go at that.'

Tallis also told him that he had been ordered to put the gun in Manuel's house by the other man.

He went on to tell the court, 'The story he had given me was that this man Watt had shot his wife, and the story I heard later was an entirely different one which led me to believe that perhaps Watt couldn't have had any connection with it at all.

'For a fortnight or three weeks I went over it in my mind. Then I had an interview with Laurence Dowdall. Dowdall asked me what I knew. I said I knew a man who had definitely gone up to Burnside to break into a house. Dowdall said that would be Tallis and I asked him how he knew.

'Dowdall said he knew all about it.'

Dowdall explained that Watt was in a very serious position, having been charged with the three murders, and he asked Manuel if he believed that a man like Watt would have anything to do with someone like Tallis.

Dowdall then put his cards on the table.

He told Manuel bluntly that he was the only person who could do something about Watt's predicament. He suggested that Manuel should go to the Procurator Fiscal with what he knew, but Manuel replied he was in a difficult position, having thrown the gun into the Clyde. After various meetings with Dowdall he was threatened that if he did nothing, Dowdall would 'get Manuel involved'. Manuel eventually wrote to the Procurator Fiscal and set up a meeting, in the course of which he told him about Dowdall's threat. He had also warned the Procurator Fiscal that Dowdall was likely to come to see him to say that he, Manuel, had sold Watt a gun, should Watt have to face a trial.

He also told the prosecutor that Dowdall had wanted him to tell a fictitious story incriminating Tallis.

Incredibly, however, the Procurator Fiscal then alleged that Manuel had actually sold the gun to Watt, but Manuel, shocked by the allegation, had protested that he had never even met him at that time!

Following the meeting with the Fiscal, Manuel heard from a police contact he had that Dowdall was working on Hendry and other police officers to persuade them that Manuel was guilty, and when he put this to Dowdall, he rubbished the suggestion and said he should realise that the police were 'just looking for information'.

Eighty minutes after Manuel had launched into his byzantine tale of treachery and double-dealing in high, low and all other places in between, Lord Cameron called a halt to the day's proceedings.

Whether His Lordship was addled by the non-stop information flow or not, the jury undoubtedly must have been.

There was still much to be said by the accused the following day – the fourteenth day of the case – and Manuel had boasted to his police escort that for every hour the Advocate Depute spoke, he would speak for two.

45

MANUEL'S EVIDENCE – DAY TWO

The *Bulletin* for 28 May 1958 reported that minutes after the court rose at the end of the thirteenth day of the trial, 'people were queuing outside to make sure they got a seat at the trial this morning.'

Heading the queue for admission to the fourteenth day of the case were two grandmothers who took up their positions in the street outside at 4.30pm, nearly an hour before the court adjourned for the day. Two younger ladies were behind them, one of whom had a perfect attendance record at the trial so far. The report ended enigmatically with the information that they were 'staying the night without relief'.

The chief court reporter observed, 'Thirty-two-year-old Peter Manuel will learn tomorrow how much his skill in defending himself in the historic eight murder charge trial at the High Court in Glasgow has impressed the jury. The end of the trial is in sight.'

Before that Manuel had to complete his evidence and to be subjected to cross-examination by the Advocate Depute.

He continued with his convoluted tale of the Watt murders and his bizarre series of meetings with Watt himself.

According to Manuel, the meetings had actually been arranged by Dowdall and after they had met in the restaurant, they had gone to a pub where Watt ordered a bottle of whisky. At that point, Watt had turned to Manuel and said that he was aware that Manuel knew that Watt and Tallis had been at Fennsbank Avenue and that one of the two of them had shot his wife.

He said Manuel could 'swing it' so that someone else would be

261

arrested for the murder of his wife, and that if Manuel helped him, he would have the best legal advice available. Indeed, Watt told him he had 'the cleverest lawyer in Britain' and that he was 'in cahoots with the highest ranking policemen in Glasgow and Lanarkshire'. Watt was 'slashing whisky' into him and had promised him 'the biggest boost in his life'. He insisted that Manuel accompany him to see his brother John, so he could 'confirm' the story about Tallis.

On the way, though, Watt suggested another drink and he stopped off at a shop where a girl was closing up. He asked her how much money was in the till, and when she counted it up as £15, he took it from her, then gave it to Manuel and told him it was a 'down payment'.

At Watt's house, he introduced him to his brother and told him that Manuel was not the sort of fellow they had been told he was.

He had referred to Manuel as 'Chief' the whole time.

When John had mentioned the events at Fennsbank Avenue, Manuel had told him that he knew one person who had been there, but as the conversation progressed, Watt mentioned Tallis and Hart.

Eventually, Watt turned to his brother and said, 'John, what happened was this. This man and Tallis went to break into the Valentes' house. They had a safe in the house and it was supposed to contain £5,000. These people went up there just to walk in and hold up these people and take the money. When they got there they looked in the window and saw the girl Valente sitting in the house and they thought it was her house. That was the time she was in my house.'

Manuel said that the two brothers argued about the situation for a couple of hours and each time Watt turned to him and asked if it was correct, he confirmed it was, exactly as Watt had wanted him to do.

As Watt had been 'rolling about all over the place' with drink, Manuel had taken him to his house in Birkenshaw in the early hours of the morning. At one point, Watt had run out of cigarettes and Manuel had gone indoors to get some, leaving him in the car, before returning with some and a pot of coffee. They had sat outside in the car until 8.30am, as he could not take him indoors, on account of Mrs Manuel probably 'throwing a fit' if she knew 'Willie Watt' was there.

They had spent the time talking about framing someone for the murders.

When he next met Dowdall, Manuel had told him that Watt had confessed to all three murders and it would be better for Dowdall if he washed his hands of him. Watt had not known his sister-in-law had been present in the house and killing her had been a mistake. He had tied his daughter up, but she had got loose, and after he had shot them, he gave the gun to Tallis.

Dowdall, however, proposed that if someone else was charged with the killings, Watt would be able to sue the authorities for a tremendous amount of money.

£5,000 was mentioned.

Watt had claimed he had primed two men, O'Neil and Hamilton, to say they had sold a gun to Tallis. However, should Manuel fail to co-operate in the scheme, they were to swear they had sold the gun to him.

When he had next met Watt, he had given him £150 in £5 notes and said, 'I want you to take this money and forget about me for a fortnight. It's coming near Christmas. Go and buy presents.'

He had taken the money and had not seen Watt from that point until he gave evidence at the trial.

Overall, then, he had definitely not broken into either 5 or 18 Fennsbank Avenue. He had known that Tallis had 'some project' in Burnside and that the rings must have come from one of those houses. As for the allegation that he had stolen stockings, 'I am sure I would not have had much interest in nylon stockings – they are objects I do not wear.' He had 'no knowledge' of, and could not say much about it, but he had not broken into the Watt house and he had not shot the three women.

Anyway, whoever had broken into number five must have had a key, otherwise how could someone have walked up and smashed the front door without waking anyone up?

*   *   *

Whatever could be said about his evidence in relation to Fennsbank Avenue, Manuel had certainly demonstrated his exceptional skill at converting a grain of truth into an elaborate maze. In normal circumstances, a legal representative would have been stopped in his tracks if he allowed his client to make important assertions that had not first been put to the relevant witnesses. As in his previous court cases, Manuel was obviously aware of the gentlemanly convention that permitted party defenders far more scope than that normally allowed.

Perhaps – and not surprisingly – Manuel had 'evidence fatigue' as he narrated his tale. Was it just coincidence that the sum of £5,000 was mentioned in connection with both the ill-planned Valente break-in and the criminal attempt by Watt to claim compensation?

His contention that he 'knew nothing' or 'could not say much' about events in Fennsbank Avenue was certainly not true, given the detailed and fabulous account he had regaled the court with.

Even so, he had spoken continuously and without notes, dealing with detailed accusations by describing exhaustive, if sometimes eccentric, scenarios. That said, some of his assertions were so fantastic that it is difficult to imagine any juror attempting to give them an airing in the jury room, without fellow jurors immediately pouring scorn on them.

The main worth of his evidence about Fennsbank Avenue is what it says about the workings of his mind. Some parts are reminiscent of the 'spy story' he recounted to Hendry at Uddingston police office in 1954.

Indeed, the 'spy syndrome' emerges in various guises.

Having failed to leave explosives at his house, Tallis eventually succeeds in leaving the actual murder weapon there.

Not only that, it had been planted on someone's orders – no less than the criminal mastermind William Watt. When Watt recruited Manuel to help cover his tracks – and simultaneously convince his grieving brother-in-law George that he, William, had nothing to do with the murders – he came up with the tale of the proposed break-in at the Valente house.

Even more sinister was the depth of the conspiracy against him.

It included McNeill mischievously enquiring how Manuel was 'getting on with Tallis' when he came to his house to search for a gun the day after the Watt murders, and then darkly hinting that he knew about it being planted when he asked Manuel directly if he had a gun.

O'Neil and Hamilton were more than just run-of-the-mill unreliable Crown witnesses; they were in on it too when they switched allegiance to implicate Manuel on orders from above.

Dowdall not only knew about Tallis's involvement, but he could secure large financial compensation for Watt if only an innocent patsy could be set up for the murders he knew Watt had committed.

In any event, Watt was in the comfortable position of offering 'the best legal advice' mainly due to being 'in cahoots with' the senior members of the local police. Despite – or because of – that, he was not above threatening Manuel that he would involve him if he failed to go to the Fiscal with what he knew – about Tallis.

And what happened when he went? The Fiscal was in on it too, carelessly letting slip that he 'knew' Manuel had sold a gun to Watt, which in itself was a lie, but served to show the extent of the conspiracy.

Should anyone be concerned about the odds he was up against though, they need not be – Manuel could take care of himself and had a contact up his sleeve in the unlikely shape of a member of the constabulary who had warned Manuel of Hendry's malicious efforts to convince fellow officers of Manuel's guilt.

On that issue, Manuel might be the underdog, but just occasionally he could demonstrate his mettle in the face of foes who underestimated his true authority. After all, he was an indispensable cog in the nefarious plans of others; they needed a man of his calibre to assist them.

Conversely, his present predicament had come from his efforts to help them but he had been dragged into their criminal enterprises instead.

Tallis had sought his help in sourcing ammunition and fencing stolen rings, Watt gave permission for him to become drawn in to Tallis's paid house-trashing enterprise, Dowdall told him he was the only person who could help Watt, and he was mysteriously given sums of money and referred to as 'Chief' just because of who he was.

His tactic of growing fictional tales from grains of truth had been occasionally effective.

Deanna Valente had been in the Watt house the night before the murders, the Misses Martin were away at the time of the break-in and a distinctive shoeprint was found at number eighteen, possibly even left by Mary Bowes.

The timing of the extraordinary Watt–Tallis meeting at the Martin house could just fit in with earlier police calculations about the journey time from the Cairnbaan Hotel. The allegation as to where Watt had parked his car before committing the evil deed was actually based on police conjecture when Watt was being investigated.

That Watt had a key which allowed him silent murderous access to his own house was not unreasonable, although Manuel's penchant for ghosting in and out of strangers' houses was evident from reading the charges on the indictment.

However, Watt having to reward Manuel from funds purloined from the till of one of his shops was not so credible.

The prospect of the tormented Mrs Manuel 'throwing a fit' should 'Willie Watt' cross her threshold is positively unlikely, she having endured her errant son's conduct for so long.

Watt casually offering Tallis and Bowes a lift into town, very shortly after a bout of frenzied homicide, seems absurd.

His own desired self-image shines through in his recounting of his daring activities, police incompetence being the other side of the same coin.

Eight or nine of them searched his house, but failed to locate the weapon so treacherously jettisoned there by Tallis at some unknown juncture immediately after the slayings.

Tallis and he had whiled away their afternoon at the pictures whilst swigging from a bottle of whisky and his capacity for strong liquor stood him in excellent stead when Watt vainly 'slashed whisky into him', the end result being that it was Watt, not Manuel who was 'rolling about' and needed help to get home. He has a ready alibi when he sees a woman home of an evening and asks what use a man like him would have for nylon stockings.

In truth, the answer to the latter point is that they come in very handy for ensuring no fingerprints are left at the scene of the crime.

Attempts at humour in any trial are ill-advised except in certain well-defined situations; trials with multiple murder charges are not, in the main, the venue for mirth. He revealed that the film he saw in Tallis's company was *The Long Arm of the Law* and the papers reported that he smiled at the jury at the paradox of it all. There are no reports of any of them sharing his mirth at the quirkiness of the contrived irony.

With the Fennsbank Avenue passage of evidence in particular, the obvious doubts nursed by the trial judge as to the accused's grip on reality clearly come into focus, as does Manuel's twisted logic.

Nightmarish images of his housebreaking style are reflected in his claim that Tallis was not only to ransack the house in question, but that he was also to make it look like someone had spent some time there, or where he claimed that Bowes, Falstaff-like, had blithely jumped into bed at number eighteen in the course of a break-in.

Both of these instances are tell-tale signs of a Manuel visit, the third, of course, being the consumption of the householder's food with the traditional ritual pouring of the dregs on the carpet.

Yet, at least there were intermittent glimpses of possible veracity in parts of his tale about the Watt charges.

His testimony about the Smart family was entirely barren in that respect.

46

MANUEL'S EVIDENCE –
THE COOKE AND SMART CHARGES

Manuel still had the last four charges to deal with.

While he was on remand, one psychiatrist who had examined him had written, 'In some respects the accused is remarkably detached from what one might regard as the realities of the situation. He shows no anxiety or apprehension about his situation and if this is a pose on his part, it indicates a remarkable capacity for self control and deception. It is not that the accused is apathetic; on the contrary, he seems to take a very lively interest in all aspects of the situation, but listening to the quiet even flow of his narrative it is difficult to feel that he is the person concerned and that he is not merely relating events of which he has been an onlooker rather than the participant.'

This 'remarkable detachment' was to come to the fore, particularly with his version of events at the Smart house.

Charge 5 – The break-in and theft at Mount Vernon on Christmas Day 1957.

He denied the crime. At the time it was believed to have been committed, he had been at home watching television. He recalled a programme about boxers and another which lasted for two hours fronted by Frankie Vaughan, who had stepped in for Max Bygraves, the original compère.

As for the gloves he had given his father and the camera he had given to Teresa, he had bought both of them in the Mail Coach Inn, about a mile from Mount Vernon, from a man who had been with two others, and whom he recognised as a regular there. In fact,

Brannan was with him at the time and he must have seen the entire transaction.

Once again he had sprung a special defence – this time of incrimination of an unknown man – without the judge disallowing it. Not that it mattered that much in respect of this charge, the main purpose of which was to ensnare Samuel and pressurise his son.

And once again, potential defence witnesses who could shed light on the truth of the matter were not traced. Like the woman he escorted home on the night before the Watt murders, the three drinkers in the pub were to remain at large, going about their various shades of business either unaware or uncaring as to the fate of an innocent accused who had crossed their paths.

Or they simply didn't exist.

His occasional detailed reference to the content of television programmes suggest that he was counting on the authorities not considering checking previous television schedules.

Given Samuel's prevarication about the gloves, the jury must have quickly concluded that rather than go shopping for last-minute Christmas gifts for his family, Manuel short-circuited the notion by allowing others to do the legwork and the purchasing of them before relieving them of the goods on the day itself.

Charge 6 – The murder of Isabelle Cooke on 28 December 1957.

Turning to this charge, Manuel revealed he could not have committed the crime as he was elsewhere at the time, namely in a picture house in Glasgow.

After his arrest, he had been locked up in Barlinnie Prison, then whisked away to Baillieston. He had asked what was happening and was told by the police that they were going there 'to look for something'. They had parked at a farm, crossed a lawn and when they came to a ditch, they all jumped over it, with the exception of Goodall, who fell into it.

He didn't know the place and he was handcuffed between two detectives.

They had stopped at a hole in a field and McNeill had told him that that was where he had originally planned to bury her. Goodall had then kicked a brick on a path but had been halted when McNeill told him he was at the wrong place. They had then picked up two shoes he had not seen before and he had been told they had belonged to Isabelle Cooke.

At another field, he had been told that that was where he had buried her.

There was a delay, however, and the police could not get their bearings properly as someone had moved a stone. The police had started digging but their shovel broke, after which he had been taken to a mineshaft where they had told him he had thrown her handbag.

He had constantly denied any involvement but they had persisted and pressed him as to where the actual murder had taken place. Goodall had told him that he might as well admit it. When they got back to the field it had been full of men digging trenches and someone had even had a mine-detector looking for 'the Beretta'.

When they returned to Hamilton police office, Goodall had been numb with the cold so he had made some tea. He had then produced a previously completed statement and had told Manuel to write a copy, but he had refused. Superintendent Brown came into the room and demanded he write it immediately. He had said, 'Look, Manuel, you are going to write this confession. You are going to read what's written down there and get it into your mind. If you don't write that confession tonight, I will have no more to do with you. I am going to fix your family. That is the only thing that will make an impression on you.'

After that, he had written out what they had wanted but 'it seemed to be so stupid' and 'it was full of details that were absolutely idiotic – murdering people and burying them in parks'.

The surprise alibi had become obligatory by this stage.

His lifetime crusade against the police has now been honed to show them as both unscrupulous and bumbling. Goodall not only fell into the ditch, but he stupidly fluffed his lines when he kicked a different brick from the one he was meant to. By the time they returned to the police office, Goodall, not Manuel, was the one who was 'numb with the cold'. At the field, the stone presumably left there on a previous visit by CID officers intent on setting the scene before Manuel's arrival had been moved and they were temporarily disorientated; when the digging started their Keystone Cops-style behaviour manifested itself in the breaking of their only spade.

Against such odds, he would have been secure in his innocence except that Brown had come in with a low blow – the threat against his family.

Charges 7 and 8 – the murders of the Smart family and the theft of their car on 1 January 1958.

He claimed that he actually knew Peter Smart and had done so since 1953. He had helped him build his bungalow in 1954 and had laid some flooring for him. He had also given him advice and assistance in installing gas in the house as he had been a Gas Board employee at that time. In fact, they had socialised together and had often gone to race meetings and boxing matches together.

However, two or three days prior to Christmas 1957, Smart had approached him and asked if he could get him a gun.

Manuel had asked him why he wanted it and he was told that he wanted it 'for about the house'. As it turned out, he could get him one but it 'wasn't up to much' and although he had four bullets for it, 'it could only be loaded by pulling back the carriage and putting the bullet up the barrel.'

Smart had not turned up to the arranged meetings so that he could examine the weapon, but he had eventually phoned Manuel on 31 December 1957 and asked if he could get the gun that night and could they meet in the Royal Oak between 7 and 9.30pm? When Manuel had gone there that night, he had been wary of the police as the office was just across the road from the pub, so he had asked McQuade, who had been playing darts, to keep a lookout for them. Then he had gone to the lavatory and left the gun behind the cistern.

When Smart appeared, they went into the toilet together and he showed him how to load a bullet and then gave him the gun and the other three bullets. He had asked for £10 for the lot, but Smart counted out £15 in new notes from his wallet, before giving him some more notes and saying, 'Here, take that. Take it all.' The notes were very thin and new and Smart had left after refusing a drink from Manuel.

When he came back into the public bar, McQuade had asked him if the business was done, which he confirmed before buying him a drink. He had stayed there until closing time.

When he went home, he said the family were not all that bothered about New Year but were celebrating it because their American cousin was there. It had been a family get-together rather than a party, and he had sat up with his brother James talking about their cousin until James had gone upstairs to bed and he had lain on the bed-chair. He had gone to bed at about 6am and he had heard his father getting up about ten minutes later.

He had got up about an hour later because everyone was getting ready to go to church and the place 'was like the Central Station and I couldn't get to sleep'.

He had made a cup of coffee for his sister and then gone out to get her cigarettes before taking a bus to Glasgow to buy some papers.

Later that day, he had gone to the Woodend Hotel with Brannan and after buying some drink he took it to the Greenans' engagement party. At the party he had discovered there wasn't enough drink to go round, so he returned to the Woodend and bought two bottles of whisky, a bottle of rum, a bottle of sherry, a dozen cans of lager and 100 cigarettes, which he took back to the party.

He had paid for the drink with the money Smart had given him. He said, 'There was no reason why I should hide it. It was just straightforward money as far as I was concerned.' After the party finished he had gone to the dancing until about 3.30am.

He now explained how he had gone into the Smarts' house after the murders had happened. When he had met him in the toilet of the Royal Oak, Smart had mentioned that a business friend called Brown was coming to see him at home on the Friday. The problem was that he, Smart, was going away to the Dumbuck Hotel the next day and so would miss him.

He asked Manuel to do him a favour. He said that because he could not contact Brown as he was on the road or something, could Manuel go to his house between 7 and 7.30pm on Friday night? It was an important engagement he couldn't put off and he would leave a bottle of whisky for them. Indeed, if Mr Brown wanted to eat, he should take him to the hotel nearby for a meal and Smart would see him when he got back from his short break. Manuel had agreed to help, and he intended to go, as planned, on the Friday night.

However, he had found himself walking along Sheepburn Road about 4 or 4.30am on the Thursday morning and it had occurred to him that he could go in for a drink to Smart's house as he remembered there was a bottle of whisky there.

He had let himself in with the key he had been given and had gone into the living room where he put the light on. At first he noticed two half-full glasses on the mantelpiece and thought this odd. On the chiffonier were three whisky bottles and a bottle of sherry. He took a drink from the whisky bottle and 'looked around', noticing that some clothing was scattered about, such as a boy's 'short pants' and a 'ladies' roll-on with the stockings attached'. Thinking the Smarts were on holiday, this had struck him as strange and he had then suspected that they must still be in the house. He had noticed that both bedroom doors were open, so he put his head round but couldn't see anything as the curtains were drawn. 'I had a good drink in me then – I don't say I was drunk – and there was something odd I could not put my finger on. I went into the boy's bedroom but could see or hear nothing. I put on the light and saw someone in the bed. Then I put the light off and tip-toed out.'

After that, he had gone into the main bedroom, put the light on, and saw Mr and Mrs Smart lying dead – very dead. The bedclothes were hanging over the edge of the bed, nothing like they were seen in the police photographs. Then he noticed that Mr Smart still had the gun beside his hand. He explained, 'When I saw it, there was no doubt in my mind. I thought he had done his son in and then done his wife in, and then himself. I took the gun.'

It had then occurred to him that his fingerprints were 'all over the place', so he 'put on a pair of gloves and an apron' and went round the house rubbing at everywhere his prints could be. On going back into the boy's room, he could see he too was definitely dead as there was blood on the pillow and the wall.

He moved on to the story about the family cat. Describing it as a 'tiger cat', he said that it had 'bolted' into the house when he opened the door with the key. He explained, 'I went back and got a hold of it. It was in an awful state. It was growling and squealing. I opened the pantry to see if there was any milk. There was nothing lying about, so I gave it a drink of water. You could see it was hungry and thirsty.'

Having found two tins of cat food in the pantry, he noticed a tin of salmon behind them. He gave the cat the salmon, explaining, 'Well, nobody will want it now.' The cat didn't seem to like the salmon so he fed it bits of meat from an ashet of stew he found, before putting it into the garden. Then he left, but did not touch the car, making his way home over a field. He had decided that he had better get rid of the gun so he parcelled it up with gloves belonging to his sister and threw it into the Clyde the following morning.

He had scanned the newspapers on the Friday and the Saturday but nothing appeared about the bodies, so he had telephoned Hamilton 561 – County Police Headquarters. When the phone was answered, he quickly said, 'There are three people dead in a house in Sheepburn Road,' before putting the receiver down. Yet still nothing happened on the Sunday or the Monday, so he thought that the police must have regarded his call as a hoax. He had decided that he should phone again, and then his brother had told him about the discovery of the bodies.

Two days after that, Samuel McKay told him that the police were asking about him being in Florence Street in Glasgow where the car was found. Manuel told him that he had not been there and denied having anything to do with it.

Then a waiter at the Woodend Hotel told him that the police were asking questions about the money he had been spending there.

The next thing was that the police came to his house; one of them was Brown, whom he did not know. Manuel admitted that he had been spending money in the Woodend on 1 January and Brown took him to Bellshill police office. When Brown questioned him further about it, he told Manuel he knew about it already because 'a mutual acquaintance' had told them about it.

Manuel replied that it was unusual for acquaintances of policemen to be acquaintances of his.

Brown explained that he was talking about McKay. Then, because he refused to talk, Brown charged him with murder. After that he had been taken into a police van and Brannan was 'slung in' as well. 'Brannan was screaming and throwing himself on the floor. He was in hysterics and was shouting, "Tell them I was not with you, tell them I was not in the car."

'I asked Brannan what the squeal was about and he said they were trying to do him for the Sheepburn Road murders along with me.'

After he had been picked out at an identification parade, Brown told him he was now in real trouble as he had been spending Peter Smart's money.

Manuel asked for a lawyer, but Brown told him, 'You are getting no lawyer. I am the man in charge of this investigation and I am not a Lanarkshire policeman. You have got these people bamboozled. They can't get you. Well, you have run into your match this time and you are getting no lawyer. You won't get away this time and I'm going to pin eight murders on you. You murdered Anne Kneilands. Then there was a little girl disappeared in Coatbridge – Moira Anderson – you were responsible for that too. You murdered Isabelle Cooke and the Smarts. Get this into your head – you are going to be held for all these murders and you are going to admit them.'

Manuel said he told him he was not going to admit them so he should just charge him, but he still wanted a lawyer present.

Brown had refused the request for a lawyer, then went on, 'We know what happened. Watt paid you to shoot his wife. He paid you £5,000 and he paid you some more to get him sprung out of jail. You twisted that case up. You twisted that fellow Hendry round your little finger. You have been seen boozing with Watt in Glasgow.'

Muncie had taken over the questioning for about an hour, firing rapid questions at him, before Goodall appeared with a different tactic. He said they knew he was mad and needed treatment. He advised him to co-operate with Brown, who was a man who tended to get his way. Brown knew that his family was his weak point and he would use them to get what he wanted. Anyway they would lock him up after he had been seen by a psychiatrist and that would be that. Goodall suggested he should write a statement out and a psychiatrist would do the rest to lock him away.

Later that day, Brown brought McKay in to see him. In front of Manuel, Brown said that he, McKay, had been in the car with Manuel and McKay said it was a pack of lies. Brown then said that it was Manuel who had said it, and McKay then said that Manuel was a liar then.

After another identification parade, Brown had told him he was going to crucify his family if he didn't write the confession out. He claimed that they had found money and cigarettes in his sister's bedroom which had come from the Smarts' house, and he had twenty-four hours to confess by writing it out or his family would be ruined.

Anyway, he said, his father had already been arrested.

He was continually threatened, then charged with the Smart murders, after which Muncie came into his cell, remaining four and a half hours until 4.30 in the morning. He had asked him lots of questions about the people who had sold him guns.

The next morning a 'young' policeman had told him his father had been taken to Barlinnie Prison, and for the first time he realised the CID were not just bluffing.

He decided that all he could do was to write out the statement they were demanding, so he asked for Inspector McNeill. He then asked him why his father was being held and McNeill said that if he would make a confession he would guarantee his father's release. Accordingly, he had written a statement but when they looked at it they said that it would not do, so he had to write out another one.

When his parents arrived Goodall told them that he was 'crackers' and urged him to confess, after which he would be certified. However, he had still refused to sign it even after the meeting.

After being taken out to the field where Isabelle Cooke had been found he was returned to the police office and Brown made the threat to 'fix' his family.

Eventually his lawyer, Mr Ferns, was brought in to see him.

At that, Manuel turned towards the jury and said, 'That, ladies and gentlemen, is what happened when I was arrested.'

47

MANUEL'S EVIDENCE – AN APPRAISAL

Manuel wrapped up his evidence with a long rambling attack on the circumstances of the 'confessions' being obtained.

At no time had he actually signed them, he claimed.

He said, 'There was no doubt in my mind at that time that I was in the hands of savage and ruthless people. They were determined to make headway somehow and that was the way they chose. They told me that they intended to do all they could to my family. They said they would cripple my family and ruin my sister. That is the reason why I wrote this confession – to get my family out of this altogether. It was hammered into my head constantly that unless I wrote this confession, they were going to charge my father with the Smart murders.'

He finished by saying that he wrote the confession for those reasons.

'By myself I would still have been sitting there yet. If they had not done that they would be there until they grew beards down to their ankles. My family is just an ordinary family. Nice people. I have given them a lot of trouble. I have given them a terrible life but at no time would I tolerate getting them into trouble on my account. I have never run them into trouble and wouldn't do it.'

Rather than finishing on a high note, though, he then undid the big build-up somewhat by covering two minor points about McKay and 'Scout' O'Neil. He denied buying a gun from O'Neil and said that if he had any connection with guns, the last person he would tell would be O'Neil – in fact he might as well tell the Chief Constable of Glasgow as tell him.

* * *

The phrase 'if he had any connection with guns' must have sounded a bit incongruous, as he had just spent over four hours explaining how he habitually handled guns and how the suicidal Peter Smart had contacted him to find him a gun so he could end it all.

This time, however, there was little in the way of verifiable fact.

True, the Smarts had built their bungalow a few years before, but that had been widely reported in the papers and Manuel avidly read about his crimes. Also true, Manuel had been an employee of the Gas Board, so it was easy to say that Smart had asked him for advice. Manuel, however, had been a general labourer rather than a technician.

However, some of the things he said are still a puzzle. Why reveal that when he innocently went into the house, clothes were scattered about in the living room? Did he add that to make it sound more credible?

His bus journey to Glasgow to buy newspapers on the morning of the first day of the year might seem odd, particularly as he had been seen on the second of January, but perhaps he had to cover the fact that he had been noticed on the bus coming home after ditching the car.

His mention of the case of Moira Anderson strikes a contemporary note.

It is more than probable that Manuel would have briefly been a suspect in her disappearance from Coatbridge in 1957 when she was eleven years old. 'Briefly' because he had been in prison at the time, but he could not tell that to the jury.

A lady called Sandra Brown, who was honoured with an OBE in 2006, set up the Moira Anderson Foundation in 2000 to campaign for children's rights. Her story begins when she discovered that her late father, Alex Gartshore, had been given a custodial sentence for raping her thirteen-year-old babysitter. Sandra investigated the possibility that he had somehow been involved in the kidnapping of Moira Anderson and that she had been abused by a paedophile ring before being murdered.

To date, the charity has helped more than 500 families to cope with instances of child sex abuse.

The murder, however, remains officially unsolved.

A constant theme throughout Manuel's evidence – in his mind at least – is the continual dim-wittedness of the police. Brown had been forced to finally acknowledge Manuel's superior wit when he told him he knew he had 'bamboozled' the Lanarkshire County CID and that he had 'twisted Hendry around his little finger'.

The 'gangster movie' which seemed to run habitually in his head appears to have been played out in the Royal Oak episode, with McQuade posted at the door as a lookout for the cops, and Manuel placing the gun behind the cistern whilst awaiting the arrival of the desperate Peter Smart. Later, in the Smart bungalow, he takes a swig of whisky from the bottle, John Wayne style, as he tries to make sense of the bewildering scene before him. When the hysterical Brannan is thrown into the police van, Manuel asks him 'what the squeal was about', a phrase culled directly from his beloved mobster movies.

Yet, it might be observed, in revealing so much of himself he simply disclosed how naive he really was.

The episode with Brannan pleading with him to tell the police he was not with him in the car is probably true. Brannan was clearly under orders to get him to confirm that when he took the car he was not with him, thereby accepting commission of the crime. On the other hand, Manuel's reference to that episode again suggests that the truth about Brannan's dual role still hadn't occurred to him.

Ultimately, there would have been no realistic chance of any sane jury going along with the vast bulk of his evidence about the Smart murders. As if:

– a man like Peter Smart would socialise with a man like Peter Manuel in 1950s Glasgow. The *Glasgow Herald* for 13 May 1958 noted that an inventory lodged with 'the Sheriff Clerk of Lanarkshire' revealed that Peter Smart left an estate of £4,899.

– a man like Peter Smart would arrange to go to the Royal Oak to buy a gun.

– a relatively successful man like Peter Smart would contemplate suicide, particularly when he was making holiday plans with his family at the same time.

– Peter Smart would give Peter Manuel a key for his house. The jury, of course, might not be fully aware of it, but Manuel did not normally require a key to gain access to premises.

– 'Mr Brown' existed. There was also the unlikely nature of the arrangement between him and Smart in that Brown was 'on the road' and could not be contacted. If their business meeting could not be put off, why was it that Manuel's deputising for Smart was appropriate?

Alternatively, if it was just a social meeting, why could that not be postponed? And where was Mr Brown and why was he not a witness at the trial? Throughout the intervening half century, he has yet to reveal himself and unburden his soul.

And:

– what happened to the house keys that Smart gave Manuel in the Royal Oak? Their production would have been decisive, and in cross-examination, Manuel lamely explained that he had lost them. Puzzlingly, he didn't allege that the keys recovered by the police from the river had been thrown there by him, presumably as that would have countered his contention that the police had set up the whole case against him. In his address to the jury, he explained that even if he had produced the keys, the Crown would allege that he had picked them up after breaking into the house. That said, he must have gained entry to the Smart house by means other than smashing a window or glass panel. Perhaps a window had been left open, as he said in the confession.

– on his account, someone else, entirely coincidentally, must have stolen the family car.

To the jury, the chapter about feeding the cat must have sounded very sinister indeed, even to confirmed cat lovers. In his version, he had just discovered three bodies, one of whom he knew well; his friend had murdered his family then committed suicide using the weapon he had sold him, yet at that point he had elected to feed the cat rather than report the situation to the authorities.

The simple truth, however, appears to be that he genuinely cared for animals. He certainly had more regard for his dog 'Rusty' than he did for any stranger, and he could conceivably have been genuinely concerned for the cat's welfare, perverse as it sounds. The fact that he stayed in the house and returned to it several times might confirm that.

Alternatively, he obviously enjoyed surveying the gruesome results of his crimes.

As with his utilitarian solution to the problem of obtaining Christmas presents, the plain truth seems to be that the Smarts were murdered so that Manuel could fund – and be seen to fund – the partying he and his family intended doing over the New Year holidays. Rather than 'having no reason to hide' the Smarts' money, he simply further illustrated his contempt for the abilities of the authorities – this time to detect or trace the stolen cash, and at the same time further demonstrated that unearthly detachment from the everyday concerns of the normal citizen.

The impression remains that he was essentially a child-like creature whose ridiculous stories were tolerated by his family. He obviously came to believe some of his own lies, otherwise it's difficult to understand why he ever thought his evidence would be believed, particularly in the Smart charges.

Whilst on remand, he wrote a letter in which he purported to explain his position after his arrest. He wrote that he had 'applied the wisdom of the old Spanish proverb "En bocca [sic] cerrada, no entra mosca," (flies may not enter a closed mouth). That was untrue, of course, and was written solely to impress a friend.

He never could keep his mouth shut.

By electing to give evidence, however, he was now subject to cross-examination by M. G. Gillies, the Advocate Depute.

48

MANUEL CROSS-EXAMINED

The *Bulletin* reported that, 'With the opening of the last act, the public caught a glimpse of a different Peter Manuel. The young Lanarkshire labourer whose dapper appearance and calm demeanour have impressed the court for thirteen days, was less composed yesterday. Under cross-examination by Mr Gillies he leaned forward with his hands wide apart, gripping the rail of the witness box and almost shouted a denunciation of Superintendent Alex Brown who led the combined force of county and city CID men in the Lanarkshire murder hunt.'

Gillies had started with a general proposition.

He asked Manuel if he was alleging that senior police officers had 'conspired to give evidence against him'.

Manuel confirmed that that indeed was his position, and he named them as Brown, Goodall and McNeill.

Gillies asked if they had compelled him to sign statements which he knew to be false, and Manuel replied that they weren't false – they were ridiculous!

He asked whether the conspiracy included leaving the newly discovered body of Isabelle Cooke for forty-eight hours so that they could 'pin the murder' on him, and Manuel readily agreed, saying that they would have left it for a week or a fortnight in order to do that.

Lord Cameron interjected.

In a reference to the sanction for committing capital murder, he asked Manuel if they had 'manufactured a conspiracy' to have him murdered.

Manuel's reply was, 'That is what it amounts to, My Lord.'

In summary, Manuel's position was:

– the keys from the Smarts' house must have been thrown into the River Calder by Inspector McNeill.

– he had not left the Smarts' car in Florence Street in Glasgow near McKay's house and the remark about the speed of an A30 was not a reference to that particular car.

Interestingly, the car, of course, was not an A30, but an A35, but nothing was made of this.

– he had not bought the Beretta from McKay in the Gordon Club.

– Peter Smart might have engineered it so that after he had killed his family and committed suicide, Manuel would enter the house and find the bodies.

– whilst all the statements were written by him, only the first and third had been signed by him, the signature on the second statement having been forged, probably by Goodall.

– he could write the statements because he had memorised their contents, in particular the information from the second one had been 'bunged' into his head by the three CID officers.

– he never kept guns or stolen property in his house.

He kept them elsewhere.

– he denied he had drawn the Webley on the piece of paper that Dowdall produced. In fact, it was not a very good drawing and if asked he could draw a better one. He offered to do it there and then in court.

– he did not shoot a cow on the Saturday before the Watt murders. What happened was that the Crown witness Lafferty and his brother were stealing electricity cables, one of which fell on it and electrocuted it.

– he denied saying, 'I don't know what made me do these things.'

– the police did not bring spades with them because they knew where Isabelle Cooke's body was beforehand, but they had to resort to digging as their 'marker' stone had been moved.

– Hamilton and O'Neil had said what they said as their evidence had been bought by Watt.

Gillies's cross-examination has been described elsewhere as 'unspectacular but effective'. He certainly had plenty of scope to put pressure on Manuel, and in parts he managed to rattle him, bringing about the change in his demeanour noted by the *Bulletin* reporter.

Gillies to Manuel: You knew (at 3 o'clock on 14 January) you could explain away the gloves and the camera?

Manuel: Yes.

Gillies to Manuel: And if you gave that explanation your father would be cleared?

Manuel: Yes.

Gillies to Manuel: You were not seriously concerned about your father's position?

Manuel: I was seriously concerned about this man Brown's threats. He was raging like a lunatic!

When Gillies turned to Manuel signing the caution at the top of the statement, production 142, he claimed that he had not bothered reading it and that he was told 'just to ignore it'.

Gillies to Manuel: You just signed that out of the goodness of your heart?

Manuel: No. Because my father was in a situation where a man, a rat of a man – a real rat of a man – was going to ruin him! I was alone with these people and they were determined to crucify my family!

The papers reported that he spat out the words 'a real rat of a man' having totally lost his self-control.

A further glimpse of the real Peter Manuel – his voice 'rising with every word' – came when he answered another of Gillies's questions by informing the court, 'I am capable of looking after myself with any police at any time! A dozen Browns, a dozen Goodalls, a dozen McNeills – I can handle them. I can laugh at them! I wrote that statement to protect my father!'

Gillies to Manuel: If you can handle dozens of policemen in the way you mention, there was no need to make a statement implicating yourself, was there?

Manuel: The statement, Mr Gillies, has been explained to you as carefully as I can explain it. I wrote it because my father was under a threat. If that cannot penetrate, I feel sorry for you.

The *Bulletin* noted, 'The Advocate Depute murmured, "Very well. You feel sorry for me," and continued his cross-examination.'

Finally, Manuel had to agree that the contents of the main statement – production 142 – fitted in pretty well with a good deal of the evidence that had been heard in court during the previous fortnight. He explained that the reason for that was because the bulk of the evidence had been perjured.

The jury's choice was stark – believe Manuel or believe the police version which undoubtedly squared with rest of the case.

Nowadays, most judges tend to clarify matters in a restrained manner and only where necessary.

It was different then and, given that Manuel was a party defender, Lord Cameron comfortably spent the next thirty minutes going over various points. Some issues were in Manuel's interests, others not. The overriding impulse, however, seems to have been to further explore the question of the prisoner's sanity. The main points were:

– there was nothing unusual in Manuel having ready cash to constantly frequent pubs, as he often got money from various sources, for example, Watt gave him £150, and McKay gave him £50 for beating up a man called Fox. He never needed to draw National Assistance, except on one occasion to help Brannan.

– Smart told him that he wanted the gun as there were prowlers about.

When the judge asked him if there was anxiety about 'unsolved crimes' in Lanarkshire, Manuel's childish boastful streak emerged and he agreed that there was – there were about ten policemen watching his house every night!

– the policeman, Constable Smith, was simply mistaken about

getting a lift from him in the A35, as he 'would never give a policeman a lift'.

– when Manuel wrote to Dowdall and referred to 'a doubly unfortunate client' – which, in context, was clearly Watt – he had actually meant himself!

When the judge explored Goodall's alleged observation that Manuel was 'not wholly responsible for his actions' and that he would receive treatment as he did not know what he was doing – and Manuel maintained that these things had been said – it seems clear that he was still not convinced that Manuel was fully in control of his faculties.

Yet Manuel still failed – or was incapable – of taking take the bait.

Lord Cameron to Manuel: Was that put forward as an additional inducement to make you sign these statements?

Manuel: No it was not that!

His testimony finished, 'Manuel left the box and once more darted across the court like an insect over the surface of a pond', as John Gray Wilson famously put it.

The net effect of hearing his responses to the allegations against him probably convinced the jury that not only was he a savage murderer without an ounce of human compassion, but he was an even bigger threat to society should he ever be freed. After all, it was now quite clear that he sincerely believed that he'd done nothing wrong.

In the white heat of facing capital murder charges, Manuel's facile scenario of world conspiracy must have sounded ludicrously infantile. The intriguing thing is that some inner belief made him think that the jury would give credence to his patently absurd and often ad hoc reactions to particular points.

The electrocuted cow and the notion that Peter Smart cleverly engineered not only his and his loved ones' demise in order that his old friend Peter Manuel might stumble across the bodies for no possible earthly reason, adds weight to the trial judge's misgivings.

Because Manuel's parents obviously spent a lifetime indulging him and giving him the benefit of the doubt, did he think the jury would do the same?

Would things have been different had an Airdrie jury not acquitted him of the Mary McLachlan charges in October 1955, or was he already too far gone by then? And what if he had settled down with Anna O'Hara?

Would he have matured, learned parenthood skills and changed his ways, so that a next generation of Manuel children would have recalled a parent with a wayward streak and a vivid imagination who told brilliant bedtime stories?

Would he have been hanged today if capital punishment still existed or would he have been sent to the State Hospital?

How could someone so obviously intelligent be so flawed?

In the 1950s, an education had connotations of social, maybe even moral superiority, and Manuel's self-taught erudition must have been perplexing for some of those who sat in judgement.

And Dr Harold Shipman was then still at school.

49

CROWN AND DEFENCE SPEECHES

'There could hardly have been a fairer opening or one more favourable to the accused – every word could have been spoken by counsel for the defence. This is in accordance with the best traditions of Scottish – and indeed British – prosecutors.'

These words are quoted from John Gray Wilson's book about the trial, and refer to the Advocate Depute's speech to the jury.

Wilson should know. Not only did he attend the trial, but he was also a lawyer, ending his career as a Sheriff. But he was a man of his times, and the above quote has a quaint, almost nostalgic ring to it.

Today's prosecutors are different and necessarily in tune with a society cynically altered by widespread drug abuse, money laundering and international terrorism. Any observer at a criminal trial today might still recognise echoes of those gentlemanly days in a random choice of prosecutors' addresses to the jury, but in truth, the fulcrum has shifted significantly.

The *Bulletin* reported that Manuel yawned several times during the prosecutor's address to the jury.

Gillies methodically pieced the Crown case together, seeking a conviction on all charges. In the Kneilands case, he made the point that if the jury thought his motive was the theft of the handbag, then it stood as a capital murder charge; if not, it was 'ordinary murder' – should such a concept exist.

On any view, however, the motive in that instance was undoubtedly not theft, but the judge was later to intervene to withdraw the charge from the jury.

Gillies then made the link between the Watt murders and the Platt and Martin housebreakings and pointed out that Manuel had told Dowdall of matters not then in the public domain. Nevertheless, he did think it necessary to rebut the case against Watt, casting doubt on the alleged sightings of him on the homicidal overnight journey home and pointing out the 'affectionate' relationship he had with his wife.

He also felt compelled to acknowledge to the court that Watt had indeed been unfaithful to her.

In the Platt and Martin break-ins, the intruder had eaten a meal and lain on the sofa; in the Martin and Watt houses someone had stubbed a cigarette out on the carpet.

The details of the Cooke and Smart murders were highlighted, as was the unlikelihood of the connection between Smart and Manuel. The jury should also take account of the fact that the clothing of Anne Kneilands, Isabelle Cooke and Vivienne Watt had all been interfered with. Manuel's apparent detailed knowledge of the interior of the Watt household was a telling factor, as was his awareness of how entry had been gained to the house.

Interestingly, Gillies again reminded the jury that if they considered the motive was not theft in the Cooke murder, it was a case of non-capital murder. He pursued the point, reminding the jury that Manuel had spoken of 'a bag snatch' in the Mount Vernon area to Brannan, yet there was money in the girl's handbag when it was recovered from an air shaft.

Needless to say, the Advocate Depute could afford to be magnanimous about the distinction between the murder charges – he still had capital charges in the Watt and Smart instances to come to.

The overnight change in Manuel's financial circumstances at New Year was highlighted, as was the sale of the Beretta to Manuel by McKay; indeed, the finding of the Smarts' Austin A35 in Florence Street in Glasgow probably had something to do with Manuel having 'some idea of pushing the blame onto someone in the Gordon Club'.

Having gone into the confession, Gillies outlined the improbability of 'a man of [Smart's] type conducting a transaction with a person in a public house on Hogmanay about a gun' or of him giving Manuel a key for his house – Smart, after all, being a building contractor's agent.

Touching on a characteristic Manuelism, he observed that food had also been eaten in the Smart house; Gillies did not specify whether he was referring to Manuel or the cat.

Summarising, Gillies pointed out that in order to accept Manuel's case, the jury would require to accept that thirty Crown witnesses had formed a common bond to commit perjury, and furthermore, the unlikelihood of that was enhanced by the 'diversity' of those involved, ranging from senior police officers, and Dowdall and Watt on the one hand, to O'Neil, Hamilton and McKay on the other.

Manuel rose and addressed the jury, speaking more slowly and deliberately than when he gave evidence. He made the following claims:

The Kneilands charge: any marks he had on his person were explained by being involved in a fight; he had worked in that area but that was all; Professor Allison had told the court about marks made by barbed wire on the girl's hands – surely they would be on the palms of her hands and yet none were found there. Why also was there no evidence led about skin and blood that could have been taken from underneath her fingernails?

A feature of the alleged 'confessions' in all the charges was that no descriptions of any of the persons mentioned was given – surely that was proof that the documents he had written were false?

Having been questioned by the police at the time, they must have been satisfied of his explanation at the time he gave it.

He finished that chapter, 'I can say this and say it sincerely – I did not kill Anne Kneilands.'

The Platt charge:

The razor had been in his house well before the time of the break-in. He had not lodged a special defence of impeachment of Tallis – as the Advocate Depute said he should have done – because he had no knowledge of this charge or the charge relating to the Martin house until the indictment was served. Anyway, the theft of the technical

instruments suggested that whoever had done this had been interested in items other than jewellery.

The Martin charge:

The special defence lodged named Tallis, which meant that 'I
didn't do it and that Charles Tallis did'. Despite being able to give
a full description of the stolen rings, Tallis claimed he only had a
brief look at them.

That women's nylons had been taken pointed to a woman being
involved in the crime.

He then made a point – described as 'shrewd' by no less than His
Lordship – when he referred to Tallis claiming that he did not know
where the rings came from until he had read about them in the evening
paper on 17 September; how could that be, when Miss Martin was
unable to say they were missing until 21 September? Accordingly,
Charles Tallis 'had knowledge about these rings and where they originated from' and he should 'be left to do the explaining of how he
knew the rings came from 18 Fennsbank Avenue'.

Logically, as the Crown case was that whoever had broken into
number eighteen had also done the same at number five and then
shot the Watts, there had to be a reasonable doubt about his involvement in both charges.

The Watt murders:

The Advocate Depute had said that Watt had no motive for killing
his wife. In that case, he had even less of a motive and there was
absolutely no reason why he should walk into their house and shoot
three people. There had been no theft or suggestion of it. Referring
to Tallis, he said that the police had come to his house 'acting on a
tip-off', so that meant that that person must have known there was
a gun in the house on 18 September.

'Broadly speaking' what he had told Dowdall in October 1956
had been correct, but he had definitely not mentioned anything
about the layout of the house. If Dowdall's claim that he had not
been given any information about the layout from Watt was correct,

then not only was Watt 'in serious trouble' but 'God help his future clients' as that was the very thing that Dowdall should be finding out about.

There were two reasons why the jury should believe him here – the fact that the police became 'abundantly satisfied' at the time about his account of his movements and secondly, that they had actually arrested Watt.

What of Watt's reaction when he heard what had happened?

He was meant to be a 'seething mass of pain, anguish and grief' but he had taken time off to tell a servant at the Cairnbaan Hotel that he had a borrowed alarm clock in his room!

He had been identified by the ferryman, Taylor and the driver, Morrison – both of whom had come forward as a result of police investigations.

Morrison had described how the lights of the car had flickered, which was consistent with the fault that had been described the week before. Manuel said they had gone off 'just like that', snapping his fingers to emphasise the point. He said, 'It may be that it is just sheer coincidence that someone bearing an amazing resemblance to William Watt crossed on the ferry that night, but it was an even greater co-incidence that a man identical to William Watt should have a dog identical to William Watt's dog.'

For those reasons, 'there can't be much doubt that William Watt was, for whatever reason, on the morning of 17 September, away from the Cairnbaan Hotel.'

He had actually seen the Webley revolver in Mary Bowes' house before it had turned up in the table drawer in his house two days after the police search. The suggestion that he should stroll into police headquarters with it, saying, 'Look what I've got' was not wise and he thought he had no alternative but to 'dump it in the Clyde'. That said, he had marked the spot by counting a number of stanchions on the bridge 'just in the off-chance that on some future date it might have to be recovered'.

His name had been linked to the gun, yet Campbell and Hamilton lived in the same area of the city, just round the corner from each other, so wasn't it 'odd that these two people who know each other' should transact the gun in the Briggait in the centre of Glasgow?

And O'Neil had been taken by Watt to the police to give a statement in May 1957, apparently so he could 'see justice done'. In that case, how could O'Neil explain why he had not gone to the police in September 1956? If he knew that Manuel had a .38 Webley, then surely the right time to disclose this to the police was after Watt had been arrested?

Watt's explanation had been that he wanted 'anyone connected with guns' to be taken to the police; if O'Neil's story had 'one shred of truth in it', it meant that Watt had given money to a man who had sold the gun which had killed his family. Not only had Watt given money to O'Neil, he had given him clothes, and that was why he had gone to the police. He had, in effect, been bought to say the things he said.

At no time had Manuel 'encountered' O'Neil or Hamilton about a gun.

At the end of his address, he returned to this charge, claiming that whoever shot these women seems to have entered the house with that specific purpose. Anyway, he argued that if he had shot the Watts it would have 'seemed silly' to have approached the accused's solicitor to furnish him with information that could prove his client's innocence.

Actually, he had taken that course of action so that there 'would be no flaw' on his conscience.

The Houston housebreaking:

– had he known that the camera and gloves he had were stolen and had he read in the papers that a girl was missing, he would have got rid of them. He explained, 'My home is a place wherein I never know the minute the police might come in and start searching.'

In any event, he had been at home that night and could give details of the television programme he had been watching. When he had bought the items in the Mail Coach Inn, he had suspected they might be stolen, but he had not realised they were linked to a murder.

The Cooke murder:

– he was at a cinema when she was murdered. The eye-witness McFarlane was mistaken when he said that he had heard a noise from the direction of the railway and had then looked up and seen him; the witness wore glasses, the place he said he had seen him at was not visible from that spot. He said there had been a full moon that night, whereas other witnesses talked of a dark windy night.

Furthermore, the jury could see from the four pairs of his shoes in court that he always wore soft-soled shoes which were noiseless.

The scattered belongings did not point to him being the culprit. What was the point of throwing her clothes away where they were found if he had done it, because it would have meant doubling back over a lower road, whereas if he had killed her he could have simply walked 200 yards along the railway from where MacFarlane claimed he had seen him and could have gone directly home.

He explained, 'If I had murdered anyone, I would take particular care I wasn't seen.' Burying the body but not the clothes made no sense – otherwise everything to do with the crime hadn't been concealed. He assured the jury, 'If I had killed Isabelle and taken the trouble to bury her body, I think I would have buried her clothing and anything connected to her.'

It was Goodall who had found the shoes, not him.

He also understood that tracker dogs had been used to search for the body – in which case they were not very good at their job. They had used 'mine-detectors' in the search, so whoever had come up with that idea must have known that the girl had a bracelet on her wrist. How did Brown get to the search area so easily without prior knowledge of it, particularly as they extinguished their lights when they heard noises?

The Smart murders:

– describing the link between him and the murders as 'extremely thin', he said it started with the allegation that he had spent certain notes in the Woodend Hotel on 1 January, but the notes produced in court were not the actual ones, but were only similar.

As for the stolen car, no-one had mentioned the obvious feature which made it stand out, which was its 'white-wall' tyres.

He claimed that Smith, the policeman who insisted that Manuel had given him a lift in it, was wrong. Anyway, Smith said he knew the car and its licence number, so why had he failed to realise it was the car when he was given a lift?

Why was it that Smith had waited until 18 January before he made the claim about getting the lift, particularly when there had been police appeals for any information as to its whereabouts for days after it had gone missing? The appeals had brought in intelligence of supposed sightings from far and wide, yet the purported journey had not been reported by Smith until much later.

The charge was murder but it had actually been suicide, and although he could not be sure of the terms of the suicide pact, either Mr or Mrs Smart had killed the boy, and then themselves.

The criticism of why he had not produced the key that Smart had given him did not take account of how far it would have helped his story, as the Crown would then simply say that he had stolen it at the same time as he had stolen the money. The only thing he had taken from the house was the gun, and there had been no car there for him to take.

The Advocate Depute had pointed out that mail and papers would have been piled up behind the door, but going into the house at 4am on 2 January meant he would not have seen a build-up of mail or papers, as there had been no deliveries on 1 January.

Feeding the cat might 'seem quite odd' he conceded, but the shock of finding three dead people means there's no accounting for your actions, particularly if 'a cat's running around'.

Dealing with the confessions, he said the police were wrong when they claimed that no pressure or threats were made to him. If all the statements made were given freely, why was it that the very first one he had made – about McKay giving him money in St Enoch Square in Glasgow – was a lie?

The suggestion he had signed the statements to release his father who was, however, on 'quite a small charge' was wrong.

That was not why he had done it.

He explained, 'The thing I had in mind was the diabolical threat by a man I considered would have carried it out to put my father in prison on a charge of being involved in the Smart murders. I mean Superintendent Brown.'

Brown was 'savage and determined' and on top of that, he had threatened to arrest his mother and sister as well.

Wasn't it curious that the versions noted by McNeill and Goodall differed in only one word? That just did not happen in real life.

McNeill managed to pinpoint the right spot at the River Calder where the Smarts' house keys were found, which was strange considering that all that he, Manuel, said was that he had thrown them in 'near the bridge'.

The evidence about Smart's money was that it was all in single notes, so where did he get the five pound notes that he was said to have been spending?

As he 'practically lived' in the Woodend Hotel at weekends, he would have been mad to have drawn attention to himself and 'thrown new money' about there.

Not being, and never having been, 'the confessing type', it was inexplicable for him to have simply confessed of his own free will; the police never produced a 'powerful reason' for that happening, whilst he did.

Then, with a simple, 'Thank you, ladies and gentleman,' he stopped speaking and sat down.

Wilson wrote: 'His speech was an intellectual feat for a largely self-educated man, but that was not what was wanted.'

Wilson thought that Manuel had been unable to destroy the 'intricate dovetailing of the Crown case' as the jury needed to hear the explanation from someone with a 'personality that would make his story seem at least possible'.

Wilson had the benefit of being there, but, with respect, there were elements of Manuel's account that would seem to preclude acceptance by any rational jury. As ever, though, with Manuel, his

preposterous explanations were peppered with genuinely good observations, some of which rang true.

His biggest worry, though, must have been that the jury was
patently uninterested in his explanations, several of them showing
definite signs of boredom in the course of his address.

They had stopped listening a long time before that.

50

REFLECTIONS ON MANUEL'S SPEECH; THE CHARGE

Ostentatious yawning by the accused during the prosecution speech is a practice not to be recommended. If done to impress the jury or the onlookers in court, it would only be effective if they were overtly sympathetic and obviously conjoining in his show of public contempt for the prosecution case.

Clearly, they were not and when Manuel addressed them, it was the jury who were restless.

In isolation, the fact that Anne Kneilands had no abrasions to the inside of her hands could have been a telling point, and sure enough, it seems that the police pathologists had failed to examine her nails for evidence of the skin or blood of her attacker.

His constant references to the police being 'satisfied' of his non-involvement in various crimes, only really amounted to a lack of hard evidence.

His explanation for failing to lodge a special defence of impeachment in the Platt housebreaking – that he had no knowledge of the charge until the indictment was served – should also have applied to the Martin housebreaking, for which he had lodged an incrimination.

Arguing that the perpetrator in the Platt break-in must have had some sort of interest in the technical instruments stolen, or that the theft of stockings in the Martin charge necessarily implied female involvement, was facile and would easily have been seen through by the jury.

299

The warped logic of the observation implies that no-one would steal anything unless they had some sort of personal interest in it.

And resetters and fences would not exist.

That said, the 'shrewd' point about Tallis's knowledge of the stolen rings before Miss Martin announced their loss was a good one.

Had Tallis and Bowes been at number eighteen, they could feasibly have been implicated in events at number five; after all, the Crown theory was that there was a strong link between the two.

Another valid comment was that the 'grief-stricken' Watt, according to Manuel, appeared to have temporarily regained his composure in order to mention the alarm clock in his room. And not only was he identified as being on the ferry, but it was remarkable that the mysterious traveller also had a black Labrador as a companion. His best point, however, was that the police felt they had a sufficiently strong case to actually arrest Watt for the murders – the implications being that either Watt was the true culprit, or if the police got it wrong once, they were perfectly capable of making another mistake.

Conversely, Manuel's claim to have carefully thrown the gun into the Clyde at a specific point in case its retrieval might be necessary was probably beyond credibility for a jury sated with horrific detail and fatigued with fantasy.

Manuel seriously lost contact with the reasonable juror by his needless and compulsive references in his speech to his criminal lifestyle.

Had he known that the camera and gloves from the Houston housebreaking were stolen, he would not have kept them in the house, as it was habitually searched by the police; inviting inspection of his shoes in order to demonstrate he always wore the 'noiseless' variety was enough to chill the spine of any property owner with an interest in retaining his possessions.

Lecturing the court on the necessity of properly concealing not only the murder victim but also her meagre possessions was less than impressive, and the point about the 'mine-detector' failing to register the presence of Isabelle Cooke's bracelet was trite, as it was clear that the police were looking for the Beretta at that stage of the enquiry. No-one, apart from him, appears to have mentioned the 'possession scattering' that he indulged in after a kill.

His reason for having dealings with McKay – that he had engaged Manuel to hospitalise a Crown witness in a forthcoming trial – was probably unlikely to win over indecisive jurors.

Manuel being Manuel, having registered some 'shrewd' points, he continually followed them up with naive or, worse, disturbing insights into the icy psyche of a serial killer.

Objectively, there has to be concern that Smith, the young policeman, appears to have been tardy in his recollection of being chauffeured in a murder victim's car by his supposed killer.

But to try to persuade the jury that the feeding of a hungry cat in the midst of a massacre amounted to normal behaviour was a pointless exercise.

Having no explanation for the Austin A35 going missing after the owner had slaughtered his family and killed himself was probably preferable to yet another fantastic tale, no doubt implicating MI5 operatives and sinister crime lords with foreign-sounding accents.

Would anyone, let alone a detective investigating multiple murder, calculatedly deposit the keys from the Smart house in a river, in order to retrieve them as and when best suited the enquiry?

Most outrageous, perhaps, was his contention that there was only an 'extremely thin' link between him and the Smart murders.

In whose eyes, and by what logic?

John Gray Wilson noted two things at the end of Manuel's address to the jury.

That he was an exponent of the 'logic' of Lewis Carroll, whereby 'what I tell you three times is true.'

And that the jury were already lost to his self-proclaimed magnetism, some of them having patently switched off well before the end.

When Lord Cameron spoke to give them legal directions – known as 'the charge to the jury' – they suddenly appeared far more alert.

The judge continued to give the fact that Manuel was a party defender top priority, and he directed that they should ensure that 'all points that can properly be made in his favour' be given 'due weight'.

Then he said something quite amazing: 'I should add this: that from what we have heard in past days, there is little doubt the accused has presented his own defence with a skill that is quite remarkable.'

Apart from being perfectly true, that statement is all the more noteworthy, coming from the formidable Lord Cameron, a man not widely recognised as being reckless with praise.

Having given the usual directions as to the burden and standard of proof, he counselled that they should be servants of the law rather than 'avengers of blood'. Significantly, he returned to the question of insanity, something that plainly exercised his mind throughout the trial. As no special defence of that nature had been lodged, it was not now a consideration. On the question of diminished responsibility, he said: 'The law of Scotland has for long recognised, though other systems have not, that aberrations or weakness of mind – mental unsoundness bordering on but not amounting to insanity – may, if established in a case of murder, reduce the quality of the crime from that of murder to that of culpable homicide. I have considered the question most carefully and in the present case, particularly in view of the nature of the charges and in view of the fact that the accused has deprived himself by his own action of the services of counsel and as I feel myself in some measure responsible for seeing that every point that can be put in his favour shall be put, I am not going to exclude that matter from your consideration – though I have little doubt as to what the result will be.

'I will direct you in law, and you must accept my direction, that, if you should come to the conclusion that the accused was responsible for more than one of the killings libelled, multiplication of killings is not by itself a fact or circumstance indicative or inferential of that aberration or weakness of mind, proof of which is essential before you can reach the conclusion that the quality of the crime should be reduced from murder to culpable homicide.'

He went on to ponder where the evidence actually was to warrant 'so merciful a conclusion'. After all, the court had heard no medical evidence, as would be expected, and he concluded, 'I especially asked his father, mother and sister if they had noticed anything abnormal and they replied "No". I did that on purpose that this matter should be as fully ventilated as it might be.

'In the past few days you have had a unique opportunity of judging for yourselves whether there is anything indicative of weakness or aberration of mind, and it is only with the greatest difficulty that I have come to the conclusion that I can leave this matter open to you in law.

'For my own part, I have had difficulty in seeing whether one scintilla of evidence can be found to warrant such a conclusion. A man may be very bad without being mad.'

In reality, that was the only possible way of dealing with the thorny question of Manuel's sanity; in short, there was nothing to say he was mad, but more as a matter of form than anything else, it was up to the jury to decide whether he acted with diminished responsibility, although His Lordship clearly decided that he didn't think so. With hindsight, we know that the jury elected not to take the soft option of culpable homicide due to diminished responsibility, but until the verdict was announced there is more than a suggestion that 'the authorities' were nervous about Manuel evading the rope, with the consequent public uproar.

Moving on to the circumstances of the 'confessions' he informed the jury that earlier in the trial he had dealt with the question of admissibility and had ruled that the question of fairness was left to them. Their task was to decide whether Manuel's behaviour was prompted by extreme threat and pressure from the police or whether there was a 'ghastly farce' involving senior police officers plotting to take him to where they already knew the girl's body was buried. He continued: 'It sometimes happened that the police erred in subjecting suspects to pressure and interrogation. But an excess of zeal to extract true information was one thing and a criminal conspiracy such as the

303

accused had alleged to force a confession was another. If the accused's story was true, not only would the senior officers he attacked be unfit to hold their positions but they should be in the dock on a charge of conspiracy to murder.'

Then he turned to one aspect of the enquiry into the killing of the Smart family.

'When the police came to his house eight days after the discovery of the bodies they "asked him to accompany them" to Bellshill police office and he was alleged to have said, "You have not found anything yet."'

At that, the judge paused and slowly added, 'One unfortunate word – "Yet".'

Manuel had queried the motive for 'confessing' and had felt obliged to let the jury know he was 'not the confessing type'.

His Lordship came up with a different theory.

Realising that the evidence was piling up against him, the judge posed the question, 'Would there not be ample motive for his real-ising that the game was up?' In other words, the pressure to confess might have come not from the police, but because of 'pressure of events'.

The first and most telling direction about the need for corrobora-tion to prove the individual charges was to direct the jury that they could not be allowed to consider the first charge involving the murder of Anne Kneilands, as there was little more than the confession itself. He told the jury that they were to return a formal verdict of not guilty. Manuel remained totally impassive and was said to have retained the same posture, sitting forward with his head downwards.

As previously noted, had that charge been the only one on the indictment, that direction might not have been so readily given; and could corroboration not have been found – if necessary – by matching up the injuries to the angle iron recovered from the river, by making more of the facial injuries he suffered about that time or by empha-sising the 'special knowledge' aspects of the confession? His Lordship thought not, and that is what matters.

Manuel's knowledge of the bullet fired during the Platt housebreaking in 1956 was imparted to Dowdall – 'a very experienced man, a criminal lawyer of wide practice and high reputation' – so how did he know that when it was not discovered until 1957?

Manuel said that the razor was brought into his house by Tallis, and that was backed up by Manuel's parents. Whilst reminding the jury that it was their duty to decide on such matters, His Lordship felt obliged to remind them that this was the same Samuel Manuel who had failed to be frank about the gloves.

The judge clearly harboured doubts about the Martin housebreaking. On one view, was it likely that Tallis and Bowes should become embroiled in a minor housebreaking the same weekend as one of the family was getting married? On the other hand, he advised the jury to think hard whether it would be safe to hold the charge proved, as there were no footprints, fingerprints or stolen items which could tie him in, and the aforementioned 'shrewd point' had to be considered.

He next turned to the Watt murders and took Watt's demeanour when he received the tragic news as his starting point; that had to be considered.

The identification by Morrison on Loch Lomondside he described as something he would personally have serious difficulty in accepting.

That statement does appear to transgress the much-breached rule that the jury should not be exposed to the judge's views. That said, he then referred to the unusual way Watt held his cigarette at the identification parade – exactly the same as the eccentrically behaved driver on that misty night.

As for Taylor the ferryman, he reminded them that mistakes of identification could occur, and that 'they had led in the past to very great miscarriages of justice.'

The frost on Watt's car was a possibly telling factor, and Manuel's information that Watt had killed his family then given the gun away was 'quite extraordinary' when he supposedly did so to none other than Tallis.

Manuel's protestation about lack of motive had to be seen in the light of his own further explanation that the safe in the Valente household was the actual target that night; the mistake may have saved the lives of those in the Valente house, but cost the lives of those next door.

John Gray Wilson noted that the judge did not acknowledge that Mrs Valente actually said that there was no safe in her house, and he points out that at that time, there were actually two houses in Fennsbank Avenue owned by families called Valente. It is to be hoped that the other Valentes suffered no ill consequences of that information being made public, as the whole story has more than a ring to it of Manuel weaving a tale around the known fact that Deanna had been in the Watt house the night before the murders.

Referring to the whole 'Fennsbank Avenue chapter', His Lordship remarked, 'One of your difficulties in this case is that so many of the witnesses are stained with some sort of crime.' He concluded by saying that in any event, should the special defence be accepted by them, they should acquit, as they should if there was a reasonable doubt.

Turning to the Houston housebreaking he directed that a conviction hinged on them accepting Brannan as a reliable witness. Why? Surely it also depended on the criminative circumstances of the finding of the recently stolen gloves and camera? In any event, whether due to misgivings over Brannan's evidence that Manuel told him about the break-in and what he had stolen, the jury eventually answered by finding the charge 'not proven'.

Even if they concluded that what Manuel had written in respect of the Cooke murder was true and given voluntarily, there would still have to be corroboration. The eye-witness identification by McFarlane could provide that, but he did not really appear to have much of an opportunity for accurate identification. The finding of the shoes and the body was entirely different and was plainly corroborative, if true. If false, it was 'a falsehood concocted with devilish artistry'. He also reminded the jury of the 'uncompleted grave of which [Manuel] gave Inspector Goodall warning'.

Their options included convicting of murder but 'not taking the further step of convicting of capital murder' if there was doubt about the alleged motive of handbag theft. He said: 'I think you may be well advised if you come to the conclusion here, that the accused is guilty of murdering Isabelle Cooke, to refuse to take the further step of convicting him of capital murder. It is for you to say.'

Turning to the Smart charges, there was no doubt in that instance that these were capital murder charges, that the weapon used was a Beretta, that the accused threw such a weapon into the Clyde, that he was in possession of new banknotes issued to Mr Smart.

Should the jury accept the alibi, or it left them in doubt, they must acquit.

Yet, the short distance between Fourth Street and Sheepburn Road meant that a small error in the estimation of time would 'throw the alibi out'.

Describing the alleged sale of the gun to Smart in the Royal Oak as 'extraordinary', Lord Cameron noted that one party to the transaction – Smart – was dead and could therefore not corroborate it. As for the other – McQuade – who had been 'employed to scout against the unwanted attentions of police officers for the price of a drink', His Lordship observed that 'his appearance and demeanour' could be 'a very ample certificate of his character'.

As happens on every occasion it's attempted, a friend 'helping out' evidentially is quickly rumbled.

The business meeting with Brown was mentioned. A neighbour had claimed that a light was on in the house on the Friday night, which might support the story, but this business acquaintance had a name that was 'the not uncommon one of Brown'.

It has to be wondered what the judge meant by that observation.

Was he postulating that Manuel's tale of the shadowy Mr Brown might have included him entering the Smart house with the bodies still *in situ*? More realistically, was the judge suggesting that 'Mr Brown' was ficititious?

Manuel's role was agreed with Smart as providing refreshment for Brown not only in the house at Sheepburn Road but also at the

Kenmure Hotel, 'and that having been done, Peter Smart and Manuel depart and they never meet again in this life', the judge observed.

It appears that His Lordship was merely reminding the jury of the defence case as he was obliged to, no matter how preposterous it sounded.

Apart from the confessions, the jury would require to find corroboration, and in that regard they had the evidence of the witnesses from the Gordon Club, the possession of the money, the finding of the car where Manuel said he left it and the remark about the speed of the car.

Without any air of irony, the judge described the lack of a weapon at the murder scene as a point in Manuel's favour, the logic being that the main reason for excluding suicide was the lack of the weapon, and Manuel had explained this.

Completely ignoring the point Manuel made in his address to the jury, the judge said that when Sergeant Frank Hogg forced entry to the house on 6 January, there was a build-up of items deposited through the letterbox since 2 January which was hardly consistent with someone entering normally with a key. Perhaps he made that statement in the light of the fact that neighbours mentioned seeing the lights on and curtains opening and closing after 2 January and it was therefore open to them to conclude that, as obviously did happen, Manuel made several trips to the house.

As for the combination of suicide and the missing car, he commented that if the jury found the accused credible, they were entitled to regard him as 'romancing' in some matters but truthful in others.

In conclusion, he explained the possible verdicts.

Apart from the Kneilands charge and his direction on that, he directed them that there are three verdicts, namely guilty, not guilty or not proven, and these could be by a unanimous verdict or by a majority. A majority in this context comprises eight which is a simple majority of fifteen, the overall number of jurors. On the capital murder charges, any guilty verdicts could be of capital murder itself or of culpable homicide, and that applied to the charge involving Isabelle Cooke, although a verdict in that instance could also be one of non-capital murder.

There was no direction that murder was an optional verdict where the charge was capital murder.

If the jury accepted the special defences they would find the accused not guilty; reasonable doubt would lead to a verdict of not proven – a direction not now given in modern trials.

He finished: 'Members of the jury, I have no doubt that as you have followed the evidence over these past many days with anxious care, you will decide this case with courage and resolution and not shrink from the consequences of your verdict in accordance with your duty, if you see your duty lies in a certain direction.'

He then invited them to retire to consider their verdicts at 2.24pm, having addressed them for four hours and ten minutes.

An interested commentator later recorded his impressions of being in court that day. Sir Compton Mackenzie later wrote an article for the now defunct *Evening Citizen* headed, 'If Lord Cameron had defended Peter Manuel.'

Like many people, Mackenzie was fascinated with the drama of murder trials and he had been an interested observer in the same court eight years before, when Lord Cameron, as Dean of Faculty, defended a serving policeman, James Ronald Robertson, on a murder charge.

He contrasted the size difference between the prisoners in the dock and the variance in their behaviour.

Robertson had been a 'wax-work' figure who sat impassively, whilst Manuel was brash and sat joking with the two police escorts in the dock before the judge took his place on the bench.

Sir Compton continued in a gloriously non-politically-correct style, noting that it was likely that Manuel had 'a Spanish or Sicilian strain in his blood' and that he had been told that 'his very dark eyes were deadly cold' but, in a Victorian-style observation, noted that 'dark brown is an unusual colour for the eyes of the deliberate murderer, whose eyes in five cases out of six are a pale, hard blue.'

When Manuel addressed the jury, Sir Compton thought they were doing their best to pay attention to 'the little man in the dock' who was fluent enough but spoke 'in a monotone thickened with a glottal accent', but the strain on them was showing. He reckoned that

Manuel's speech was a disappointment in the light of the reviews his cross-examination had received, and that when the judge started to address them, the jury visibly perked up, causing him to ponder the title of the article.

He too wondered whether the point of no return was the McLachlan trial in Airdrie, where 'he elected to defend himself and to the regrettable sound of public applause was acquitted.'

Whatever the answer, Manuel's was the voice of somebody who was 'incapable of grasping the fact that he had committed any act which he was not perfectly entitled to commit', to the point whether he wondered if even Manuel was aware that the 'spatulate finger he pointed at the jury to emphasise a point was the one which had pulled the trigger for seven murders'.

Given the number of murders by shooting he was attributing to him, it appears that Sir Compton had personally convicted Manuel of the murder of Sydney Dunn.

The title of the article begs the question. Could anyone have successfully defended Manuel?

It's worth noting that Cameron's client in 1950 had been executed, but the received wisdom is that Robertson, in a final contrast to Manuel, instructed a low-key approach to his defence, which at least retained a modicum of dignity for his and the victim's family.

Of course, His Lordship would have been all too aware of a previous 'miracle' acquittal referred to earlier. In the present case there was also a particular phenomenon he undoubtedly had regard to – the well-catalogued reluctance of some juries to convict of capital murder.

In 1938, Cameron himself had also defended Patrick Carraher when he was convicted of culpable homicide despite the evidence pointing strongly to murder, and it was noticed that a pattern of such verdicts developed over the years. Some commentators blamed the fact that women were now on 'mixed' juries and that they were responsible for taking the softer option. They also pointed to a series of hangings in 1945–6 which seemingly 'curbed the enthusiasm' of post-war hoodlums in Glasgow, according to police anecdote.

But in every case, no matter the apparent strength of a prosecution case, there is always room for uncertainty.

Either outcome would affect Cameron.

Should Manuel be convicted of non-capital murder, or worse still, culpable homicide, the judge would have to re-examine his role in the proceedings, as happened to Lord Pitman in 1938 in the first Carraher trial; should it be otherwise, he would have to personally ordain the execution of a fellow human being, albeit that it happened to be Peter Thomas Anthony Manuel.

51

THE VERDICTS

On Friday 30 May 1958 almost all newspapers ran the same banner headline:

MANUEL TO HANG

Following the verdict, he had been whisked away in a police van through a jeering, booing and shoving throng of about a hundred women in the Saltmarket, most of whom had waited all day behind a cordon of policemen, some on horseback. The prisoner was remanded to the grim condemned cell at Barlinnie Prison, and the date of execution was fixed for 19 June 1958.

Most papers featured the famous fixed-stare head and shoulders portrait of the condemned man which has come down to us today in the numerous articles and stories that have been published since.

The *Bulletin* went one better with an artist's impression by none other than the famous caricaturist Emilio Coia, who studied him for several days in court. Coia accompanied his impression with the comment that he was 'a small dark man with a big personality attractive to women, a thrusting dominating profile, fleshy nose, restless sensuous mouth and deep-set black eyes that are the coldest that I have ever seen. He had the short stubby hand of the super confident and the vanity which is found in men lacking stature.'

Within the court building, it was noted that there were many magistrates and councillors, wearing the traditional lapel flower given out at the fortnightly meetings of Glasgow Corporation, and lawyers,

312

senior policemen and reporters all milling about waiting for the verdicts.

After such a long and complicated trial, it was anyone's guess when the jury would come to a decision on the charges.

However, after an hour's seclusion, a buzzer was heard to operate in the court, leading to an almighty scramble for the prime observation points of the next stage of the proceedings.

It was a false alarm.

The Macer turned the impatient rabble back at the door, informing them that it had not been a signal for 'the resumption of proceedings'.

At 4.45pm, two hours twenty-one minutes after their retiral, a bell sounded, signalling the jury's verdict and an end to the current proceedings.

In the course of the trial, a woman juror claimed to have lost a stone in weight through the stress of the ordeal.

Manuel was brought up from the cells below.

For most accused, awaiting the jury's verdict is an extremely nerve-racking time. Unlike the lady juror, Manuel appeared to have suffered no noticeable anxiety and had snoozed as the jury deliberated. Back in court, he whiled away the normally tense time waiting for the judge to come on the bench, by chatting amiably to the escorting officer on his left whilst sitting with one knee raised and clasped between his hands.

The summer sun was streaming in the massive windows.

After the buzzer sounded, every seat had been immediately occupied and the *Scotsman* reported that when the verdict was delivered, Manuel sat impassively, surrounded by six policemen, a further nine stationed at the North door and seven at the South door. All the standing areas were taken by reporters, lawyers, court officials and councillors who had been unable to secure seats for the occasion.

The Clerk of Justiciary asked who spoke for the jury and the 'burly balding middle-aged' foreman rose from the foreman's bench and said that he did. At 4.50pm, the clerk asked if they had reached a verdict and he confirmed that they had.

When asked what the verdicts were, the foreman donned his glasses and read from 'a marked typed foolscap script' as follows:

Charge 1 – (the murder of Anne Kneilands) – Not Guilty, unanimous

Charge 2 – (the Platt break-in) – Guilty, unanimous

Charge 3 – (the Martin break-in) – Guilty, majority

Charge 4 – (the Watt murders) – Guilty, unanimous of capital murder

Charge 5 – (the Houston break-in) – Not Proven, unanimous

Charge 6 – (the Cooke murder) – Guilty, unanimous, of murder

Charge 7 – (the Smart murders) – Guilty, unanimous of capital murder

Charge 8 – (the theft of Smart's car) – Guilty, unanimous

After the verdicts had been delivered, the clerk sat down for a full five minutes, writing them out in longhand prior to reading them back for the jury to confirm that they were their true findings. During that time, the court sat in total silence, all eyes on the condemned man, all that is, apart from the members of the jury, none of whom even glanced at him.

They had clearly accepted he had committed the murders they had been asked to consider; curiously, they were not unanimous as regards the break-in at the Martin house, and paradoxically, they acquitted unanimously of the charge which effectively cracked the investigation, the break-in at the Houston house.

Manuel, understandably, was now noticeably flushed, his hands clasped in front of him and his fingers moving nervously.

The clerk passed the minutes to the bench and there was a hushed conversation between him and the judge. The judge then invited the Advocate Depute to proceed and he duly moved for sentence, but only on the fourth, sixth and seventh charges.

There was no mention of previous convictions, now an academic issue.

The judge then addressed Manuel at 4.58pm:

'Peter Thomas Anthony Manuel, in respect of the verdict of guilty of capital murder and of murder done on a different occasion, the sentence of the court is that you be taken from this place to the prison of Barlinnie, Glasgow, therein to be detained until the 19th day of June, next, and upon that day, in the said prison of Barlinnie, Glasgow and between the hours of eight and ten o'clock, you suffer death by hanging, which is pronounced for doom.'

Accompanying the last few words, the infamous Black Cap was held slightly above his head for a few seconds before being replaced in the special shelf on the bench.

His Lordship was seen to be 'visibly moved'.

Manuel reportedly turned smartly and ran down the steps to the cells below as spectators muttered and craned forward to gain a last glimpse of the damned prisoner.

The awful spell was abruptly broken as the Macer sprang to his feet and bellowed, 'Sit down and be quiet!' The judge turned to thank the jury for discharging their difficult and onerous duty, before informing them that he was issuing instructions that given the length of the case, they were to be relieved of jury service for the rest of their lives.

They were now free to return to their families to try to pick up the threads of their lives. A newspaper report in May 1959 gave details of a jury reunion which had been proposed one year after the event. It was claimed that 'at least one QC' was going to attend the dinner and address them about the case itself. When word got out, however, the idea was shelved, presumably on grounds of good taste.

Manuel now had ten days in which to lodge an appeal and speculation surrounded whether he would do so or not. His solicitor, John M. Ferns, told reporters that he and his assistant Ian Docherty had waited at the High Court until Manuel had been taken away, lest he should indicate that he wanted to see them, but no such indication had been received.

Normally, the convicted person is visited by his legal team as soon as possible following conviction; perhaps there was an etiquette surrounding a post-conviction consultation with a condemned man – now lost on today's practitioners – which allows him time to compose himself before discussing any next desperate step to save his life.

Alternatively, Ferns and Docherty had been exercising discretion as they were dreading the meeting.

The papers noted that Watt had not been present at the verdict. Some journalists had tried to contact him, and it was reported that he was not at his lodgings, nor at his brother's house nor indeed at the nursing home he had been recuperating at following the road accident.

The universal and significant conclusion of the press was that the verdict had 'cleared his name', implying that had it not been for the unanimous finding of guilt against Manuel on the fourth charge, Watt would continue to be considered a newsworthy suspect who had probably escaped justice.

The judge had invited Detective Superintendent Brown, Detective Inspector Goodall and Detective Inspector McNeill into chambers after the court rose. There was speculation that he had wanted to thank them personally for their efforts in the case, but none of them was later prepared to reveal what His Lordship had said to them in private.

We can be assured that he was not enquiring if the officers nursed any doubts about the conviction and sentence.

Wilson wrote:

'His first murder trial as a Judge was over. It is hard to conceive of a more difficult initiation; and hard also to imagine a task better done.

'Throughout the whole trial he was firmly in control and he controlled it in the great Scottish tradition of fairness. When the accused dismissed his counsel, Lord Cameron unhesitatingly shouldered the additional burden which that placed on his shoulders and Manuel, in a sense, had the great criminal experience of Sir John

Cameron KC, Dean of the Faculty of Advocates at his service. He and the Scottish legal system were alike fortunate in that.'

Whether Manuel would have readily concurred in that sentiment at that stage is unlikely.

52

THE APPEAL

Today, 'ultimate justice' is often decided in Strasbourg, but in 1958 a condemned man had two options.

Should the judges in the Appeal Court decide there were no grounds of appeal, a plea for clemency to the Secretary of State remained.

For Manuel, the latter was improbable.

Apart from the miserable Mrs Manuel, there was no movement for mercy and no public outcry that the condemned man be reprieved. Some American airmen based in Norfolk, England tried to drum up support for a wildly misguided campaign to save 'a fellow countryman', which never progressed beyond a curious historical footnote.

The final hope for him was that somehow there had been a miscarriage of justice.

The Dean of Faculty now had a decision to make.

Manuel's solicitor had intimated an appeal against conviction and the execution was necessarily postponed. The condemned man had dismissed the services of two senior and one junior counsel at his trial, but the appeal undoubtedly required the input of someone skilled in drafting the grounds of appeal and then appearing in court to argue them.

A recently appointed silk, R. H. MacDonald QC, together with the defence 'trial junior' Alistair Malcolm Morison, later known as 'Tiger' Morison when appointed to the bench, were appointed to present the appeal.

The major issue for the media was whether Manuel would try to take over again, but the fight had gone out of him and he made no effort to become involved.

Thereafter, speculation revolved around whether he was going to actually appear in court.

He was taken to the Appeal Court in Edinburgh from Barlinnie Prison in Glasgow on the morning of 24 June 1958 for the appeal hearing, but never actually appeared in the court room.

His fatalistic state of mind at that stage can be gleaned from his easy acquiescence in MacDonald's advice that 'it was in his best interests not to appear', the court thereafter accepting the competence of the appeal hearing proceeding in his absence. A few weeks before, Manuel would have turned the tables on his counsel and rejoiced in the opportunity to demonstrate his nascent legal skills to a willing press corps.

It might have been that he finally realised that there was now no prospect of evading the death penalty; even if all the grounds of appeal were unexpectedly successful on all counts, the conviction on the Smart murders could still stand.

The legal personnel were relieved and the watching media disappointed that the unpredictable and dangerous prisoner was not now going to pull one final rabbit out of the hat.

Lord Justice General Clyde, Lord Carmont and Lord Sorn heard the appeal.

The Lord Advocate, Milligan, appeared with Gillies, the trial Depute and Sutherland, the junior.

Six grounds had been formulated:
1. The written and verbal 'confessions' should not have been admitted.

This ground was the most far-reaching and was argued last.

2. The judge had misdirected the jury as to the burden of proof relating to the special defences.

The basis of this ground was that the judge had apparently made it appear that an accused had to 'prove' his special defence, when, of course, the law provides that an accused person does not have to prove anything, the onus being always on the prosecution.

The proposition was that there had been insufficient emphasis that an accused might still be acquitted even though his special defence had not been established.

The court pronounced that they were satisfied that there was no substance in this ground of appeal. The trial judge had dealt with each special defence correctly, outlining not only 'the limited burden of proof that lay on an accused' but also directing the jury that even if a special defence failed, if it raised a reasonable doubt, that should be given to the accused.

The appeal point would have more validity today. Lord Cameron's direction that 'a special defence of any kind brings with it a burden of proof which lies on the shoulders of the person accused' sits uneasily with the modern – certainly from 1973 – approach.

3. The verdict in the Martin housebreaking was 'contrary to the evidence'.

The proposition advanced was that as the judge had 'made it clear' that there was insufficient evidence to convict in this instance, the jury should have acquitted, the corroboration coming from the witness Charles Tallis being unacceptable.

The court studied what the trial judge had said in his charge to the jury and concluded that the combination of the evidence of Tallis together with what Manuel said in production 142 – that he and three others had broken into number 18 that night – was thin but sufficient.

4. The jury were misdirected as to the question of motive regarding the Watt murders.

The Lord Justice General expressed puzzlement as to exactly what this ground meant. MacDonald said that he 'shared the difficulty' to some extent, explaining that this ground of appeal had been framed before he was instructed in the appeal.

Perhaps not the best start to a persuasive presentation.

His 'understanding' of the point was that the judge had 'engaged in an excursion into the realms of fantasy' by his reference to Watt mentioning the Valente girl being seen at the window of the Watt house and the misconception arising that there was a safe therein containing £5,000.

That observation amounted to speculation as to a possible motive and, it could be suggested that such 'excessive speculation' would be a valid reason for quashing the conviction.

The court said little about this ground, except that the trial judge had properly left the question of what inferences could be drawn from that chapter of evidence. It was noted that Watt had given evidence about Manuel relating the story of the 'mistaken break-in' to him; in reiterating it in his charge, the allegation appears to have been that the judge – if this ground of appeal can be fathomed – had unwittingly elevated Manuel's story to a possible motive.

This ground does not appear to have been seriously or strenuously advanced.

5. The judge failed to summarise the evidence of the witnesses Taylor and Morrison fairly in support of the special defence of impeachment of William Watt.

The allegation here was that Lord Cameron had not been impartial in overstressing the dangers of misidentification when it came to the evidence of Taylor, the ferryman and Morrison, the other driver, both of whom had been defence witnesses. The assertion was that he had spent a lot of time warning the jury about the unreliability of such evidence, but had spent little time, for instance, making the same comments about the evidence of the part-time policeman McFarlane, who claimed to have seen Manuel at the railway line on the night of the Cooke murder.

The court dismissed this ground on the basis that the judge was correct in drawing the attention of the jury to 'the vagueness' of the identifications by the two witnesses, pointing out that there was nothing wrong about a judge 'laying out' his greater experience in such matters before the jury then qualifying that course of action by reminding them that it was the jury who made the decision, not him.

Was that really fair?

What the judge said in his charge went pretty far; he informed the jury of his 'grave difficulty' in accepting Morrison's identification.

Why should His Lordship feel he had to inform the jury of his personal misgivings?

After all, the real force of Morrison's identification was that the mystery driver 'crooked' his finger over the cigarette he was smoking in the manner of a pipe smoker, exactly as Watt had been the only one to do at the identification parade.

Although not an identification issue, the car he had seen coming erratically towards him also appears to have had faulty lights.

On the other hand, when rehearsing Taylor's evidence, the trial judge reminded the jury that he had identified the man as Watt and that the man had a black dog in the car, which however, Taylor had wrongly stated was a Wolseley, not a Vauxhall.

Not only was that a reasonable summation, but, it has to be said, the judge also made a very good defence point – the fact that despite massive publicity for the time, no-one had come forward to identify himself as the man who, incredibly, not only looked like Watt but also had a black Labrador with him and was following a route that could easily have been taken by Watt had he paid a night-time visit to the family home.

Much more so than with Morrison's evidence, perhaps the trial judge was right to have doubts about Taylor's testimony, although his expression of those doubts in his charge could have been problematical.

6. The judge misdirected the jury in directing them that the finding of the body and shoes in the Cooke murder could be regarded as independent evidence capable of corroborating the alleged confession.

The issue was whether the finding of the shoes and the body of the victim had an independence from the alleged statements; the submission was that these actions were merely an extension or repetition of the statements. The court summarily dealt with this ground, referring to a passage from Alison's *Criminal Law*. The Lord Justice General observed that it 'might have been written with this case in mind':

If a person is apprehended on a charge of theft and he tells the officer who seized him that if he will go to such a place and look under such a bush he will find the stolen goods, or if he is charged with murder and he says he threw the bloody weapon into such a pool in such a river and it is searched for and found, without doubt these are such strong confirmations of the truth of the confession as renders it of itself sufficient, if the corpus is established aliunde, to convict the prisoner.

Accordingly, the trial judge's charge was 'proper and correct'.

These observations by Lord Clyde were apposite in an unexpected way.

They were to be the basis for the controversial concept of 'special knowledge' confessions, the first real case taking twenty-five years to emerge, and the river rather than the judicial title being the link, when a youth made a 'special knowledge confession' to driving a bulldozer into the Clyde. His rambling explanation for his actions led to him being convicted 'out of his own mouth' following legal debate that cited the case of Manuel v HMA.

Turning to the main ground of appeal, the first one, the court heard the submission from the appellant's counsel that for a statement to be admissible, there had to be no suggestion that the accused had been subjected to any hint of inducement to make the statement. He maintained that any proper examination of the statements made showed there had been evidence of a deal of some kind. Furthermore, not only was Samuel Manuel taken to the police station to meet the appellant, but Samuel's later release pointed to the deal actually being given effect to. In those circumstances and context, subsequent 'formal warnings' about self-incrimination were meaningless. Indeed, in more serious cases, the police should be very careful in accepting 'confessions' and in this instance, which was unique, they should have taken a back seat and employed the services of a 'neutral' official such as a magistrate to note the terms of the confession.

What had happened amounted to the 'breaking down' of a suspect who had had no legal representation. It was significant that the appellant's 'uncharacteristic' remorse should occur at a time when he had had no contact with the outside world. In that situation, regard had to be taken of the prisoner's mental and physical capacity and to the gravity of the charges. Accordingly, the conclusion must be that the statements had not been given voluntarily, or at least there was grave doubt on that point.

MacDonald's closing argument was that if Their Lordships were with him on this ground, it would lead to all charges except the break-in at the Platt house being quashed.

That last point does not bear close scrutiny.

In the Cooke murder, the 'unfair' confession which led to the subsequent finding of the body must necessarily have tainted that evidence, in some respects, and its exclusion could have led to that conviction being quashed.

However, in the Watt murders, Manuel's bizarre behaviour and the specific criminal knowledge he exhibited during his meetings with Dowdall and Watt certainly focused suspicion on him and could have been regarded as an element in the case against him which was separate to, and independent from, the circumstances surrounding the giving of the statements to the police. There was also the 'Platt bullet' and its strong evidential link to the crime, which again had an independence from any alleged bullying and pressure exerted on the suspect at the police station.

The 'no case to answer submission', which clarifies the question of sufficiency, did not exist in 1958. Should an accused elect to remain within the confines of the dock rather than give his version of events, there was no second tactical opportunity to tackle the prosecution case.

Nevertheless, at Manuel's trial, the trial judge's decision to repel the defence objection to the admission of the statements would have had no bearing on any further defence submission along the lines of a no case to answer submission, had it existed. In any event, a different 'sifting' process at that time was the widely held view that on a charge of capital murder, the evidence had to be 'especially' water-tight in all respects.

What would have remained of the Smart charges, had the confession evidence been excluded?

There was still the evidence about the stolen car, the possession of the stolen money and the accused's geographical proximity to the scene of the crime.

And what of Manuel's tale about finding the bodies of his 'friend' Peter Smart and his family? Certainly a modern appeal court would have no difficulty in taking the evidence given by an accused at his trial into account when considering the bigger picture.

And Manuel's remarkable performance at his trial effectively destroyed any suggestion that he was psychologically incapable of looking after himself whilst 'in the hands of the Philistines' in police custody.

As it was, however, Their Lordships engaged only in a 'brief conference' on the bench, before pronouncing on all the grounds before them.

Not only did they deem it unnecessary to grace the proceedings with a short adjournment to 'consider' the arguments before them – particularly in a sensational case of this kind – but they also decided not to call on the Lord Advocate to answer any of the grounds of appeal!

Perhaps even more telling is that the court felt it necessary to give their reasons for repelling the grounds of appeal, only, it seems, 'in recognition' of the fact that MacDonald had argued the submissions 'cogently' and in the light of the service he had 'faithfully performed' in presenting the appeal, and not, it seems, in order to set down clear guidelines as to the development and state of the law of criminal evidence.

With hindsight, and in the days before transparency and public accountability, the appeal proceedings had the air of a 'deal' having already been done before a word was publicly uttered.

As for the statements being unfairly obtained, they held that the trial judge had correctly followed the Chalmers guidelines and had heard from the appellant's family outwith the jury's presence before rejecting the allegation of unfairness; the police officers could not have made an arrangement with Manuel as his father was outwith their control and in the hands of the Procurator Fiscal, an independent body. Unlike Chalmers, the appellant was 'thirty-two years of age' (sic) and in full possession of his faculties; he seems to have deliberately decided to unburden his soul and reveal the dark deeds outlined in such convincing detail in production 142.

Rather than pressurising the appellant, the police conduct appeared to be 'a model of propriety and fairness'.

All matters were fairly put before the jury and no advantage had been taken of the appellant's decision to defend himself.

Looking at it from today's vantage point, it's difficult to imagine that the appeal judges were privately unaware of the situation.

In one sense, Manuel probably considered that he was being cute when he made the statements and wrongly believed that they would all be swept under the carpet at a later date.

Nevertheless, certain qualms remain as to exactly why Samuel Manuel was charged and remanded over the theft of the gloves, then 'allowed' to see his son whilst both were in custody. MacDonald's contention that proof that the 'deal' existed could be gleaned from the fact that it was acted upon seems reasonable.

In truth, Manuel's Achilles heel had been exploited, but public policy had to prevail.

Beyond that, it would undoubtedly have been a social disaster had he won his freedom at any time after his arrest on 14 January 1958, as he had embarked on an unstoppable homicidal slide; if society and the legal process had failed to stop him, no doubt a figure from the underworld of Glasgow or London would have.

53

BRIDGET'S STORY

The now obsolete *Empire News and Sunday Chronicle* for 1 June 1958 reported that after being sentenced to death, Manuel had the privilege of being allowed to speak to his parents for twenty minutes in the office of the prison's deputy governor. No physical contact was allowed and he spoke mainly about the fact that the judge had failed to ask him if he had anything to say, as was traditional, after he had sentenced him. Manuel told his parents that he had wanted to say something and was disappointed at not being asked.

His mother said that perhaps the judge felt that he had said enough already.

Manuel told his father he did not know what to do about an appeal and an eavesdropping prison officer told them that Mr Ferns had already arranged to visit him to discuss it.

Manuel enquired after his sister, and his mother said she was well but she didn't know where she was at present.

Mrs Manuel herself later arranged to go to a convent to seek peace of mind.

The Manuels had returned from staying at their seaside hotel at Prestwick, courtesy of the newspaper, to speak to their son.

A bizarre adjunct to an already surreal situation was added when Mrs Manuel agreed to 'tell her story' to the journalist Bill Knox. He explained: 'She has undergone an ordeal which no other mother of a man convicted of murder has ever done in this country – she has stood in the dock and been cross-examined by her son in his own defence and by the prosecuting counsel striving to present a case which would mean the death of her son.'

It was said that Manuel's composure had deserted him during the trial, and just before the end, prison warders had heard him weeping bitterly in his cell. When he emerged, though, his insouciant exterior had returned and by the time he met his parents again, contact was on a formal basis.

His mother had attended early morning mass every day after she had finished giving her evidence not, as she explained, to pray for her son's acquittal but 'for his soul'. What grieved her most was that he had fallen away from the faith she practised. She said she had felt no great pressure when giving evidence as she was being truthful and was without fear or favour even though it was her 'own beloved boy' who was on trial. The real judge was the Superior One who would ensure that all of us would answer to him one day. She said that her 'greatest comfort' was that Peter had put his family's welfare above his own throughout the trial, echoing a point that Manuel himself had made in his evidence. She now sought peace, as did Samuel, who, characteristically, still retained some sort of residual faith in his condemned son, claiming he was 'something of a genius' with a flair for music, the arts, decorating and writing.

Unconvincingly, however, he said that he had tried everything to get through to him – from cuffing him to persuasion to cajolery but none had worked.

Knox claimed that other prisoners had been told that Manuel intended to poison himself rather than meekly submit to execution. When his father delivered sandwiches to Barlinnie, Manuel flew into a rage when he heard that they had been rejected by staff as a precaution. The prison authorities also searched for a phial of poison rumoured to have been smuggled in by a fellow inmate.

Outside of the prison, daily life in Lanarkshire and its environs became more relaxed in Manuel's absence. Knox reported a skipping rhyme then popular in playgrounds:

Mary had a little cat, she used to call it Daniel
Then she found it killed six mice, and now she calls it Manuel.

Like other commentators, he was concerned that Manuel might become something of a folk-hero in the eyes of young impressionable types who might have approved of his apparent ability to 'baffle' the police and because he had 'astounded a nation by showing that a *labourer* could possess such skill and aplomb'.

The Manuels' neighbours were surprisingly sympathetic and generally reluctant to visit the sins of the son on the parents, who had decided to come home and tend to the garden rather than hide at the seaside. Their second twenty-minute visit had again been a formal affair, but since Manuel was no longer untried but convicted, his privileges had been withdrawn and the staff had returned cigarettes and matches to which he was no longer entitled to his parents who had brought them.

Perhaps surprisingly, the Manuels expressed bitterness about certain aspects of the Crown case, in particular the chapter dealing with the Watt murders, as they had thought that the jury would have doubts about that charge.

Another talking-point was that some witnesses from the trial had received threatening letters from an anonymous member of the public, the witness David Knox being one of them. The Manuels decided that they were the work of a crank and when they discussed it with Peter, he agreed.

Whoever the author was, he now had official sanction from an expert.

Words of comfort from Brenda Gordon arrived via Bill Knox to Mrs Manuel. Her son, Ian, had been convicted of murdering a judge's daughter in Northern Ireland and he had thereafter been remanded in a mental hospital. His mother vowed not to give up the fight to prove his innocence and sanity. She said she empathised with what the Manuels were going through.

Gordon later did establish his innocence, an option not open to Manuel and straining the comparison.

She said that it was the family who bear the greatest strain when someone is charged with murder and she offered the comfort that the public's memory 'soon dies'.

Wrong again.

Three days before the appeal hearing, the *Empire News* ran the story about Manuel frothing at the mouth and being rushed to the prison hospital. Tests showed no irritants and he was returned to the condemned cell after three hours. The rumour-mill, however, reported that he had swallowed cleaning fluid in a suicide attempt, blithely ignoring the fact that he was under observation with no access to such items.

The inside pages contained Bridget Manuel's story about his life, so that the 'world would know him' as she did.

The journal was silent as to what fee, if any, was paid.

To modern eyes, any 'human interest' story about a serial killer is per se distasteful; in the days of capital punishment, a different attitude existed.

After all, he was about to pay for his crimes.

Even so, what the murder victims' relatives thought of the concept and the content can only be guessed at.

Bridget Manuel had been nineteen and Samuel was twenty when they married in 1922. After a while, Samuel had gone to Detroit to look for work. His mother and brother already lived there, and for two and a half years he had sent money to Bridget and their son James back home in Scotland. When she went out to join him there, she had left James behind to make it easier for her to seek work. After the couple had moved to Manhattan, she discovered that she was pregnant again and when Samuel went down with scarlet fever, she became worried for her unborn child. She needn't have, as Peter was born a 'lively black-haired nine-and-a-half pound bundle', which the nurses christened 'Jack Dempsey' as he always fought to free his hands from the bedclothes.

The family prospered when Samuel got a charge-hand's job in

the Briggs car body factory in Detroit and they moved into a white-painted bungalow in the Harper district. One day when the family was decorating the house, they left Peter to his own devices and later discovered that he had painted their dog green, pink and lavender!

After Samuel suffered a ruptured appendix and peritonitis, the family decided to return home, as there was no national insurance scheme in America.

They sailed for Glasgow in June 1932.

On the way over, Peter had tried to escape through the cabin port-hole, but his parents had caught him 'just in time'.

The Depression years meant little or no work and after Peter attended primary school in Motherwell for a while, the family again moved, this time to Coventry in 1937. He had a strong American accent but had successfully made friends and settled at school in Motherwell.

According to his mother, the real problems with Peter began after they moved to England. He had already been behind with his lessons, but when he went to school in Coventry, it was all too much for him, particularly as he had been placed according to age rather than ability.

One day he returned home from school and told his mother that he didn't know what the teacher was talking about and that he was not going back. Shortly after that, he tried to return home and was caught at Coventry station trying to buy a ticket to go to Motherwell to see his grandmother. Then he started staying out all night and seemed immune to his parents' efforts to discipline him; he would never say he was sorry. His only solace was in reading and he won a limerick competition in a boys' magazine after his anti-social behaviour had started.

One day a policeman had brought him home. He had broken into a shop and stolen £12, which had been found in his pocket, and because of that, he had been placed on probation, although he had gone back to school – briefly.

Out of parental control, he was then sent to a remand home at

Coleshill in Warwickshire and when Bridget walked three miles to visit him one wild, windy day, she arrived to discover that he had run away.

He was eleven years old.

From there he was sent to a home run by the Christian Brothers in Suffolk. In a visit one day, he told his mother that he had seen a German bomb explode near the home and that he had lost his sight for a few days and he claimed that another boy who had been looking out of the window with him at the same time had been blinded.

He told a vaguely similar story to a psychiatrist in 1958, but it can be safely assumed that the truth content, if any, was very low. Perhaps he had heard reports of a bomb landing a few miles away.

As Peter was moved about, he always ran away.

The Manuels had got on with their lives, but decided to return to Motherwell after their Coventry home was flattened by a German bomb – a real one this time. When Peter was finally allowed to return home, he was eighteen and sullen. He had no friends and could not relate to his parents in any way. For a while after that, he had stayed at home, sketching and sometimes baking. The family never asked what had happened to him in 'the seven lost years' and he never referred to them.

The lack of a realistic relationship persisted to the end; throughout the series of articles, Bridget calls Peter 'the boy', despite the fact that he was thirty-one years old when he died.

When his call-up papers arrived he protested, claiming that he could not be drafted as he was 'a citizen of the United States'; if he can be believed, he won his case and the British army lost interest.

Charged with the twenty-two housebreakings in 1946, Peter returned home after Samuel posted bail of £60. His mother described him as showing 'no shame' and having no apologies to make. She explained that when he told them he was 'staying with a friend' overnight, they had wanted to believe so much that he actually had a friend, that they never questioned him further.

And she was pragmatic, to say the least, about her son's talent for property violation, explaining that it was not the money that interested him, but it was the 'the joy of showing how expert he was at it' that made him do it.

For those families who had to repair structural damage, replace stolen items and clean and replace bedding and carpets, this observation was cold comfort. Thankfully, she stopped short of explaining her son's homicidal tendencies in the same superficial manner.

When challenged about the break-ins, however, he reassured his mother that he wasn't doing anything wrong.

After he had been charged with rape in 1946, Bridget said she had offered to be a witness for him at the trial, but Peter refused on the basis that 'the things the police were saying were too horrible' for her to hear.

He had also refused to allow her to visit him in Peterhead.

Released from prison in 1953, he briefly gave her some hope that he had mended his ways when he paid £32 for a typewriter and began composing short stories. Some would be thrown straight into the fire, others would be sent off, but none were ultimately accepted for publication. He had never talked about rejection slips, but carefully filed them and the stories away in a briefcase which the police took but never returned.

Are they still lying in a cupboard somewhere?

A briefcase can be seen in the back of a police van in one of the photographs of the police seizing his clothes and possessions at the time of his final arrest. Was that the one?

About that time, she thought that Peter would have a better chance in life if the family moved back to the United States but, surprisingly, he was totally against the move and described it as 'going off into the unknown'.

As a Labour councillor of the sixth district committee of Lanarkshire, Samuel had offered his resignation after his son was jailed, but colleagues dissuaded him from taking it further. He served another nine years before he resigned due to 'pressure of work'.

Mrs Manuel told Knox that 'not one person she knew has expressed anything but the deepest sorrow at what has befallen our family.'

One night Superintendent Hendry asked her what she would do if Peter told her that he had murdered someone. Would she tell the police? Bridget said she wouldn't – she would seek guidance from her priest and would do what he suggested.

She said that when he came out of Peterhead Prison she thought he might 'go straight' when he got a job at the gasworks where his father worked. After six weeks he left after a row but landed another job as a shunter at British Railways.

At that time, he had spent most nights at home reading cowboy books and thrillers. Then he had started going steady with Anna O'Hara. Bridget had seen it as 'a real chance' for him to live an honest life, but she soon realised that he needed to come clean about his past if it was going to work.

When he broke up with Anna, he was upset for the first of only three times she knew of, and that occasion was the only time he was sorry for himself. The next time had been when she had to tell him that his dog Rusty had been killed, and he was miserable at losing the pet he had lavished so much care and attention on.

The final time had been when she was taken to Hamilton police office to hear him confess to multiple murder.

When he was remanded for the assault on Mary McLachlan, she said that the family had asked the solicitor who was then acting for him to have him examined by a psychiatrist, but when Peter had found out, he became angry and refused to co-operate. They had then made the same request of the prosecutor and it had been duly arranged, but nothing emerged from the examination which suggested mental illness.

After his surprise acquittal, she said he had simply 'slid back' into family life as if nothing had happened and as if he never doubted the outcome.

Bridget confirmed that one night a large American car actually did come up the street and a man with an American accent came to their door for him. He left with him in a hurry and when he returned three days later, he told her that he had flown the Atlantic with the Secret Service so he could help them trace a man he had known in Peterhead and who was a traitor to the United States.

She knew he had been fantasising but had pretended to believe him.

On the night Anne Kneilands was murdered, Bridget and Samuel had gone out leaving him at home. As they left, he had mentioned a 'great play' on the television which he suggested they would be back in time to see, but when they returned, Samuel had felt ill and had gone straight to bed. As a result, Bridget later claimed, she could not rememeber whether Peter had been at home or not that night. When the police had eventually called at the house, she remembered he 'mesmerised us all' by calmly breaking off from their questioning, going into the kitchen and making a cup of tea, behaviour later mirrored by her in the final police raid in 1958.

Bridget's story had been serialised, starting a few weeks before the execution and ending sixteen days after it. It must have been difficult for her to tell it, but the impression emerges of someone unable to grieve any more and confident in a higher authority.

She rarely doubted his guilt, instead pointing out that she had done her best to get him some sort of psychiatric help, and whenever he went out of the house, she dreaded what might happen.

Despite that, she remained resolute in her belief that he had been at home on the night of the murder of Sydney John Dunn in County Durham in December 1957, and it has to be wondered why she should say that, particularly in the light of her realism about the egregious crimes he had already committed by then. It would have made little difference to her peace of mind if he had been found to be innocent of that crime, but the finding of the coroner's jury may have given closure to Dunn's family.

She had some interesting things to say about her perception of her son's activities when it came to the tricky problem of Christmas presents for the family. On Christmas Eve 1957, the family attended

335

midnight mass, leaving the house about 11.30pm with Peter electing to stay at home 'to watch Mass on television'.

When the family returned home about 1.30am on Christmas Day, he was asleep in bed. Three weeks later, she found out that the 'yellow leather gloves' he'd given to his father and the camera he'd given to his sister – soon to be the main pressure point in the enquiry – had been stolen from the Reverend Houston's house about a mile away.

His alter ego had seemingly emerged in that two-hour window, and, mission accomplished, he could play the dutiful son and present wonderful gifts to his family on Christmas Day despite having no means of support.

The Reverend Houston had in fact identified the stolen gloves as being sheepskin and he testified at the trial that the break-in was during daylight hours on Christmas Day; either Bridget was understandably confused or a housebreaking from 1957 remains unsolved.

A further post-trial insight was revealed when Bridget wrote about the family gathering at Hogmanay 1957.

What did not emerge at the trial was the fact that James was 'very short sighted and doesn't wear glasses' and that rather than James being able to speak to the crucial timings that morning, Bridget tells us that it was Peter who had told James that the time was 6 o'clock and that James had simply taken his brother's word for it. Her view was that James would have been unable to see the clock, let alone the time.

Another concession she made was that Peter could have committed the Smart murders and returned without anyone in the Manuel household knowing, as there was always an emergency key hidden in the garden in case any of the family was locked out.

On the night of the Isabelle Cooke murder, she recalled him going to the pictures at about 5pm, and when he returned home, his clothes and shoes were unblemished. The police later told her that he must have had a stash of clothes hidden somewhere outside the house that he changed in and out of, and Bridget agreed.

The area had been 'buzzing' with the news of the Smart murders, and when James spoke about it, Peter had commented that from what he'd heard it was 'a case of murder and suicide', a foretaste of his future defence.

On 14 January 1958, the police had arrived in force at the house.

Initially shocked when they told her that their visit was in connection with the murders at Sheepburn Road, she had become hysterical when they arrested Samuel. She revealed that stress and worry had caused her to lose four stones in weight for the two years up until that date; in contrast, she describes Peter in his last moments of freedom and as the house was being systematically turned over, 'dressing, shaving and knotting his tie as if he was about to go somewhere to be entertained', and casually saying, 'Make these men a cup of tea, will you Maw?'

Inured to Peter's outrages, she had been distraught when Samuel appeared at Airdrie Sheriff Court on a charge of breaking into the Reverend Houston's house on Christmas day and stealing a pair of gloves, a camera and £2. Bail had been refused and he was remanded in custody – quite remarkable in itself.

The whole charade ended farcically when the charge against Samuel was dropped the day after Peter confessed.

As she had done in court – with the occasional evidential wobble – she confirmed that she had heard Peter confess his guilt. At their meeting, there had been preliminary exchanges with him asking, 'Is your job alright, Daddy? Why didn't you tell them I gave you the gloves?'

He had then turned to the detectives there and told them that his father was one of the best men at the gasworks and 'should he lose his job because of this carry-on . . .', at which point McNeill had butted in to remind him that he had asked to speak to his mother.

Manuel had then spilled out his story about not knowing 'what made him do these things'. He had told her that he didn't want his family to suffer on his account and Bridget had replied that his spiritual welfare was her only concern. She then made him promise that he would make a 'good confession' and make his peace with God before he left this world, for his own peace of mind. After she embraced him for the last time – and he didn't respond – she shed her last tear; before that night she couldn't stop crying and after that night she could cry no more.

After his release, Samuel had come home and they both had tried to come to terms with the full horror of the situation. Samuel recalled a Saturday night when Peter had been sitting at home and he had offered him money to go to the pictures. Peter had refused it. He told them he 'had a reason for staying in' and that he 'didn't want to go out on Saturday nights'.

His parents later discussed what he had said and collated it with what they now knew.

The crimes he had committed or been charged with had all occurred at weekends or on holidays when he had time on his hands. That Saturday night, he had been fighting 'the terrible thing' he had spoken of in the police station.

By implication, then, a life or lives had been saved by his refusal to take the money from his father that night.

Referring to one of her final visits to her son, Bridget concluded:

'As he talked, I knew I would always be glad I was kind to him, that I didn't put him out of the house when he got into so much trouble.

'For, as I believe, he was really sick in his mind, then it was right that I should do all I could to make my boy happy.

'Why have I told Peter's story?

'Because I want to tell of the boy I knew . . . I don't know the other Peter who did these dreadful things. I know the little boy who learned his prayers at my knee, the Peter who was always kind, gentle and thoughtful.

'Peter has paid the penalty demanded by the law for the crimes of which he was found guilty. But I will always remember and pray for the son I knew – a good kind son he was to me.'

54

THE EXECUTION

As the death sentence had already been imposed, the court confirmed HM Prison, Barlinnie, Glasgow as the place, and 8am on 11 July 1958 as the time and date of the execution.

Considering that the movement towards the abolition of capital punishment was slowly gaining ground – the Homicide Act of 1957 being part of the process – it's commonly assumed that Manuel was 'the last to hang' in Scotland, but that's not the case.

That unwanted distinction belongs to a Henry John Burnett, who was executed at Craiginches Prison in Aberdeen on 15 August 1963 for shooting his girlfriend's husband. She had told him that she was planning to leave him to return to live with her husband, whereupon Burnett armed himself with a pistol, went to where his rival lived and shot him in the head. Burnett then dragged his terrified lover away from the scene, car-jacked a local driver and fled, somewhat curiously, to Ellon in Aberdeenshire, where he later surrendered to local police officers.

At the trial, there was a special defence of insanity, with the alternative of diminished responsibility, neither of which was accepted by the jury. Oddly enough, whilst a plea for clemency was made by both Burnett's and the victim's families, Burnett did not lodge an appeal and the sentence was duly carried out.

He was twenty-one years old.

The Royal Commission on Capital Punishment reported its findings in 1954. Part of its remit was to explore whether the sentence of capital punishment for murder should be modified to a sentence of

339

(life) imprisonment in certain circumstances. The Craig and Bentley case had caused anguish because of its patent unfairness, and the Commission had regard to the deterrence – or otherwise – of execution, particularly in the light of the experiences of other countries, and indeed, whether forms of execution other than hanging would be more humane.

Only one of the Commission's recommendations, however, would actually apply to Manuel. The necessary rehearsal for a hanging involved repeated operation of the trapdoor the condemned man was soon to drop through; given the traditional proximity of the execution block to the condemned cell, the Commission suggested that rubber silencers be attached to the trap in order to muffle the dreaded noise reaching the prisoner, and that was duly done to the apparatus at Barlinnie shortly before the sentence was carried out.

The executioner was a forty-seven-year-old publican from Manchester called Harry Bertrum Allen, who was assisted by his twenty-three-year-old son Brian. He had become the 'number one' executioner after Albert Pierrepoint resigned and had been on the Home Office list since 1941. Overall, Allen carried out twenty-nine executions and assisted in another forty-four in the United Kingdom, and his services were also occasionally required abroad.

Apart from dispatching Manuel, Allen also executed James Hanratty at Bedford prison in 1962. Up until DNA evidence appears to have 'clinched' the case in 2002 – if such an observation is appropriate post-execution – Hanratty's friends and family, together with several high-profile campaigners such as John Lennon, protested his innocence.

Allen also took part in the last executions in Britain at 8am on 13 August 1964 when he hanged Gwynne Evans at Strangeways Prison in Manchester and Evan's partner in crime, Peter Allen, was simultaneously hanged at Walton Prison in Liverpool.

The *Bulletin & Scots Pictorial* for 12 July 1958 reported that Manuel had been dressed in his black blazer and flannels as he calmly went to his death. He had wakened at 6am and partaken of his last break-fast with a glass of whisky chaser – something that would have appealed to his gangster self-image. His final handshake was with the prison governor before his hands were shackled behind him. He had also bade farewell to the prison nightshift as they left the building, many of whom had spent the days between the failed appeal and the day of reckoning playing card games for matches and talking about football and other topics with him, whenever he wanted to, which, apparently, was not a lot.

He would probably have been unaware of a recent question in the Commons by Hector Hughes QC, Labour MP for Aberdeen North to the Lord Advocate seeking details of the proposed compensation for William Watt.

The other prisoners in 'D' Block were not sent to work until later that morning, and despite their purported loathing for the condemned man, they were described as being 'solemn'.

The paper also reported that a petition for last-minute clemency, based on Manuel's mental state, had been turned down by the Scottish Secretary, John Maclay. It had been organised by an abolitionist, a Mr Edward Bond, and was signed by him and fifty-eight others under the umbrella of 'The Manuel Appeal Committee' based at the Blythswood Hotel in Glasgow's Argyle Street. Among the signatories were several American servicemen and 'Battling Bessie' Braddock, the redoubtable Liverpudlian MP known for her willingness to champion the rights of prisoners in the country's jails and detainees in mental institutions.

Mr Maclay said he 'regretted' he had been unable to find suffi-cient grounds to consider granting the crave of the petition.

Behind the scenes, Maclay had been advised that there were several letters favouring a reprieve for the condemned man, the most impor-tant of which had been written on behalf of sixty teachers following a meeting they had to air their views, the starting premise being that 'the condemned man is abnormal to a degree where his responsi-bility for acts of violence is diminished' and that 'the common feature of his crimes is their irrationality'.

They also believed that the argument that executing the 'mentally unfit' in order to save public funds was contrary to Christian views, and that 'if by some fine effort, [psychiatrists] should, in time, redeem a human wretch from his affliction – what triumph!'

Interestingly, Maclay's advisers decided not to trouble him with any of the other letters, two of which were based on simple opposition to capital punishment, two – apart from the teachers' letter – based on the condemned man's supposed insanity, three in which the grounds of opposition were not clearly stated, and a surprising six on the grounds of Manuel's innocence.

That said, the latter category contained letters from 'one anonymous sufferer from delusions about Freemasonry, address unknown'.

It's worth noting that eight days before Manuel's execution, Maclay had found it necessary to allay civic fears by publicly announcing that the introduction of the Homicide Act of 1957 had not led to the widely predicted increase in the number of murders.

It all depends, of course, where you start counting from.

A possible combination of jurors reluctant to take the responsibility for condemning an accused man, and would-be killers wary of the ultimate sanction – although there is no genuine reason for supposing the latter statement to be either true or empirically provable – meant that there were no judicial hangings in Scotland between August 1928 and February 1946. Prior to Manuel's execution, there had been none since 1954. Yet when capital punishment was suspended, as it were, in 1965, there was a rise in 'capital crimes' of 125% between then and 1969.

As has often been observed in various studies, there seems to be less crime in jurisdictions where a 'fear culture' has grown out of the certainty of execution for specific offences.

Despite there being no special defence of insanity nor a plea in bar of trial concerning Manuel's mental state, the Scottish Secretary still had to ensure that they were not about to execute a mentally ill man. Down the years, the courts had come to terms with the concept that there was some middle ground between sanity and insanity and that there might be circumstances in which an accused's responsibility for his criminal acts was diminished.

In the course of an appeal in 1923, Lord Alness said, 'Formerly there were only two classes of prisoner – those who were completely responsible and those who were completely irresponsible.

'Our law now has come to recognise in murder cases a third class ... who, while they may not merit the description of being insane, are nevertheless in such a condition as to reduce their act from murder to culpable homicide.'

It was, of course, Lord Cameron who had acted for Patrick Carraher in his 1938 trial. The appeal arising from the 1946 trial decided that 'a psychopathic personality disorder' should not be regarded as definitive grounds for concluding that a person was of 'diminished responsibility'.

A large measure of public policy appears to have come into play here, given that Carraher was on his second murder trial, having previously escaped execution.

Should a murderer be diagnosed as having such a personality – and realistically murderers might be expected to be reasonably well represented in that category – he would evade the consequences of his actions, and in practice, psychiatrists appeared to be uncovering increasing numbers with such a disorder.

The Royal Commission on Capital Punishment, however, had made a recommendation which ran contrary to the Carraher appeal findings when it suggested that the courts in Scotland 'give rather greater weight to psychopathic personality as a ground for reprieve than has sometimes been the practice in the past'.

Was there any danger of Manuel escaping the noose?

Three psychiatrists reported that there was no good reason to think that Manuel was insane 'either at the time of the offences or at the present time' (2 July 1958). They found him to be 'an abnormal man' with many psychopathic traits but that these were not of such a degree as to diminish his responsibility.

One of the three, Dr Angus MacNiven, apparently did think that Manuel had a psychopathic personality but agreed with his colleagues that a reprieve was not appropriate.

It's of historic interest to note that the Scottish Secretary 'in accordance with practice' consulted with the Home Office as to whether the course of law should be interfered with; the paternalistic sounding response was that had it been an English case, there would have been no hesitation in advising the Home Secretary that the law should take its course.

Lord Cameron, who had asked some pointed questions about his mental state at the trial, reported that he had no doubt as to Manuel's guilt on the charges he was convicted of and there was nothing to indicate that Manuel had behaved abnormally either before or after the crimes. His Lordship also let it be known that he had watched Manuel carefully during the trial and, as a layman, he could see no signs of mental illness.

And there was more.

He suspected that the prisoner was trying to lay the foundations for a reprieve on mental health grounds *but not in front of the jury*.

His defence of the likes of Carraher had clearly imbued the judge with a healthy cynicism and his conclusion, unsurprisingly, was that Manuel was a dangerous criminal who was fully responsible for his actions.

In order to observe the proper process for the execution to proceed, the authorities would accordingly have to decide – as the Lord Advocate did – that 'there is very little evidence at the moment of psychopathic personality: Dr MacNiven's opinion is about all that there is.'

Would today's psychiatric practitioners tend more to Dr MacNiven's view or would they agree with the contention that there was 'little evidence' of psychopathic personality?

The Lord Advocate also observed that he got an impression 'of great versatility, of a man who can change his personality at will and who is shrewd and dangerous'.

He then continued in language refreshing to our politically correct era, 'For myself I am inclined to look on Manuel as a really bad man.'

Two Baillies, the Depute Town Clerk and a policeman had been required to witness Manuel's hanging in order to give evidence at the Inquiry at

Glasgow Sheriff Court later that day when the Procurator Fiscal Depute led the formalities. The policeman's role was to inform the presiding Sheriff that he had – by means of visual identification – confirmed that the executed prisoner was the same one that he had witnessed being convicted. Dr David Anderson, who had examined Manuel after his admission to prison in January and found him to be of sound mind and fit to plead, spoke to certifying death at 8.01am that day.

During his last days, Manuel's mood oscillated wildly. Conscious of his image, he initially feigned indifference, but at one point, and as a final combative throw of the dice, he even managed to summon sufficient enthusiasm to complain that he had been assaulted by prison officers.

There was also the report that he had drunk cleaning fluid and foamed at the mouth in an attempt to simulate madness, but that story appears in the context of press speculation that he would be wily enough to concoct some way of avoiding execution.

What actually happened was that Manuel behaved normally until a few days before his appeal. On 20 June, he was seen to be frothing slightly at the mouth. His stomach was pumped but nothing unusual was found and from then until a few days before the execution, he refused to talk to anyone, twitched and contorted himself.

The psychiatrists concluded all this was 'consciously motivated'.

Immediately after the appeal, he was morose and taciturn up until a few days before the sentence was carried out. When he finally realised that he was definitely not going to avoid the rope, he reverted to normal behaviour and played cards, smoked and chatted to his guards. He also spent time alone with Father Smith, who may have heard his confession. No-one is sure, although he seems to have convinced his mother at least that his mortal soul would now be in safe hands.

When the actual time came there was a surreal touch to the sombre proceedings, when a nearby radio could be overheard playing the popular tune of the time, 'Tea For Two'.

MANUEL

He is said to have suggested to his executioner that they 'quickly get it over with' and he walked the twelve paces, briskly and unaided, from the condemned cell D.2-27 into the execution chamber, where the traditional white hood was slipped over his head seconds before the trapdoor was sprung.

Later that day, his brother James appeared at the prison with flowers which were placed on the grave inside the prison.

As a brother, Peter had been a true ally yet a source of puzzlement, embarrassment and shame to James; as a citizen, he was seemingly destined to die on the gallows and be buried 'within the confines of prison walls'.

And it's thought he's still there today.

55

THE FINAL RECKONING

Whilst in Peterhead, Manuel let it be known he was in for safe-blowing rather than rape. It was the 'glamour' crime of its day and the cover-up crime of choice for those convicted of other less savoury matters.

The 1955 film *The Ladykillers*, starring Alec Guinness, Peter Sellers and Herbert Lom, probably mirrored the underworld view of the times, in that the only real consequence of a 'caper' such as an armed robbery was that the victim's insurance cover rose very slightly.

When twelve of the Great Train Robbers were given sentences totalling 307 years at Buckinghamshire Assizes in 1964, there was something of an outcry, with many members of the public thinking that they had been harshly dealt with. The judge felt it right to point out that the crime was 'not romantic' as some people thought, and that the train driver, Jack Mills, had suffered serious injury.

Unlike today, 1950s Zeitgeist was not wholly condemnatory of some types of villainy. Just a few years before in the Second World War, the armed forces had carried out dangerous missions and been praised for their courage and initiative. Post-war Britain still sneakingly admired certain non-aggressive criminals, the safe-blower Johnny Ramensky having a mythology all of his own. Like Manuel, he was sentenced to Borstal training and to stretches in both Barlinnie and Peterhead; unlike him, Ramensky was from an impoverished background, was non-violent and was a genuine safe-blower who had perfected his 'skills' whilst working in the mines. To blur the issue further, during the war Ramensky was drafted into a commando unit and dropped behind enemy lines, where he used his expertise to blow a safe and capture Nazi documents. He received the Military Medal for his actions and despite returning to crime at the end of the war, he was still largely respected by most who knew him. His funeral in 1972 was attended by many of the policemen who had spent much of their careers trying to catch him.

No-one admired Manuel.

It has often been observed that rape is a 'power crime' primarily about control – even 'temporary ownership' of another person. At no time has society lauded a man who has been convicted of rape; the secret information that an attacker had ejaculated before he could achieve his goal is less than mitigatory and gives greater insight into the mind of an assailant, particularly one who progresses to murder.

Much better then to build up a heroic alternative.

As has been said before, the most convincing witness is not necessarily the most truthful one, but is often the one who actually believes what he says. If no one else did, Manuel believed that he had been jailed for being detected at the scene of a safe-blowing. He had fled the scene, jumped into a fashionable getaway car and a lengthy car chase had ensued. When his vehicle eventually crashed, a copper, naturally, had gone through the windscreen.

That was his Peterhead story and that was what he was sticking to.

Lest that was insufficient for proper respect, he told tales of foxy ladies who adored him, of his prowess in the boxing ring and of a long-standing invitation from a top London mob who were desperate to recruit a man of his calibre immediately on his release.

When the American servicemen based in Norfolk tried to garner support for Manuel's reprieve, it can only be assumed that they were not in possession of the full facts.

Almost unanimously, the rest of society saw his execution as the only possible solution with neither punishment nor revenge necessarily being the prime reasons.

There was simply nothing else to do with him.

Had he remained in society he would have needed to kill again to feed his self-importance, and it's more than probable that some underworld inadequate would have killed him just to make a name for himself.

He was certainly unmourned by the villains whose approval he so desperately craved.

The press, who had shown such reverence to the legal process at the beginning of the trial, later started to show signs of disquiet about police methods, and by the trial's end many newspaper editorials were asking why it had taken so long to bring him to justice and what could be done about such crimes in future.

Chronologically, the first crime on the indictment was January 1956 but he had not been arrested until January 1958 and between those dates seven others were murdered.

Whilst acknowledging the difficulties that the Lanarkshire force faced in an unprecedented situation, the general view was that some form of re-organisation was needed for the smaller forces to keep up with unexpected events. Some called for Scotland Yard to be extended so that 'murder squads' could tour the country on demand, without regard to the different legal systems between Scotland and England. The perceived problem was that local forces had limited manpower and were geared up for maintaining essential services and that, whilst unique for the time, another Manuel might arise like a spectre to haunt a helpless community policed by a hard-working but restricted force. A national police force was talked of – as it sometimes is today – and it was not lost on observers that Manuel's arrest had happened only eight days after the City of Glasgow CID effectively took over.

The former Deputy Chief Constable of the City of Aberdeen, John Westland, was asked to report on what, if anything, could have been done to expedite the case against Manuel. Starting with Locard's Principle – that the perpetrator always leaves some traces of his presence at the locus – he then posed the question why it should be that some crimes remain undetected. His answer was that if some investigators were inefficient in identifying those traces where there was a recognised technique for doing so, that was culpable. Manuel himself had made the point at the trial that no scrapings had been taken from Anne Kneilands' nails.

It has to be assumed that had that been done, small particles of tissue belonging to the accused man would have been discovered.

And should Manuel's clothes have been scientifically examined for evidence traces? Given that he seemingly hid clothes elsewhere for the purpose of housebreaking and murder, that would have been a pointless exercise. Forensic reports which were lodged at the trial were neutral in that respect, a fact which bolsters the 'hidden clothes' theory.

The detective training college in Scotland only provided training for a month every year in 1958, which was obviously inadequate, and knowledge of forensic techniques and presentation had to be improved.

A centralised CID for Scotland was one suggestion, as there was a general view that entrenched loyalties, local 'pride' and straightforward jealousy had hampered the Manuel enquiry; better surely to blend local knowledge with officers trained in modern investigative techniques?

Interestingly, there still exist regional forces in Scotland; however, when the need arises – as in the extreme example of Pan Am Flight 103 exploding over Lockerbie in December 1988 – 'outside' help is quickly drafted in. Indeed, part of the folklore surrounding Lockerbie insists that first on the scene were American secret servicemen rather than the steady constables of Dumfries and Galloway Constabulary.

Ironically, and despite all the perceived flaws and operational criticisms, Manuel was convicted mostly on the strength of a confession, extracted, it has to be said, using methods based entirely on knowledge of the suspect's probable psychological weaknesses.

The question remains of how many murders he actually did commit.

The self-interest of newspapers cannot be disentangled from the known facts and almost all of them 'exclusively revealed' similar stories.

The *Sunday Pictorial* for 13 July 1958 proclaimed the figure to be twelve and that he had made a condemned cell confession about killing Anne Kneilands – as if the original confession should be doubted. The article surmised that on top of the eight he was charged with, there should be added Sydney John Dunn and another three names. In sensational mode, it also reported that he 'planned to kill another three' in the days leading up to his arrest but that the police would 'never disclose their names'. Despite official silence, it takes little by way of detective training to suppose that this was a poorly veiled reference to Brown, Goodall and McNeill.

The pre-execution 'confession' to the Anne Kneilands murder was purportedly the result of a conversation between an alleged visitor and the condemned man. A reporter called Peter Kennerley wrote: 'The news of [the confession] was given to me exclusively by a man who was one of his last visitors in Barlinnie Prison.

'This man was led by two warders to the death cell – three cells converted into one.

'As the green painted cell door swung open to admit the visitor, he saw Manuel lying on a bed smoking.

'For ten days Manuel had maintained a complete sullen silence.

'"How are you today?" asked the visitor.

'No reply.

'"Now all hope is passed, did you do it?"

'No reply.

'"Was the police confession produced in court true after all?"

'A long silence.

'Then suddenly Peter Manuel hurled himself off the bed.

'"YES **** you, IT WAS!" he yelled, "**** them all."'

How much was some 'friend' of Manuel paid for that piece of information?

How did the 'friend' get to speak to the doomed man?

Did the 'friend' exist?

Last-minute 'confessions' were time-honoured journalistic devices for boosting circulation.

So were reports of 'other murders'.

Surprisingly, John Gray Wilson wrote that Manuel had confessed to three other killings. He appears to have taken that fact from the *Sunday Pictorial*. Surprising, because Wilson wrote a detailed, careful and reliable account of the trial. Yet at no time did the paper report that Manuel confessed to three other murders. It certainly ran a story that 'Manuel Did 12 Murders', but at no point in the article is there any hint that Manuel 'confessed' to any crimes – other than the ludicrous 'Kneilands' scenario above.

What in fact the newspaper did was to say that it was 'able to disclose' that he had committed the following crimes:

1. The murder of fifty-six-year-old Anne Steele at her tenement flat in Aberfoyle Street, Dennistoun, Glasgow on 11 January 1956.

Someone had broken into her third-floor flat and attacked her by hitting her on the head with a poker. The noise of the blows and the screams of the dying woman caused neighbours to listen outside, then batter on the door. The attacker was heard to run from room to room before he climbed out of a window then down a drainpipe and escaped. No-one was charged with the crime.

2. The murder of forty-two-year-old Ellen Petrie, known as 'English Nellie', in West George Lane, Glasgow on 15 June 1956.

She was a prostitute who was found lying in a pool of blood having been slashed in the thigh. It appears that she had been 'working' in the area and that she had gone into the lane with a customer who had attacked her and fled. No-one was charged with the crime.

3. The murder of Helen Carlin, known as 'Red Helen', in Pimlico, London in September 1954.

She was a prostitute who had been found strangled with a nylon stocking. No-one was charged with the crime, but it was known that Manuel was in London around that time, desperately trying to become a member of any London 'mob' that would take him. None did.

According to the journalist Kennerley, senior police officers had told him they regarded the murders of Sydney Dunn, Helen Carlin and Anne Steele as now 'solved'.

On what basis?

Manuel was obviously capable of all of theses crimes, but beyond pious hope and possible geographical proximity there exists nothing that has come down to us today to link him with two of them at least. Even Manuel's protest that the police were trying to 'prove that I did in Anne Steele and English Nellie' was quoted in one article as if it amounted to a false denial.

Mention has already been made of the disappearance of Moira Anderson in February 1957. In the course of his evidence, Manuel referred to the police trying to 'pin' the crime on him, but of course he could not reveal in court that he was in custody at the time of the offence.

The *Empire News and Sunday Chronicle* for 13 July 1958 mentioned other murders over which a question mark would remain 'at least in the public mind'. These were:

1. The murder of thirty-two-year-old Mrs Jean Chalinder, found battered to death on September 1956. She had left her home in Albany Road, Cardiff to go picking brambles. Her body had been mutilated and her shoes had been removed and placed under her.

2. The murder of a Maltese girl found strangled in a Soho street in 1955.

3. The murder of a Mrs Maitland, who was attacked as she cycled through a park in Cranfield, Middlesex. No date was given for the crime.

4. The murder of eleven-year-old Sheila Martin, who was strangled in woods near her home in Fawkham Green, Kent in July 1946.

For these crimes to linger 'in the public mind' as potentially the work of Manuel has to suggest that 'the public' were privy to far more information than the readers of the *Empire News*.

Not only is there no geographical link suggested, in the case of the Martin murder in July 1946 it's well documented that Manuel was serving a sentence of twelve months' imprisonment for house-breakings from 21 March 1946, soon to be followed by an eight-year sentence for rape on 25 June 1946.

In 1958, as now, mention of a link with a serial killer, no matter how tenuous, helped sell newspapers.

As with the famous 'Dundee Man Lost at Sea' headline ascribed to the Dundee *Evening Telegraph* in 1912, the reader only finds out post-purchase whether a genuine story exists or not; unlike the speculation surrounding Manuel's 'other murders', which in effect were non-stories, the 'Telly' did follow the headline up with a real one.

The sinking of the *Titanic*.

56

WHY?

Like Manuel himself, the term 'serial killer' originated in the United States, and was first used to describe certain high-profile murderers in the 1970s such as Ted Bundy and Peter Sutcliffe. It applies to someone who has killed on at least three separate occasions, with 'cooling-off periods' in between the murders.

Like all such labels, it can withstand only a certain amount of scrutiny. A serial killer's motives can develop as he progresses through the arc of violence he has become embroiled in, and in time he may become 'a spree killer'. Manuel appears to have evolved from serial to spree between December 1957 and January 1958.

The spree killer does not have the same cooling-off periods in between attacks and seems less concerned about detection, possibly due to a growing belief that he has become uncatchable. Based on behavioural probability, a profile might emerge which can lead to the killer's identification and apprehension.

Of course, no criminologists in 1950s Britain would have heard of such classifications and very few would have been able to have a reasonable insight into the serial killer's motivation. Indeed, lunar influence was one contemporary explanation offered for Manuel's conduct.

He was hanged a mere thirteen years after the end of the Second World War and it would be wrong to suggest that the population who lived through the revelations of Nazi atrocities were unschooled in the less attractive side of human nature.

Did the fascination with Manuel stem from the fact that his crimes happened in post-war Britain?

How could this sort of thing happen here?

A contemporary reference point is the Homicide Act of 1957. Whilst section 6 of the Act suggests that the death penalty could have applied to Manuel on the basis of 'repeated murder', the prosecution do not appear to have relied on that.

Fifty years on, the 1957 Act's attempt to proscribe homicidal behaviour in the classification of capital and non-capital murder has the appearance of a limited legislative reaction to the 'Craig and Bentley' case. The enduring image is of the jury being solemnly informed that if they thought that Manuel's motive in both the Kneilands and Cooke murders was *robbery*, it would be appropriate for them to convict him of capital murder.

Perhaps it just hadn't occurred to the legislature that someone like Manuel could exist. The intervening half-century has, however, allowed criminologists to build on their knowledge and make certain other observations. One of the strangest is the number of occasions that a figure like William Watt comes under the police microscope in the course of a major enquiry. From the Jack the Ripper case to the tragic Timothy Evans, there have been many instances of so called 'plausible suspects' coming under the spotlight, the most recent, it seems, being Barry George, his conviction for the murder of Jill Dando being overturned on 1 August 2008.

Damage to the brain's temporal lobe is another area explored in the context of serial killers, spree killers and mass murderers. The Texas State University killer, Charles Whitman, was said to have been suffering from a brain tumour which might account for his shooting spree; most commentators now regard unusual social factors in his upbringing as more significant.

The possibility of brain damage is raised only because Manuel claimed to have been hit by shrapnel from a German bomb. On the one hand, he does appear to have had a scar on his head possibly consistent with his narration of events, but on the other, the teller of the tale was Peter Manuel.

Manuel wrote to whomever he thought he might impress. His many letters seem to raise another issue. His handwriting varies greatly and would appear to depend on how he signed his letters, be it 'P. Manuel', 'Peter Manuel' or any variation using his middle names or initials. Perhaps the Lord Advocate was on to something when he observed, *'I got an impression . . . of a man who can change his personality at will.'*

Nevertheless, there are some similarities in the profiles of serial killers, most of whom are white, male and under thirty-five. It's been observed they are often good actors, capable of rapid improvisation; they are usually more intelligent than the general population and are motivated by the need to exercise control over a situation they have created. They are *not* psychotic and appear quite normal in their everyday social context. They are unlikely to be abusers of alcohol, drugs or even cigarettes; they generally care for their appearance and are often 'fastidious' about their dress. They have no ability to experience any feelings for their victims, whom they regard as mere obstacles in the way of their pleasure. Most of them have served a burglary 'apprenticeship'. They are unable to admit to their abnormality, usually sexual – to do so would expose their eccentric *raison d'être*. Above all, they are 'made' rather than born, in respect that there is often a dysfunctional upbringing.

The spectre of sexual abuse has to be considered in Manuel's case even if only to be dismissed, as there was never any suggestion of it at the time. That said, evidence of such abuse often either surfaces many years later – or not at all.

Up until the Smart murders – leaving aside the Dunn case – Manuel's victims were exclusively female, something that might be significant to modern profilers and suggesting that he was possibly battling real or imagined maternal disapproval. On that thesis, the motivation for the 1946 attacks, the McLachlan incident and even the Kneilands murder was *not* sexual relief but was temporary respite from a confidence-sapping inadequacy.

His ever-indulgent father was both an ally and a weakness. When Samuel completed an enquiry form into his son's suitability for Borstal training in 1946, his answers were revealing. Asked about his son's level of education, he replied that he really couldn't assess it, but that he 'seemed very intelligent'. He went on to explain that his son would not now attend church, having received 'Communist tuition' during his first spell of Borstal training. He was 'to[o] brilliant for his age', was a gifted artist and he even offered the authorities a book of his son's drawings for their consideration, should they so wish.

He also said that his son had a violent temper, a vivid imagination and took mental blackouts, but added that he was 'very obedient until he was aged eleven' after which time he was 'in the hands of the authorities'.

For a developing psychopath, it must surely have been a telling factor that his own father was of the opinion that 'the authorities' were responsible not only for warping his son's mind with the great social bogey of the age – communism – but were also the real cause of his later criminality. Samuel's attitude would amount to a perfect foundation for Peter negating responsibility for anything he did in later life.

Of course, although nothing can be regarded as certain when assessing the influences which shaped him, it is tempting to consider what the impact of his return to the United Kingdom meant to the young Manuel. He had been the focus of his parents' attention until then. On his arrival, he met his older brother for the first time and from that point on, there was limited social contact for the social misfit with the strange accent, as the family continually moved about in search of work.

Whatever fuelled his rage, it's probable that he fantasised about his attacks beforehand; during them he would have experienced some temporary relief and afterwards would have basked in the satisfaction of their success.

The Platt mattress bullet must have been a fantasy-based rehearsal. The three sex attacks in March 1946 increased in gravity until his goal was achieved and it's significant that the Watt killings were a mere two weeks away from an anticipated eighteen-month sentence.

FBI profilers often link magazine and film scenarios with criminal acts – known as 'the eroticisation of violence' – and at the risk of overstretching a point, Lanarkshire CID may have suspected he was influenced by fantasy when they seized a copy of *True Detective* magazine along with items of clothing from his bedroom two days after William Watt was released from custody on 3 December 1956; it's to be assumed that it was not taken for training purposes. Manuel was also an avid film-goer and his surviving sketches speak for themselves.

Stress factors are sometimes regarded as a trigger for violence. The obvious example in Manuel's case is the attack on Mary McLachlan in 1955 on the day he was supposed to marry Anna O'Hara. The modern profiler regards such instances as significant, as in the case of Richard Cottingham, who attempted to kill a prostitute in 1990 in New York on the same day as his divorce hearing. Manuel's 'January murders' may simply have been triggered by the stress of being a misfit at holiday time.

Manuel additionally suffered from a machismo-sapping combination of sexual deviance and lack of height. Following an incident in Peterhead Prison in the 1950s, fellow prisoners complained about the patent unfairness of the diminutive Manuel being manhandled by a well-built prison officer.

If only they knew.

The phenomenon of paraphilia – defined as 'the need for abnormal stimulus in order to achieve sexual arousal or orgasm' – has a long social history and may even be a dark facet of humanity's propensity for violence. A British war correspondent, reporting on the 1877–8 conflict between Russia and Turkey claimed to have witnessed Turkish troops taking sexual advantage of dying soldiers on the battlefield. He did not report whether the victims were exclusively Russian or not, and was informed that the practice was 'a matter of expert timing'.

Jack the Ripper was sexually aroused by the mutilation of his victims, as was Peter Kurten, 'the Vampire of Düsseldorf', who was executed in 1931; Reginald Christie needed his victims to be semi-conscious before he could experience arousal or ejaculation.

Investigators of aberrant human activity have come a long way since the shocked war correspondent filed his report and several aspects of serial killer behaviour are now seen to be surprisingly similar. Things just happen to them as if by chance. Manuel's explanation about the night he 'met' Anne Kneilands tells how she approached and pestered him to the point where her own foolishness sealed her fate. Ted Bundy offered instances of victims virtually asking to be murdered, and serial killer Richard Macek from Chicago set the scene for a murder by describing how he was driving along the road when *the car* 'turned and went toward' the crime scene.

Serial killers appear to be motivated by the need to control, and maintain control of, a situation they have created in order to achieve sexual gratification and empowerment. Their behavioural similarities manifest themselves in various ways.

The violated property – the need to desecrate, remain or return

There is often bizarre behaviour in and around the house that has been entered. Manuel's 'signature' was to consume food, pour liquid on floors, stub cigarettes out on carpets and wipe his muddy shoes on bedclothes. As a youngster, he found a hiding place and remained there, sometimes for days; as an adult, he slept calmly in other people's couches or beds. A serial killer called William Heirens in 1940s Chicago also broke in and stayed in properties, stole women's underwear, then urinated and defecated on floors before leaving.

Why? Profilers suggest this demonstrates mastery over something temporarily belonging to him. Some analysts even suggest that it amounts to some sort of animalistic 'territory marking', effectively challenging and showing contempt for the owner's social values.

Another example was Andrew Philip Cunanan, best known for his slaying of Gianni Versace in Miami in 1997. That same year he murdered businessman Lee Miglin in the garage of his house, then went into the house, made himself some food and slept all night in his bed. In the morning he stole money, clothes and Miglin's car, all without appearing to be concerned or aware that Miglin's wife just happened to be away on business that night. So why take the risk?

Again it seems that it is simply an extension of the desire to exercise control over someone else's life and possessions, the main purpose being to extend the pleasure of the initial, sexually exciting act. It's also thought that more pleasure is gained if the victim is materially wealthy.

In terms of the risk of detection, though, revisiting violated properties is clearly irrational. Manuel's repeat visits to the Smart house after his first deadly visit were further demonstrations of his mastery and control, in which he was eking out the residual thrill of the original crime. He moved the bodies and possibly revisited both the Kneilands and Cooke crime scenes.

In 1990 in Bellevue, Washington, George Russell killed three women. After each murder, he stayed with the victim for increasingly long periods, arranging the crime scenes in order to shock those unlucky enough to find the bodies.

Serial killers Bundy, Dahmer and Nilsen all spent time with their dead victims, although the latter two took the notion of 'pleasure extension' a stage further in dismembering and storing their victims' body parts, some of which Dahmer ate, in and around their own flats.

The comfort zone

The serial killer is often comfortable within a certain geographical zone, as it follows that he stands a greater chance of escape if he is familiar with the lie of the land; confidence increases as crimes go undetected and in the event of a challenge to his presence in a particular area, he is safe in the knowledge that he can offer a plausible explanation.

For twelve years until his execution, Manuel's crimes were all within a few miles of his home addresses, excepting the murder of Sydney Dunn.

The unsolved murder of Anne Steele in January 1956 would suggest an incipient 'spree' following the Kneilands slaying and could probably correspond geographically. However, other aspects of the *modus* are less convincing, as the assault took place in a top-floor flat and was noisily executed and the escape route was difficult.

Much more typical of Manuel was the nocturnal dexterity he displayed when taking the police to the makeshift grave of Isabelle Cooke, demonstrating to them that he knew his patch well both by day and night.

Studies show that as many as 90% of killers are familiar with the locus of their crimes. Moreover, there is a 50% chance that the killer actually lives within a circle drawn on a map connecting the two crimes furthest away from each other.

Accordingly, homicidal behaviour is also situational. Many serial killers are model prisoners, and as with Manuel, Sutcliffe and many others, their families do not appear to have been in any genuine danger of the treatment meted out to complete strangers. A 'them and us' view of the outside world exists, which is only apparent if certain conditions apply, the comfort zone being one of them.

The final insult

Apart from repeat visits to crime scenes, serial killers often like to show their subjugation of, and power over, their victims, often by witnessing their terror. Peter Smart was discovered lying on his back having been shot in the head. He would have known nothing of his fate beforehand. His wife, though, was found lying on her side, her arm extended over her husband as if vainly trying to comfort, or seek the protection of her husband whilst she awaited a similar fate. Michael Smart had been shot through his left temple as he lay on his back. Like his father, he did not appear to have had a chance to react, and as a child in a child's bed, was obviously no threat to his killer. Manuel never appears to have worn a mask and by that stage there was no question of witnesses living to testify against him anyway, but ten-year-old Michael could only have amounted to being a removable irritation to Manuel.

His two male victims were speedily dispatched but more time was taken with some of his female victims. There is a suggestion that he 'toyed' with Isabelle Cooke, if his confession is to be believed, and that she was still alive when he threw her bag away.

Given her injuries, Vivienne Watt may have wakened from the unconsciousness brought about by the blow to her head to the nightmare of Manuel contorting his face and outlining her proposed fate, as per the McLachlan scenario.

The absence of semen is today regarded as significant in that the perpetrator either fulfilled his goal spontaneously at the crime scene or achieved it later with the aid of mementoes from the victim. The power of life and death over a conscious victim seems to temporarily banish the killer's deep-seated feelings of inadequacy.

Richard Cottingham deliberately left a gun within reach of a victim he had been torturing so that she would seize it, point it at him and pull the trigger, hoping that within the space of a few seconds she might be free of him. Of course, her hopes were quickly dashed when she discovered that the weapon was a replica. Cottingham explained that it gave him 'extra' control over her.

Controlling the enquiry – the trophies

The recognised phenomenon of 'possession scattering' following a murder seems to be a combination of an effort to somehow control the direction of the subsequent police investigation and to pander to the killer's whim of keeping some – and disposing of other – 'trophies' belonging to the victim.

Many other serial killers have indulged in this, as did Manuel in both the Kneilands and Cooke murders, investigators finding personal items and pieces of clothing scattered around the crime scenes. Indeed, Isabelle Cooke's ring, vanity case, shoes, coat and petticoat were all found in the area between her house and his. Anne Kneilands' purse with the spools inside was craftily placed at the Simpsons' house to try to send investigators in the wrong direction.

Yet the key to 'cracking' the Manuel case was ultimately down to him irrationally retaining stolen goods. The gloves stolen from the Reverend Houston's house and the incriminating banknotes from the Smart house led to his final arrest. Not only did he not make any real effort to distance himself from these items, but he seems to have made a perverse point of ensuring that he *could* be tied in with them.

What made him do that? At least part of the explanation might be that he genuinely believed that he could talk his way out of almost any situation and, of course, could totally rely on his father agreeing to say or do anything to 'assist' him when matters came to a head.

But there was more to it than that.

Unlike the scattering phenomenon, the victim's possessions are actually retained as trophies. Even more difficult to comprehend is the idea that someone subject to continual police interest should make gifts of stolen goods to family members, and yet it's a common occurrence with serial killers.

Again, the killer is somehow extending the pleasure of the memory of the original act, so that by ostentatiously spending the money Mr Smart withdrew for the holidays on drink, taxis and cigarettes, Manuel was inwardly draining the last vestiges of pleasure from murdering the true owner of the money. His dark secret was enhanced by the fact that the unwitting bartender or shopkeeper who accepted the money was totally unaware of the pedigree of the cash, thus under-lining the killer's superiority and boosting his ego.

To some extent, even the press coverage and general gossip which followed his murders allowed him to gain satisfaction from situations he had created and which he privately believed belonged to him.

Controlling the enquiry – getting involved

The serial killer often imagines that he is both invisible during the commission of the crime and invincible after its commission, and in that context, risk-taking corroborates his self-image. He's so ahead of the game, he becomes concerned that the rest of society might not be aware of the genius in their midst. Getting the authorities to acknowledge him bolsters the truth of that belief and contacting the police, the prosecutor and other public figures causes him to imagine he is 'on a par' with them and that secretly they are filled with admiration and respect for his achievements.

Dennis Rader, the president of a church congregation in Wichita, ensured his own conviction in 2005 when he contacted the police to 'claim' a murder which had not been attributed to the 'BTK' killer (for 'bind, torture and kill'), after which he was quickly identified and apprehended. His murders spanned thirty years and on at least one occasion *he* reported a murder he had committed to the police. He also wrote several letters asking what he had to do to rate a mention in the newspapers.

At his sentencing hearing, which decided that he would be eligible for parole in a mere 175 years, Rader undoubtedly relished being the centre of attention and it became evident that he regarded the investigation into the ten killings he was convicted of as a contest between him and the police, who he imagined acknowledged him as a worthy opponent. Disbelieving victims' relatives even heard him express admiration for the way that some of his victims met their deaths.

Manuel made the 'anonymous' call to the police in 1955 which suggested that he was the mastermind behind a robbery. In the Kneilands enquiry a year later, he butted in when a policeman was speaking to a work colleague at the initial stage of the enquiry and later told police he chased a suspect near the locus, thereby drawing unnecessary attention to himself and getting his picture and his story into the newspapers. He was a police informant, although, naturally, his information was heavy with self-aggrandisement and fantasy.

Above all, he assumed a self-appointed lead role in his dealings with Watt and Dowdall.

At the time, commentators were baffled as to why someone like him would deliberately flag themselves up and run the risk of detection, but today it's seen as another aspect of the serial killer's 'controlling' impulse.

He dropped hints that the police were looking in the wrong place in their search for Isabelle Cooke, offered an opinion that the Smart case was actually a double murder and a suicide, and he gave a policeman a lift in the car stolen from the Smarts' garage, all behaviour which reinforced his self-importance and enhanced the thrill of possible detection. In reserve, there was his unshakeable belief that he would easily persuade a jury that his actions were only those of a concerned citizen who should be rewarded rather than punished.

The enquiry – rewarding the police

Manuel showed the police where Isabelle Cooke was buried and where guns, keys and other items had been jettisoned. What could trigger such uncharacteristic co-operation with his sworn enemies? As often happens *post facto* when major incidents have occurred, the police in the Manuel enquiry came in for criticism, some of which was possibly justified.

The police certainly got one thing right, though – playing to Manuel's ego.

The serial killer likes to dictate his 'terms of surrender' and the process is greatly assisted if he thinks that he has negotiated from a position of strength. In Manuel's case, the police exploited his odd relationship with his parents to put pressure on him, but he was still able to convince himself that he was in charge of the situation and could honourably co-operate with them. What the police didn't know was that he had his legal argument about fairness up his sleeve; what Manuel didn't know was that it ultimately counted for nothing.

Seattle police sought help from the FBI when they were faced with an arson epidemic in the 1990s. As a result, they followed suggested profiling guidelines when they brought a suspect called Paul Keller in for questioning. In order to boost his self-importance, they arranged for a police convoy with blaring sirens to bring him in and hinted at his brilliance during questioning, a tactic which helped clear up enquiries into seventy-eight deliberate fires. Keller explained that none of it was actually his fault and that the real culprits were the property owners who were remiss enough to leave combustible material lying about beside their houses and factories.

Like Manuel, Keller was allowed to meet with his father before interview, but there was one important difference – Keller senior told his son it was the right time to confess, whereas Manuel junior held the initiative in that respect, and no doubt saw himself controlling the behaviour of the police in order to ensure his father's release. By that stage, however, it was the police who held the initiative, Manuel almost acknowledging as much when he expressed approval of Inspector McNeill's tactic of making him wait for two and a half hours before interview.

One matter remains. In December 1956 police took a black jacket and a pair of flannels from 32 Fourth Street for examination. They found semen on the inside of the trousers and a small smear of blood on the jacket, the trademarks of a successful Manuel night out. The blood-stain was too small to be tested properly but given modern technology it might be possible to identify the source, in theory at least, as being any of Anne Kneilands, Marion Watt, Vivienne Watt or Margaret Brown.

There's only one problem.

He was hanged wearing a black jacket and flannels.

Did they give him comfort *in extremis*?

> '*A good man can be stupid and still be good, but a bad man must have brains.*'
>
> Maksim Gorky, *The Lower Depths* (1903)

BIBLIOGRAPHY

Allison, *Principles and Practice of the Criminal Law of Scotland* (Edinburgh 1832 and 1833)

Berry-Dee, C., *Talking With Serial Killers* (John Blake Publishing Ltd, 2003)

Bingham, J., *The Hunting Down of Peter Manuel* (Panther Books Ltd, 1975)

Canter, D., *Mapping Murder* (Virgin Books, 2005)

Douglas, J. and Olshaker, M., *The Anatomy of Motive* (Pocket Books, 1999)

Dowdall, L. and Marshall, A., *Get Me Dowdall!* (Paul Harris Publishing, 1979)

Keppel, R. D. and Birnes, W. J., *Signature Killers* (Arrow Books, 1998)

Knox, B., *Court of Murder* (John Long Ltd, 1968)

Lindner, R. M., *Rebel Without a Cause* (Other Press, 2003)

Morland, N., *Pattern of Murder* (Elek, 1966)

Morrison, H. and Goldberg H., *My Life Among the Serial Killers* (John Wiley and Sons Ltd, 2004)

Muncie, W., *The Crime Pond* (W & R Chambers Ltd, 1979)

Notable British Trials Series, *The Trials of Patrick Carraher* (William Hodge and Co. Ltd, 1951)

Wilson, C., *A Criminal History of Mankind* (Diamond Books, 1993)

Wilson, J. G., *The Trial of Peter Manuel* (Secker and Warburg, 1959)

Newspaper references 1956–8

Evening Citizen (Glasgow)

Scottish Daily Express

The Glasgow Herald

Daily Record

Empire News and Sunday Chronicle

The Bulletin & Scots Pictorial

Sunday Pictorial

News of the World

Durham County Advertiser

Evening Chronicle (Newcastle)

The Northern Echo

Newcastle Journal

Evening Telegraph (Dundee)

The Scotsman

INDEX

INDEX

INDEX